BISHOPS AND WRITERS

D0993795

for
GARRETT SWEENEY
Master of St. Edmund's House, Cambridge
1964–1976

Garrett Sweeney,

BISHOPS AND WRITERS

ASPECTS OF THE EVOLUTION OF MODERN ENGLISH CATHOLICISM

Edited by
Adrian Hastings

ANTHONY CLARKE
WHEATHAMPSTEAD — HERTFORDSHIRE

First published in Great Britain in 1977 by
ANTHONY CLARKE BOOKS
WHEATHAMPSTEAD — HERTFORDSHIRE

© St. Edmund's House, Cambridge

ISBN 0 85650 045 3

*Made and Printed in Great Britain by
Chapel River Press, Andover, Hampshire*

Contents

Acknowledgements

THE following chapters first appeared in the *Clergy Review* and are here reproduced by courtesy of its editor: *The Forgotten Council*, October 1971; *The Primacy: the small print of Vatican I*, February 1974; *The 'Wound in the Right Foot': Unhealed?*, September 1975.

Preface

WHEN Canon Sweeney announced his intention of retiring from the mastership of St. Edmund's House, its Fellows decided that the most appropriate way of thanking him for all he had done in those richly fruitful twelve years, in which St. Edmund's had passed from a house of residence for student priests to full collegial status as a post-graduate 'Approved Foundation' of the University of Cambridge, would be the publication of a *festschrift*. The idea that came to us was of a rather special sort of *festschrift* in which half the book would contain some of his own writings while the other half would consist of a number of essays contributed by members of the House past and present. Naturally each writer is alone responsible for what he has written, but we wanted the book to have a unity and a single central theme and decided that this could best be that of the intellectual evolution of modern English Catholicism, because this is both the context in which St. Edmund's has itself developed and a primary academic interest of Canon Sweeney.

No one who has been a member of St. Edmund's House during the years of his mastership will question the dry, clear-sighted, profoundly humane quality of Canon Sweeney's leadership through the long years of a difficult transformation when it was several times far from sure that the House would continue at all. The subtle conversion of a traditionally clerical establishment into a predominantly lay one without any sell-out of the positive qualities of the old regime was a rare achievement in Catholic history. Perhaps no one less clerical than Canon Sweeney could have managed it without shipwreck, identifying profoundly as he could with both the academic and the ecclesiastical viewpoint. He saw the goal and he did not falter in the pursuit, but most of us will think of him still more as a priest of utter integrity and naturally conservative tastes, governed by a model of the most exigent service to others and the loyalties befitting a diocesan priest and a learned clerk. The quality of his unconcern for himself was almost painfully emphatic and few men can ever have left a Cambridge mastership with fewer material rewards. If St. Edmund's was in his time — as it had been in that of many of his predecessors — a conspicuously happy community, much of that happiness was somehow owed to the shy, rather awkward man who presided over it.

This volume is offered as a token of the enduring sense of gratitude that Fellows, members and friends of St. Edmund's are united in feeling for Garrett Sweeney, former Master, friend, and — now — parish priest in his own diocese of Nottingham, on whose history he has already collected numerous materials and about which we hope he will some day find time to write.

A.H.

An introduction

Freeing the papacy

John Coventry S.J.

No reader of these essays, which touch on aspects of English Catholicism from Newman onwards, can fail to be struck by the degree to which Catholics in this period are pre-occupied with Rome and the papacy. The exception is the period of revival in the thirties of this century treated by Fr. Adrian Hastings. For all its limitations and even defects this revival was at least concerned with capturing and expressing the spirit of Catholicism. And focus on the papacy is by no means an obvious way of doing that. Rather would one attempt to bring out an emphasis on tradition and a sacramental understanding of christian community, christian life and christian worship; a conviction that all man's creative arts and all God's created world could find a rightful place in mediating the saving action of God; an optimistic view of the power of Christ's presence and self-gift to transform men and women and their world into his kingdom. Vatican II and the years that have followed it have done much to renew the search for a fuller Catholicism. But they have also in their own way brought to the fore the question of the papacy, not only within Catholicism, but for a Catholicism actively engaged in the search for christian unity. The agreed statement on Authority recently published by the Anglican-Roman Catholic International Commission[1], while it falls short of solving all the problems, shows an approach to the subject by Catholic theologians in many ways transformed beyond recognition from anything that could have been imagined in the century before the Council.

Modern historical studies have enabled us to chart the ever growing dominance of the papacy in the Western Church, and its ever increasing claims. Its history puts many challenges to theological evaluation. A broad view of the emergence of christian ministry from the beginning shows how the very diversified ministries of the early Church, attested in the New Testament, are gradually absorbed into the ordained ministry. The Church becomes progressively clericalised, leaving a laity no longer thought to have a share in Christ's ministry in his Church. Whatever the precise origins of their office, this pattern is seen to continue in the development of bishop and presbyter: the bishop absorbs in principle all the functions of the presbyter, who becomes his delegate.[2] The increasing dominance of the papacy can then be seen to be a continuation of this same principle: the papacy moves far in the direction of absorbing the functions of episcopacy in its assumption of overall responsibility for the Church, and bishops begin to look like, and to behave like, delegates of the pope. The Declaration of the German Bishops in response to Vatican I, and at the prompting of Bismarck, and the counter-protestations from Rome, themselves attest how far the process had gone. Though Vatican I represents an apogee of theoretical statement about papal absolutism, it came at a time when actual papal power in the political sphere had declined from its highest point. It is interesting to note that, as its effective political power over the affairs of 'christian nations' diminished, so the acknowledged position of the papacy in ecclesiastical jurisdiction and in teaching authority grew. 'In the eighteenth century the papacy's power (both inside and outside the church) was definitely on the decline. It was only the shattering influence of the French Revolution and Napoleonic rule that opened up the possibilities for papal recovery of influence in the nineteenth century.'[3] These factors set the scene for the nineteenth century preoccupation with the papacy, considered in juridical and constitutional terms, which culminated in Vatican I. This Council itself set the tone and pace in the years till Vatican II for an astonishing growth in actually effective control over all areas of church life of a papacy equipped with a powerful bureaucracy.[4] It is difficult for Catholics today to realise how rapid and how recent this growth has been.

What we are now witnessing is the beginning of a reversal by Vatican II of these centuries old trends of absorption, both of episcopacy by papacy, and of the Church's ministry by ordained ministers. The Council moved in this direction by the establishment of regional or national Episcopal Conferences and by introducing the concept of collegiality. It also laid the foundation for a subsequent development in Roman documents of a theology of the local Church.[5] We are therefore in the very early stages today of a process of devolution or decentralisation, both in the way the Vatican understands its functions and in theological understanding of the nature of the Church.

A study of the historical growth of the papacy, and the resulting awareness of the intricate relation of this growth to changing cultural and political environments, raise the theological question of what in the papacy is essential to Catholicism and what is changeable and relative to the contemporary needs of the Church. More precisely the question must be posed: What is there about the papacy that could be put forward as a matter of faith?

The difficulties that arise against giving any simple answer to this question come from a number of quarters. In the first place there has been a considerable shift in the understanding of faith itself, and of the correlative concept of revelation.[6] If one may now refer summarily to ground that has often been covered before, it was characteristic of the period of Vatican I that faith was considered to be primarily in doctrinal statements and revelation was correspondingly said to be 'contained in' Scripture, tradition, conciliar definitions, the teaching of the Church. In this perspective

3

it could be envisaged that 'articles of faith' could grow indefinitely, as the Church developed and clarified her system of doctrines. By contrast, it is now commonly recognised that revelation is always, and is only, an act of God communicating himself, and faith is in him: christian faith is a response of the whole man to Christ recognised as the definitive self-communication of God.[7] The statements of the New Testament and the authoritative statements of the Church are not themselves directly revelation, but a faithful witness to God's personal self-communication, a faithful statement of man's grasp of that communication, i.e. of his faith. We are therefore bound to ask, Can there be a statement about the human structures of the Church, however exalted and essential they are seen to be, which can strictly engage our faith? Faith is in Christ. Faith can only have God as its object, God personally grasped and encountered. Even if there were clear evidence that Jesus gave instructions about the ordering of the Church — and study of the New Testament convinces one that he gave none — could even his instructions on such a matter engage our faith? Only, perhaps, and in so far as, such ordering involved essential ways in which he, the Risen Lord, was present and active in his Church. And even then faith would be in his presence and action, and not in its human embodiment as such.

Vatican I itself insisted, in its discussions and in its formal Constitution on the Catholic Faith, on a distinction between what may be known by natural reason and what can only be grasped by faith. 'There is a twofold order of knowledge, distinct not only in its principle but in its object: in its principle, because in the one we know by natural reason, in the other by divine faith; in its object, because, apart from what natural reason can attain, there are proposed to our belief mysteries that are hidden in God, which can never be known unless they are revealed by God.'[8] The concept of 'natural reason' here used causes difficulties, as it appears to mean 'unaffected by grace' and not simply 'reason unaided by christian revelation', as it does in the famous statement earlier in the document that 'God, the beginning and end of

4

all things, can be known with certainty from the things that were created, through the natural light of human reason'.[9] But the purpose of both conciliar paragraphs is to indicate that it is the mystery of God and of man's destiny revealed in Christ that is the object of faith.

Vatican I left many problems unsolved, notably that of the theological criteria for what can be said to be revelation and what cannot. If it be granted that there is responsibility, and therefore authority, in the Church to define matters of revelation,[10] then the Church must have some way of knowing what is and what is not revelation, before knowing whether it can be defined. The Church cannot simply make matters to be matters of revelation by defining them.[11]

It is clear that, to guard the unity of the Church and the integrity of the Gospel, the Church has found it necessary to formulate binding statements of its central faith, which are not themselves directly the object of that faith. Their exact status has been under much discussion, notably in England with the Report of the Doctrine Commission of the Church of England.[12] A further question arises over doctrinal statements about matters that are seen to be intimately connected with the central realities of faith and belong to the category of mystery, but are derivative and are not themselves the centre: one might instance angels, purgatory, the role and privileges of Mary. But yet another problem arises with doctrinal statements about matters like the Church's ministry which may be essential to the Church's task of preaching the Gospel, but are not themselves about the Gospel: they are further removed from being the object of faith. The point can be made by saying that the structures of the Church are not part of the Gospel.[13] The ministry of the Church exists to serve Christ, not to take his place. The authoritative organs of the Church exist to serve the voice and the lordship of Christ: they are not his voice and his lordship. The responsibilities of leaders in the Church are serious responsibilities, but they are the human responsibilities of Christians: they belong, not to the Gospel, but to the Church's obedience to the Gospel.

5

Questions about the papacy need to be seen and to be treated within this broader perspective of the Church's ministry. It is a matter of faith that Christ's ministry has been, is being, and always will be exercised in the Church. (It must surely be obvious, and indeed a matter of faith, that it is never exercised perfectly.) It must, however, be questioned whether any particular ways in which it is exercised can themselves be objects of faith. That they mediate Christ's ministry is what engages our faith; but they cannot in their own historical and changing forms themselves be absolute. In treating Order as a sacrament Catholic tradition has seen ordained ministers as effective signs of Christ's ministry: this does not imply that any particular form of the sign is either perfect as sign or fully effective; but it does make clear that it is not the sign as such, but that of which it is a sign, which is the object of faith. A serious belief in the Incarnation, as the revelation of God's involvement in our human history, does not exclude, but rather implies, the realisation that God is present and active in our human reality precisely as in that which is changeable and transitory. The quasi-platonic views of Incarnation to be found in some patristic writings, according to which the Word assumed some timeless and perfect Form of human nature, fall short of that true christian belief that the Word became flesh precisely in order to gather this earthly reality into his kingdom.

To say that structures of the Church's ministry are not matters of faith is not to say that they have little value or importance. It is surely right to see in the emergence and long persistence, first of episcopacy, then of papacy, the guidance of the Holy Spirit for the Church's life and the fulfilment of her mission. The theological values of these structures have been a matter of christian experience for centuries, and have often been spelled out. But two qualifications are needed. The emergence of particular structures and the varying manner of their functioning attest not only the guidance and faithfulness of God's Spirit; they also attest the all too human limitations of man. For instance, the authority that derives from christian responsibility is all too easily confused with the merely human possession and use of power. And, secondly, if the Spirit can lead the Church into certain structures relevant to the conditions of culture in which it exists, the same Spirit can thereafter lead the Church to modify its forms of ministry in later and other historical circumstances. Not only are the forms of the Church's ministry not themselves objects of faith; it is hard to see how they can become theologically absolute on the basis of christian experience. The only theological absolute that could be formulated would be the obligation of the Church at all times so to shape her ministry, in the light of Scripture and christian experience (tradition), as to enable her best to fulfil the mission entrusted to her by Christ.

It has been characteristic of Roman Catholic theology to see the existence of the papacy and some details of its authority as theologically absolute because based on the direct institution of Christ. (It has similarly been characteristic of some Protestant theology to see other patterns of ministry as mandatory on New Testament evidence.) The concept of *ius divinum* came to be used to convey this notion of something the Church cannot change because it is a matter of God's law (Christ's personal instructions interpreted in the apostolic age under the guidance of the Spirit) and not of ecclesiastical law.[14] This notion antedates modern biblical and historical studies and needs to be reconsidered in their light. The origins of episcopacy have often been studied in recent times and there is now agreement that there was no general pattern of mon-episcopacy in the first century. It had taken firm shape in the Antioch of Ignatius early in the second century, but there is not sufficient evidence for us to know when it became universal. (It is not certain that there was a Bishop of Rome before the second century.) These facts alone show that the first generation of Christians, to whose understanding the New Testament bears witness, did not themselves think that Jesus had given his followers any instructions about the christian communities being led by bishops as 'successors of the apostles'. Or, to broaden the

idea of institution by Christ, it is clear that the first generations of Christians were not guided by the Spirit to understand any received sayings or doings of Jesus in this way.
The matter would not even be relevant to a primitive Church
eagerly expecting the Second Coming in the near future.
Further, the very complexity of ministries attested in the
New Testament makes it clear that there was no awareness
of any instructions from Christ about the ordering of the
Church's ministry. The eventual patterns emerged slowly,
possibly on Jewish models, precisely as an adjustment to the
developing historical (social, political, cultural) conditions
in which the Churches found themselves.

Of particular interest, as far as the papacy is concerned,
have been the studies of the Lutheran-Roman Catholic
dialogue in America.[15] The central insight of these studies
is that the New Testament itself shows that the image of
Peter grows in the early Church after his death, as do the
images of other historical figures, notably Paul, John and
Mary. One is able to see a projection, or trajectory, of these
figures as the reflection and experience of Christians came to
regard the historical persons as symbols of elements inherent
in the Church itself. In the case of Peter this insight is
founded on such factors as Matthew's addition in chapter 16
of elements of post-resurrection experience to the Marcan
account of Peter's profession of faith at Caesarea Philippi;
the figure of Peter as it appears in the Fourth Gospel (in-
terestingly intersecting with the trajectory of John); the
writing of letters by later Christians under the name of
Peter, something paralleled in the case of Paul. But the idea
of a 'trajectory' implies that the trajectory can continue.
It does not lead to any set constitutional pattern, or justify
the fixation of the petrine office at any point in its history in
terms of a definitive set of rights, privileges, functions. It does
not provide a basis for a *lex fundamentalis ecclesiae* of the
papacy. It implies, rather, that the idea of primacy can be
variously fulfilled according to christian insights and needs
in varying historical conditions. In this perspective the
concept of *ius divinum* must cease to be operative, at least in

its traditional and more obvious sense. It could, however, be argued that some notion of a petrine office has been integral to the Church's self-understanding almost from the first, and is attested in Scripture as the Spirit's guidance for the Church.

The main purpose of these reflections has been to suggest that there is need of a distinction, drawn as firmly as it is possible to do so, between matters of faith and matters of deep christian conviction; between what of their nature can be matters engaging christian faith, and what of their nature cannot, though they are susceptible of solid theological argument. But such matters must remain open to discussion and can only be accepted on the strength of the theological considerations adduced for them. Without such a distinction Catholics will be claiming too much, with the inevitable result that too little will then be conceded by those whose christian tradition and experience makes it impossible for them to accept a Catholic conviction as a matter of divine revelation commanding the assent of faith.

The Anglican-Roman Catholic statement on Authority concedes (n. 12), with what may be thought to be a measure of urbane understatement, that: 'Sometimes functions assumed by the see of Rome were not necessarily linked to the primacy: sometimes the conduct of the occupant of this see has been unworthy of his office: sometimes the image of this office has been obscured by interpretations placed upon it: and sometimes external pressures have made its proper exercise almost impossible. Yet the primacy, rightly understood, implies that the bishop of Rome exercises his oversight in order to guard and promote the faithfulness of all the churches to Christ and one another. Communion with him is intended as a safeguard of the catholicity of each local church, and as a sign of the communion of all the churches.' Without being insensitive to the facts of history, Catholics can nevertheless commend the papacy with deep conviction as the visible and effective sign (the sacrament, in the broader sense of the term) of the unity and universality of the Church. The strongest arguments for episcopacy are that the

communion of bishops has in fact served the unity of the
Church in faith and mission throughout many centuries of
threats to that unity; and that the single episcopal figure
more readily and effectively represents to the local community the lordship of Christ and his continuing care for his flock
than any synodal body can do, notably when he celebrates
that lordship and that care in the Eucharist. The same arguments apply to the papacy. It has served the unity of the
Church in faith and mission, even if not perfectly; and at
various levels christian communities have experienced the
need for a primatial figure to be the centre of their world-
wide communion. The more weight one gives to a eucharistic
ecclesiology, the more necessary it seems that there should
be a president of the Eucharist of the universal Church, to be
not only a mere symbol but an effective sign of that unity of
the Church which Christ instituted the Eucharist to celebrate, to preserve and to deepen.

But the ways in which the papacy can effectively fulfil this
role remain open to christian insight in the changing conditions of history — a christian insight that needs to be guided
by the essential God-given qualities of christian life, and to
detach itself as wholly as possible from the particular human
and historical embodiments in which the ideal has found
expression in the past. Human expression in concrete historical circumstances is a necessity for all christian ideals; it is
an outworking of the Incarnation with its inbuilt scandal of
particularity. It is always inadequate, it is always a threat
to the very ideals it embodies; but God works and triumphs
in and through the human limitations.

The ways, therefore, in which the idea and ideal of papacy
or petrine office have found expression in the past can and
must be open to honest and critical assessment. In particular,
Catholic theologians today are seriously questioning the
application of the concept of jurisdiction to Church ministry.
It was the growth of ecclesiastical business and the growth of
the Church's involvement in civil affairs in the middle ages
that led to the distinction being made between *potestas
ordinis* and *potestas iurisdictionis*. The concept of episcopal and

papal jurisdiction over the Church (and even over all human
society) developed in the context of conflicts between ecclesiastical and civil authority, in order to preserve the independence of the Church. Once in use, it gained its own
momentum for internal use as a theory of the relationships
between bishops and people, and then of that between
bishops and pope. After the Reformation it came to be
applied to papal and episcopal authority in teaching within
the Church, partly perhaps because the old conflicts between
sacerdotium and *imperium* had lost much of their relevance.[16]
Clearly, in the exercise of oversight there must be authority
somewhere in the Church to regulate various matters,
whether exercised by episcopal persons or synodal bodies or a
combination of the two. But the weaknesses of the distinction
in such a context between *ordo* and *iurisdictio* are twofold.
Firstly, it implies that there must be some authority in the
Church in addition to and other than that stemming from
the sacramental nature of the Church and of its ministries.
And, secondly, once given an independent existence of its
own, the concept of jurisdiction grows independently and
leads increasingly to thinking of the Church and ordering its
life in legalistic terms and in terms of power. Though
political analogies may have their place in thinking about the
Church, such thought models cannot be applied literally to
what is, certainly, a human society but is never merely a
human society. The sacramental thought model, as a theological one, is the only apposite category of thought and
must remain predominant.

To free our understanding of the papacy from the essentially transitory categories in which it has found expression
in the past is to free it for its future. That future is one which
the Church is free to construct, indeed is called on by Christ's
will for unity to construct, in obedience solely to the Gospel.

NOTES

1 *Authority in the Church: a statement on the question of authority, its nature, exercise and implications*, jointly published by the C.T.S. and the S.P.C.K. (an ecumenical landmark in itself!), 1976.

2 For this pattern see the most recent and comprehensive survey: Bernard Cooke, *Ministry to Word and Sacraments*, Philadelphia, Fortress Press, 1976.

3 So Bernard Cooke, op. cit., p. 505, referring to R. Greaves, *New Cambridge Modern History*, Cambridge, 1961, Vol. 7, pp. 113–22.

4 See Cooke, op. cit., p. 504. For the casual and largely unwanted growth of papal control of episcopal appointments see the essay in this volume by G. D. Sweeney, *The Wound in the Right Foot: Unhealed?*

5 'A diocese . . . constitutes a particular Church, in which is truly present and operative the One, Holy, Catholic and Apostolic Church of Christ' (Vatican II, *Decree of Bishops*, n. 11.) This line of thinking is developed in the Unity Secretariat's *Ecumenical Collaboration at the Regional National and Local Levels* (1975), chap. 2; and in Paul VI, *Evangelii Nuntiandi*, 1975, nn. 62–65.

6 See J. Coventry, *The Theology of Faith*, Mercier Press, 1968; Paul Surlis (ed.), *Faith: its Nature and Meaning*, Gill and Macmillan, 1970.

7 See Vatican II, *Constitution on Divine Revelation*, especially n. 5; and G. O'Collins, *Theology and Revelation*, Mercier Press, 1968.

8 Denzinger-Schoenmetzer, *Enchiridion Symbolorum*, (DS) 3015.

9 DS. 3004.

10 DS. 3011.

11 Cf J. Coventry, *Christian Truth*, Darton Longman & Todd, 1975, pp. 84–85.

12 *Christian Believing*, S.P.C.K., 1976.

13 See Robert Murray, S. J., quoted below by G. D. Sweeney in his essay, *The Primacy: the small print of Vatican I*.

14 The phrase *ius divinum* is so interpreted by Vatican I in its canon on the primacy, DS. 3058.

15 R. Brown and others, *Peter in the New Testament*, Chapman, 1974. This is summarised in R. Brown, *Crises Facing the Church*, Darton Longman & Todd, 1975, chapter 4.

16 See Cooke, op. cit., pp. 88, 449–50, 486–87.

PART I

Newman's attitude to ultramontanism and liberal Catholicism on the eve of the first Vatican Council

J. Derek Holmes

THE movement of Liberal Catholicism, in so far as it was a movement, largely depended on local factors as well as on the situation in the Church at large. French Liberal Catholics were mostly concerned with political developments and the Church's response to the revolutionary principles of 1789. Liberal Catholics in Germany were not uninterested in problems of Church and State, but were more concerned with the need to reconcile traditional teaching with recent findings of scientific and historical research, and the defence of academic freedom. The *Risorgimento* became the crucial issue in Italy where the territorial possessions of the pope prevented the unification of the country. Originally, Liberal Catholics were also ultramontane supporters of papal supremacy, but the 'liberal' and the 'papal' elements of the Catholic revival later diverged on both the political and intellectual levels. In Italy, it became clear that the pope could not support the advent of democracy or the unification of the nation without jeopardising his own secular authority and the papacy eventually not only refused to distinguish spiritual and temporal authority, but even used the former to defend the latter. In due course, the temporal power of the pope became the test of political conservatism and reaction both outside as well as inside the Church.

The Ultramontanes increasingly emphasised the necessity of dependence on the Holy See and manifested a strong personal devotion to the Holy Father, seeking his guidance in practically every sphere of human activity on almost any possible occasion. An antithesis between liberalism and ultramontanism replaced the earlier contrast between the freedom of ultramontanism and the erastianism which gallicanism had frequently involved. As a result, German Liberal Catholics ceased to be ultramontane, while French Ultramontanes ceased to be liberal; ultramontanism became clerical and anti-democratic rather than popular and anti-gallican.

Liberal Catholics in England had originally hoped to improve the social position and intellectual quality of their fellow Catholics, though most of their bishops and co-religionists became more concerned with threats to the papacy abroad or administrative problems and public relations at home. The attempt to prevent the social or intellectual isolation of English Catholics or a divorce between Catholicism and educated opinion was closely associated with controversies over the provision of higher education for Catholics and the publication of *The Rambler*, the most important English Catholic review to appear during the nineteenth century. But these particular issues must also be seen in the context of the widening divisions between Liberal and Ultramontane Catholics.

As English Ultramontanes such as H. E. Manning, F. W. Faber and W. G. Ward became more extravagant in devotion and unquestioning in belief and obedience, *The Rambler* reacted by becoming more aggressive and was involved in a series of conflicts with the bishops on education and the state of English Catholicism as well as on theological questions such as original sin. John Henry Newman, the leading convert from the Oxford Movement, was the symbol of the hopes of English Liberal Catholics. He had already shown his awareness of the need for higher education and academic freedom, and had himself described the important role which educated laymen might play in the life of the

Church. Convinced that *The Rambler* was too valuable to be lost by conflicting with ecclesiastical authority, Newman devoted himself to the task of preventing a final break when the magazine became involved for a third time in a controversy with the bishops over the control of Catholic education. In an effort to save the magazine, Newman became editor and thereby provided, according to the historian of the English Liberal Catholic Movement, the last opportunity of preventing a final break between Liberal and Ultramontane English Catholics.[1]

In submitting to the bishops' decision on the controversy over education, Newman argued that their pastorals did not contain any particular reference to *The Rambler* and that the author of the article in question had not opposed their decision since this was not known when he originally wrote on the subject. However, Newman went even further and pleaded for greater consideration to be given to lay opinion on the grounds that the faithful were consulted even in the preparation of dogmatic definitions. This statement was challenged and in his second and last issue as editor, Newman published his famous article 'On Consulting the Faithful in Matters of Doctrine'. He pointed out in his discussion of the role of the laity in preserving dogmatic truth that, following the Council of Nicaea, the laity had defended the orthodox tradition, whereas the bishops had tolerated Arianism. The content of this article did not appeal to the Ultramontanes, but the conscious and explicit recognition of the theological significance of history was equally important since the Ultramontanes tended to be unhistorical in their understanding of theology. An English bishop informed the Roman authorities of the content of Newman's article. They in turn demanded an explanation from Newman and although Newman himself was reassured by Manning, his reply was never actually received in Rome. As a result, Newman remained under suspicion until 1867 when he first heard that his letter to Cardinal Wiseman had not been forwarded to the Roman authorities.[2]

Meanwhile, Newman resigned as editor of *The Rambler*.

He continued to sympathise with the views expressed in the magazine, but not with the editors' tone and several events increased the division between Newman on the one side and Sir John Acton and Richard Simpson on the other before events finally came to a head over the issue of the temporal power. In general, Newman wanted *The Rambler* to become more political and to avoid theological discussions which might occasion the intervention of ecclesiastical authority. This advice, however, was difficult to follow at a time when the pope and the Ultramontanes were deliberately confusing the theological with the political, as the attitude of a Catholic to the temporal power of the pope became the touchstone of loyalty and orthodoxy on other issues.

The Roman Question united the majority of Catholics who increasingly adopted an attitude of fundamental opposition to the 'liberalism' of the age. English Catholics in common with Catholics throughout the world became emotionally involved in the trials and sufferings of the pope and their devotion to him was manifested in trivial as well as in more extreme ways. Roman customs were introduced and became increasingly popular. English priests began to use Roman vestments or the buckled shoes and knee-breeches of Roman ecclesiastics as signs of the true Roman spirit. Every papal word or phrase became important and addresses were sent to him by every type of group on every possible occasion. It became customary to drink the health of the pope at Catholic gatherings, while pilgrims to Rome treasured his slippers or pieces of his cassocks which were brought home as relics.

Newman was the most famous English Catholic who eventually refused to support the cause of the temporal power. He suspected privately that the temporal power had an adverse effect on the spiritual life of the Church and in 1860, Newman was even more opposed to the temporal power than Acton himself who still believed that territorial sovereignty was necessary for the freedom and independence of the Church. In fact, Acton later expressed the opinion that it was 'Newman's influence made the Rambler anti-

Roman.'³ The temporal power was the issue on which
English Catholics finally divided.

In his work on Edmund Campion, Simpson offended
many Catholics by condemning the popes, especially Pius V,
for encroaching on English political rights and exposing
English Catholics to the hostility of their fellow countrymen.
This was not unreasonably interpreted as a veiled allusion to
Pio Nono's defence of the temporal power. In 1861, *The
Rambler* came out in support of Ignaz Döllinger's opinion
that although the temporal power might be legitimate and
useful, it was not essential for the Church which might even
be strengthened by its loss. Before the end of the year, the
Roman authorities issued a most critical rescript and the
Catholic publisher refused to produce the next number unless
it was issued under Manning's control. Acton's suggestion
that Newman might resume the editorship was rejected on
the grounds that he was so unpopular with the Ultramontanes that he would jeopardise the magazine's chances of
success. Consequently, the editors were forced to employ a
Protestant publisher and *The Rambler* became *The Home and
Foreign Review*, though policy and personnel remained the
same. A circular letter was then sent from the Prefect of
Propaganda to the English bishops who were required to
issue the pastoral letters within three months warning the
faithful against the review. All the English bishops except
one issued the letters strongly disapproving of *The Rambler*
and its successor. *The Home and Foreign*, therefore, ceased to
be a representative organ of English Catholicism and its
financial position was already critical as a result of falling
circulation when the editors finally decided to cease publication on account of events abroad.

In 1863, the Roman authorities criticised Charles de
Montalembert's two famous speeches at the international
congress of Malines in which he had urged Catholics to
accept the principles of liberal democracy and religious
toleration. Later in the same year, a papal brief to the Archbishop of Munich implicitly condemned Döllinger's speech
at the Munich Congress. This brief was not an infallible

statement, its language was vague and ill-defined, but the intention was clear and the censures capable of extending to *The Home and Foreign Review* which had endorsed Döllinger's views.[4] Acton believed that the Munich Congress had been a serious attempt to deal with contemporary intellectual difficulties, while recognising the significance of ecclesiastical doctrine and authority. *The Munich Brief*, however, insisted that scholarly research should be conducted with respect and deference to ecclesiastical authority. Catholic thought should be guided by the ordinary *magisterium* of the Church and the teaching of theologians as well as dogmatic definitions. The brief implied that Catholic scholars must respect the decisions of the Roman Congregations, including the decrees of the Index, together with contemporary theological opinions acceptable to the bishops.

Acton's decision to end *The Home and Foreign Review* effectively ended the English Liberal Catholic 'Movement' as such; English Liberal Catholics from then on could only act as individuals. Newman for his part had become increasingly critical of ultramontanism and modified his earlier enthusiastic opinions about the Holy See as a result of recent events and his own personal history. Newman had previously believed that the popes enjoyed 'a gift of sagacity' in practical affairs as well as infallibility in doctrinal questions. History seemed to show that papal policies had been expedient for the Church at particular times, but this impression 'has been very considerably weakened as far as the present Pope is concerned'.[5] By 1863, Newman claimed that English Catholics were under the 'arbitrary, military power' of Propaganda which acted like a man of business with a civil service. Its attitude made any attempt to solve contemporary problems like fighting under the lash or with a chain on the arm. Later, Newman expressed his fears that ultramontane attitudes might not only lead to hasty, inadequate or even ignorant ecclesiastical decisions, but have a narrowing or restricting effect on the Church itself which he described as a sort of Novatianism.

Immediately after Newman's conversion in 1845, his

views on the papacy were clearly ultramontane, and not simply because of the climate of opinion in the Catholic Church, but as a result of his own apologetic approach. Newman believed that the task of the Christian apologist was to approach the evidence in favour of the Church as a whole without becoming involved in specific points at issue. Once a particular Christian community had been identified with that of the early Church, the teaching of that Church had to be accepted as a necessary consequence.

> 'I have made the Papacy a *doctrine*, which may fairly be taken on faith without a bit of evidence in its favour, on the *Church's warrant*, supposing there be no great antecedent objection to it, and no facts clearly irreconcilable with it — or, which is rather the state of the case, supposing there is much for it, and some things apparently against it — whereas Allies, I believe, takes it as a primary and elementary point, to be proved simply by historical evidence in order to the determination *which* is the Church. This is just the reverse to my mode of reasoning in my book.'[6]

A few weeks earlier, Newman had made a few notes before reading Allies' work. These notes centred on two main points — whether the development of the papal system from the patriarchal system was a greater development than that of the Athanasian from the Apostles Creed and secondly since the earlier was interpreted by the later in the case of the doctrine of the Trinity, why this should not also be done in the case of the papacy. Newman felt that Allies failed to appreciate the main argument of *The Essay on Development*,

> 'that there was one organized integral body or Church in the beginning, and that it has gone on to this time by a continuous tradition of life, and that the Roman communion and none other is it; that there is an unbroken connexion between the present Roman Church and the primitive — so that the present Roman may be accounted its legitimate heir and representative".[7]

On the 21 May 1847, Newman wrote a series of notes 'for (R. A.) Coffin' arguing that the papacy was the episcopate, for there was but one episcopate in the Church, and that the papacy was essentially a matter of jurisdiction and not of order or priesthood. The episcopate, primacy, monarchy and papacy belonged to St. Peter and came to the pope as a result of the fact that he was bishop of Rome. The notes 'for Coffin' use the same arguments which are to be found in much more detail in other later notes which Newman prepared for his lectures on the Church and the Pope.[8] These notes illustrate Newman's familiarity with classical Catholic theologians and his arguments tended to be almost exclusively ultramontane. Newman defended the monarchical government of the Church on the grounds that monarchy was the best form of government. He refused to make any distinction between the essential and accidental rights of primacy; primacy either meant a great deal more or a great deal less than Gallicans would admit and Gallicans could not escape becoming Ultramontanes except by becoming Protestants. Newman argued that the pope, unlike bishops, had universal jurisdiction because bishops were generic successors of the apostles as a whole, whereas the pope was the specific successor of St. Peter, and because the universal jurisdiction of the apostles was extraordinary and not transmitted, whereas St. Peter's jurisdiction was ordinary and transmitted. Newman maintained that the pope was above a general council as a bishop was above his diocesan synod and that in times of schism, general councils did not have jurisdiction over rival popes, but merely the power of declaring which was the true pope and the duty of promoting reconciliation.

Newman was less explicitly ultramontane in his discussion of papal infallibility, though he argued that infallible authority was a necessary consequence of the pope's responsibility to preserve the unity of faith and communion. Newman naturally rejected the opinion of Jean Gerson that the pope could teach heresy if he attempted to define doctrine apart from a general council, but he did admit that the pope

even with a general council might err in questions of fact
depending on testimony, or even make a mistake in matters
of faith and morals when teaching as a private theologian.
On the other hand, the pope could not err when dealing
with faith and morals in general council and he should be
obeyed in doubtful cases when he was acting alone or with a
particular council.

In 1864, as a result of the success of *The Apologia* in the
controversy with Charles Kingsley, Newman secured the
sympathetic attention of the English nation. Acton urged
him to take this opportunity to defend the Church as a
whole as well as his own honesty, especially in the light of
recent events involving *The Home and Foreign* and *The
Munich Brief* which as Newman himself had claimed, 'tied
his hands' as an apologist.[9] The defence of the Catholic
system with the discussion on ecclesiastical infallibility and
intellectual freedom in the last chapter of the *Apologia* was an
implicit attack on the Ultramontanes; so also was the criticism of foreign devotions as unsuitable for England as well
as the praise and sympathy for the Church of England and
things English which Newman's work revealed. Newman
affirmed his own loyalty and accepted the doctrine of infallibility, but pointed to its negative and limited nature, and
condemned the violent party which would turn opinions into
dogmas and destroy every school of thought but its own.
Newman defended the value and necessity of academic freedom and independent speculation, and explained that the
purpose of infallibility was to prevent members of the Church
from going to extremes, not to reduce the freedom and
vigour of human thought. In the event, Newman argued,
there would be few infallible pronouncements which would
be limited to faith and morals, statements of existing beliefs,
and only made after long investigation into the actual
beliefs of Catholics.

The reactions of the English Ultramontanes to the
Apologia revealed the extent of their hostility to Newman and
attempts were made to criticise his work in Rome. Manning
complained that Anglicans regarded the *Apologia* 'as a plea

for remaining as they are'; Herbert Vaughan found 'views put forward which I abhor, and which fill me with pain and suspicion', while Coffin apparently maintained that all Newman's Catholic writings should be put on the index.[10] On the other hand, H. J. Coleridge, the future editor of *The Month*, believed that Newman was 'perfectly and exactly right,' and suspecting that W. G. Ward was preparing a counter-attack, Coleridge remarked,

'It seems to me that there is a danger of the Dublin's being made the vehicle of its editors' idiosyncracies . . . I have the most profound distrust of Mr Ward as a theologian, — a distrust I believe very widely spread indeed. I would never let him touch a theological subject if I could — but at all events, it is important that he should be checked in his desire to pitch into others, especially such a man as Dr. Newman — who can make an example of him as he did of Kingsley if he chooses. It is a great misfortune that the theology of the Dublin should be in his hands.'[11]

Coleridge was responsible for the review of reviews which appeared in *The Dublin Review* and he wanted to devote the whole section of the January issue to a defence of Newman and a refutation of misrepresentations of the *Apologia*. Ward and Manning, however, were opposed to the idea and in December 1864 the sub-editor, who had supported Coleridge, resigned in protest. Aubrey de Vere wrote,

'I need not say how sorry I was to hear that the Dublin Review is taking such an extraordinary course as that of refusing to allow Dr. Newman a defence against misrepresentation. I should have thought any Catholic writer of eminence might have looked for such an opportunity of vindicating himself against erroneous or unjust attacks. As for Dr. Newman, considering him, as I do, not only the greatest man in England, but one to whom Catholicity in England owes more than it has owed to any one else since the days of St. Augustine of Canterbury, it is inconceivable to me that he should be treated at once with such ingratitude and injustice. I do not see how you could do anything but sever your connection with the Review under such circumstances. I certainly could not write for it . . . I am one of that large number who, (humanly speaking) would never have been Catholics, but for Dr. Newman and I should not wish to be connected with anything that treats him with disrespect. We must of course have always different schools of thought among us: but I should have thought that Catholics of all schools would have thought Dr. Newman's reputation to be part of our common possession and joined in any defence of him against misrepresentation.'[12]

In 1865, Newman again publicly criticised English Ultramontanes in his reply to Pusey's *Eirenicon* when he refused to identify their opinions with the teaching of the Catholic Church. In the *Letter to Pusey*, Newman clearly dissociated himself from the theological views of Manning, Faber and Ward particularly on the question of devotion to Our Lady, but also and explicitly on the issue of papal infallibility.[13] Manning was now urged 'as the advocate of Roman views' to fight 'because every Englishman is naturally anti-Roman. To be Roman is to an Englishman an effort. Dr. Newman is more English than the English. His spirit must be crushed.' Manning reported that Newman,

'has become the centre of those who hold low views about the Holy See, are anti-Roman, cold and silent, to say no more, about the Temporal Power, national, English, critical of Catholic devotions . . . I see much danger of an English Catholicism of which Newman is the highest type. It is the old Anglican, patristic, literary, Oxford tone transplanted into the Church. It takes the line of deprecating exaggerations, foreign devotions, Ultramontanism, anti-national sympathies. In one word, it is worldly Catholicism, and it will have the worldly on its side, and will deceive many.'[14]

Ward apparently wrote a reply to Newman's *Letter* on the grounds that it was impossible to ignore the 'slur' which

Newman had cast on foreign Catholics and necessary to correct several anti-Catholic statements in his 'Protestant' letter. However, Bishop W. B. Ullathorne of Birmingham and Bishop William Clifford of Clifton both refused to read Ward's article and their action effectively prevented it from being published. The same two bishops also wrote to defend Newman whose work had occasioned a controversial correspondence in *The Tablet* and *The Weekly Register* where the great majority of correspondents took Newman's side. But this particular controversy was again only one aspect of a more significant controversy which was occasioned by events taking place in the Church at large.

In December 1864, *The Syllabus of Errors* and the encyclical *Quanta Cura* had been sent to bishops throughout the world. The last document would probably have been given a hostile reception, but would not have caused a sensation. It condemned most of the teaching condemned in *The Syllabus*, but in more obscure, moderate and conventional language. *The Syllabus*, on the other hand, was an index of condemnations torn from their contexts and, simply referring to the relevant documents, listed those dangerous and perverse ideas which were considered to conflict with Catholic doctrine. Earlier ecclesiastical decisions such as the criticisms of Montalembert and Döllinger had prepared the way for *The Syllabus* which was regarded throughout Europe as a quixotic attempt to defend the temporal power and the old order, and it provided the secular press with further opportunities of abusing and ridiculing Catholicism. The method of promulgating the document as well as its content was a further victory for the Ultramontanes who were lavish in their praise and another defeat for Liberal Catholics who were embittered or alienated, diverted into safer fields of activity or occasionally driven out of the Church altogether.

Those who would defend Pius IX have pointed out that *The Syllabus* was obviously a technical document, enumerating previous condemnations to be understood in their original contexts, and that it should have been interpreted theologically rather than discussed as the subject of a public debate.

However, the pope himself used harsh and categorical language, and adopted a form which was unsuitable for discussing, let alone condemning, 'errors' of such gravity. Furthermore, if the positive teaching of *The Syllabus* was difficult to determine, its context was hardly known outside Italy. Yet although the Italian situation occasioned *The Syllabus* which had specific reference to Italy, publication was not restricted to Italy, so it is hardly surprising that the hostile reaction was also universal. Bishop Félix Dupanloup's interpretation of it distinguishing between thesis and hypothesis, the ideal and the possible, was therefore welcomed with a profound and widespread sense of relief by Catholics throughout the world, though neither the pope nor the Ultramontanes seem to have been satisfied with the bishop's explanation that ideal claims rather than practical policies were being condemned. Both contemporary and later interpretations of the Dupanloup type do seem to have obscured the original aims and intentions of the pope who could at any time simply have pointed out that he had been misunderstood.

The immediate English reaction to *The Syllabus* is to be found in the newspapers and only one reaction was to be expected from the non-Catholic press. The intensity of hostility might vary, the criticism in some might be more objective than the offensive sarcasm of others, but all the newspapers agreed that the encyclical was among the most unreasonable fabrications that the Holy See had attempted to foist on an astonished world during the nineteen hundred years of its existence. Catholic publications were unable to answer this barrage of criticism because they appeared less frequently and even when they did appear they simply greeted the papal statements with extravagant praise without attempting to interpret them within the English context. William Monsell told Newman that the Catholic press apparently believed that eighty new propositions had been added to the Creed. *The Dublin Review* maintained that the doctrinal declarations of the encyclical 'possess absolute infallibility',[15] while *The Tablet's* Roman correspondent claimed that the Holy See was now committed to the principles of legitimate sovereignty. Of course, the papal condemnations of 'liberalism' were also used as another weapon against the Liberal Catholics. It is therefore hardly surprising that the dogmatic significance of *The Syllabus* should have become such a crucial question between 1864 and 1870. And it was at this time, between 1865 and 1867, that Newman wrote a series of 'Notes in preparation of my proposed Second Pamphlet to PUSEY on the Pope's Powers which was superseded by Ignatius's Pamphlets to Ward'.[16]

Almost at the same time that Newman published his *Letter to Pusey*, W. G. Ward published his *Authority of Doctrinal Decisions* (1866) which proposed to extend papal infallibility to most doctrinal instructions in the pope's official public letters and even private letters intended for general guidance. Incidental statements were not infallible, though minor censures were. Even Monsignor George Talbot, the pope's secretary, thought that Ward might have gone too far, though he maintained that this was unimportant on the grounds that it was safer to believe too much than too little and impossible to be mistaken in always following the guidance of the Holy See;

> 'No one better than I can know the care with which all the Pope's Encyclicals and Allocutions are prepared, and as the Pope is no great theologian himself, I feel convinced that when he writes them he is inspired by God. As for myself, I have always read them on my knees and do all I can to assent internally with every word contained in them.'[17]

Henry Ignatius Ryder, a priest of the Birmingham Oratory and Manning's nephew, challenged Ward's opinions. Ward argued that any form of doctrinal instruction must be accepted as infallibly true under pain of mortal sin. Ryder maintained that doctrinal instructions only obliged in virtue of *pietas fidei* and must be directly or conclusively shown to be infallible in each individual case; they demanded obedience or assent, but were not necessarily infallible or binding under mortal sin. According to Ward, the teaching of *The Syllabus* and its infallibility must be accepted under pain of mortal sin. According to Ryder, Catholics must accept *The Syllabus*, but its infallibility could only be probable, at most. Although Ward never changed his personal belief in the infallibility of *The Syllabus*, he eventually admitted the possibility of another interpretation, and McElrath has argued that, in the last analysis, Ward's habit of imposing obligations where none certainly existed was perhaps the crucial point in the controversy, rather than *The Syllabus* itself.[18]

In 1867, Manning himself declared that *The Syllabus* and *Quanta cura* were among the greatest acts of Pio Nono's pontificate and part of the supreme and infallible teaching of the Church. The Jesuit theologian, Father Paul Bottalla, went even further, maintaining that the encyclical *Mirari vos* which condemned liberal democracy in 1832 as well as *Quanta cura* were 'evidently utterances *ex cathedra*'.[19] But not all English priests and Jesuits supported Ward and his allies. Coleridge, for example, complained about the way in which Ward wrote, but more particularly of the fact that he had never been taught and never really studied theology;

'He is a self educated man — and all self educated men, as a rule, are wanting in balance, adjustment, tact, discernment of "perspective" as it were — much more in theology. My impression of him is not my own, it was taught me at Rome. Dr. Manning asked me (in 1854 I think), as he was leaving for England, to take round to some Roman theologians Ward's tract on the Sins of the Obdurate. It was most amusing to see how they treated it. The 'red-tape' theologians as it were, would not read beyond the first page or two. There are some *sproposito* at every line. Three or four of our own best theologians, such as Passaglia and (?) read it carefully through, and gave a clear opinion — The authorities were ignorantly and badly selected, and they did not think the *logic* good, the conclusion did not follow from the premises. Now this is just what one might expect in a man who had studied under no guidance but his own, and had never for an hour sat on the benches of a Catholic lecture room as a disciple. It is the same still — when I ask some one of our trained theologians like Fr. Jones or Dr. O'Reilly, they say that it is not theology — it is all distorted and confused. He does more harm to his own side than to that against which he writes. Then, besides, there are of course certain personal characteristics — a great tendency to exaggeration, and an utter inability to understand two sides of a question. In short, is not his mind utterly undisciplined?'[20]

Liberal Catholics like Acton simply rejected *The Syllabus*, Ultramontanes such as Ward proclaimed its infallibility, whereas Newman and Ryder were prepared to submit to *The Syllabus*, but rejected the notion that it was infallible. The two Oratorians adopted very similar attitudes on its content and dogmatic significance and Ryder followed Newman's advice and used the *Apologia* in his controversy with Ward. Ryder himself was responsible for the original idea and the composition of his pamphlet attacking Ward, but Newman first suggested the specific area of attack — how untrustworthy Ward was.[21] Newman's attitude to *The Syllabus* was consistent with his criticisms of Propaganda and *The Munich Brief*, and he was less concerned with the content than with the spirit or methods of the Roman authorities who seemed determined to make the position of English Catholics as difficult as possible. In fact, Newman explained that he did not even understand some of the condemnations since specific censures were not included and undefined terms like 'liberalism', 'progress' and 'recent civilization' were simply the newspaper cant of the day.

The Syllabus was not, of course, an infallible statement and its tone was in some respects even modified by the first Vatican Council. But the close association between *The Syllabus* and the Council of 1870 can be seen in the fact that members of the doctrinal commission preparing for the Council were given various sections of *The Syllabus* to serve as the basis of a report or *votum*. When Vaughan edited *The*

Year of Preparation for the Vatican Council, he reprinted the text of *The Syllabus of Errors* and the encyclical *Quanta cura*. Acton thought that Döllinger would not have had any clear objection to the definition of infallibility, if it had not been for *The Syllabus* and the same would also seem to have been true of himself.

On the eve of the Vatican Council, therefore, Newman found that it was 'not at all easy to break that formidable conspiracy, which is in action against the theological liberty of Catholics'. He condemned the tyranny of the Roman authorities who tried to exclude intellectual or educated Catholics from the Church, to restrict Catholic action to the obsolete and effete, and to create 'a dreadful breach between society and religion'. Furthermore, he wrote,

> 'It is intolerable that we should be placed at the mercy of a secret tribunal, which dares to speak in the name of the Pope, and would institute, if it could, a regime of espionage, denunciation and terrorism . . . the danger is as great as the evil is intolerable.'

Newman compared contemporary Catholic theologians and philosophers to old nurses who smothered children in blankets and closed windows in order to prevent their exposure to fresh air; 'they think they do the free Church of God service, by subjecting her to an etiquette as grievous as that which led to the King of Spain being burned to cinders.'[22]

Although Manning apparently attempted to exclude Newman from the Council, the Pope himself invited the Oratorian to Rome as one of the consultors to the Council. Newman, however, felt that by accepting such an invitation he would lose his independence without gaining anything. Newman was also invited by Bishop Brown of Newport who had previously delated his article on the laity, an event which Newman now used as an excuse for declining. Newman received another invitation from Bishop Clifford and described Bishop Dupanloup's intended invitation conveyed through Montalembert as the act of 'a noble independent Bishop, who dares do what he thinks right.'[23] But it is difficult not to conclude that, in the event, Newman's presence in England where the voice of moderation was seldom heard, would ultimately prove more important than his attendance at a Council where the voices of moderation were so often ignored.

NOTES

1 J. L. Altholz, *The Liberal Catholic Movement in England. The Rambler and its contributors 1848–1864* (London, 1962), pp. 70, 98, 213.

2 C. S. Dessain (Ed.), *The Letters and Diaries of John Henry Newman* (London, 1961–), vol. XIX, pp. 289–90, 333–34; vol. XXIII, pp. xv, 213–14, 226.

3 H. A. MacDougall, *The Acton-Newman Relations. The Dilemma of Christian Liberalism* (New York, 1962), p. 75.

4 See, W. G. Ward, 'Rome and the Munich Congress', *Dublin Review*, vol. III, n.s., (1864), pp. 64–96.

5 *Autobiographical Writings* (London, 1956), p. 320; *Letters and Diaries*, vol. XX, pp. 391, 447; vol. XXII, pp. 314–15; vol. XXIII, pp. 217, 274; vol. XXIV, p. 120; vol. XXVI, p. 27.

6 *Letters and Diaries*, vol. XI, p. 239, see also p. 69; Newman was referring to his own *Essay on Development* and T. W. Allies, *The Church of England cleared from the Charge of Schism* published in 1846.

7 Newman's remarks on 'Allies's Book', 26 June 1846, Birmingham Oratory Archives; I am most grateful to the Fathers of the Oratory for permission to use their archives. Newman wrote another *Memorandum* along the same apologetic lines on 15 July 1846.

8 See, G. Biemer, *Newman on Tradition* (London, 1967), pp. 177–9.

9 W. Ward, *The Life of John Henry Cardinal Newman* (London, 1912), vol. I, p. 585; *Apologia Pro Vita Sua. Edited, with an Introduction and Notes, by Martin J. Svaglic* (Oxford, 1967), pp. 235–6; E. Kelly, 'The Apologia and the Ultramontanes', in V. F. Blehl and F. X. Connolly, (Ed.), *Newman's Apologia: A Classic*, Reconsidered (New York, 1964), pp. 26–46; Altholz, *Liberal Catholic Movement*, pp. 230–1; MacDougall, *Acton-Newman Relations*, pp. 90–3; for Newman's own analysis of *The Munich Brief* see, Ward, *Newman*, vol. I, pp. 640–2 and of the later *Syllabus*, *Certain Difficulties felt by Anglicans in Catholic Teaching* (London, 1907), vol. II, pp. 276–98.

10 E. S. Purcell, *Life of Cardinal Manning Archbishop of Westminster* (London, 1896), vol. II, pp. 323, 326; *Letters and Diaries*, vol. XXII, p. 328; J. G. Snead-Cox, *The Life of Cardinal Vaughan* (London, 1910), vol. I, p. 215; C. Butler, *The Life and Times of Bishop Ullathorne* (London, 1926), vol. II, p. 308.

11 Coleridge to Thompson, 13 October 1864; I am most grateful to the Catholic Record Society for permission to use this correspondence which is now deposited in the Archives of the Archbishop of Westminster.

12 Aubrey de Vere to Thompson, 6 December 1864; another correspondent also commented on the bias of *The Dublin* and its editor in favour of Wiseman and Manning, Teebay to Thompson, January 1865, A.A.W.

13 *Difficulties of Anglicans*, vol. II, pp. 16–17, 21–5, 117; *Letters and Diaries*, vol. XXII, pp. 44–5, 157; Ward, *Newman*, vol. II, pp. 110–12.

14 Purcell, *Manning*, vol. II, pp. 309, 322–3; see also, Butler, Ullathorne, vol. I, pp. 358, 363–8; D. McElrath, *The Syllabus of Pius IX. Some Reactions in England* (Louvain, 1964), p. 147.
15 Quoted by McElrath, *Syllabus*, p. 103; *Letters and Diaries*, vol. XXI, p. 383.
16 Pusey's second letter to Newman on reunion was published in 1870; *Letters and Diaries*, vol. XXV, p. 15.
17 McElrath, *Syllabus*, pp. 135–6.
18 McElrath, *Syllabus*, pp. 152, 330–1; see also, Butler, *Ullathorne*, vol. II, pp. 41–4; Purcell, *Manning*, vol. II, pp. 320, 323, 349, 389.
19 P. Bottalla, *The Pope and the Church* (London, 1870), p. 386; 'The Centenary of St. Peter and the General Council' (London, 1867), p. 38.
20 Coleridge to Ryder, 30 October 1867, Birmingham Oratory Archives.
21 See: *Letters and Diaries*, vol. XXI, pp. 378–9, 385–6, 391–2; vol. XXII, pp. 19–23; vol. XXIII, pp. 227, 233; vol. XXIV, p. 3; *Autobiographical Writings*, pp. 265–7; MacDougall, *Acton-Newman Relations*, pp. 97–8; McElrath, *Syllabus*, pp. 112–13, 127, 138–41, 204–5; Ward, *Newman*, vol. II, p. 241; see also, M. Ward, *The Wilfrid Wards and the Transition* (London, 1934), p. 32, for some of the most offensive attacks on Newman at this time.
22 *Letters and Diaries*, vol. XXIII, pp. 187, 193; vol. XXIV, pp. 248, 316–17.
23 *Letters and Diaries*, vol. XXIII, p. 396; see also, vol. XXIV, pp. 48, 161–2, 361–2, 367–8; vol. XXVIII, p. 439; Purcell, *Manning*, vol. II, pp. 422–3; F. J. Cwiekowski, *The English Bishops and the First Vatican Council* (Louvain, 1971), pp. 72–8, 105–9.

2

The later Acton: the historian as moralist

Hugh MacDougall

MOST commentators on Lord Acton have noted a radical shift in his thinking in the period following Vatican Council I. Up to 1870 he held to the hope that the official church would play a significant role in meeting the challenge to Christian belief posed by the new secular culture that had come to dominate European thought since the end of the eighteenth century. By the mid-1870's it seemed clear to Acton that Rome's response to modern culture was to retreat behind ancient defences that were inadequate to the challenge. Rather than accept change and becoming as the basic reality of history — a fundamental principle informing the modern spirit — official Catholicism chose to remain rooted in old forms and structures fashioned in patristic and medieval times, insisting on their unchanging nature and fixed permanent value.

Acton had returned to England in 1857, after seven years of study in Germany, eager to present to the English Catholic community some of the fruits of continental scholarship. He believed that German scholarship in particular had made significant advances of which English Catholics were only dimly aware. He saw it as his mission to bring them up-to-date.

The 1850's were years of promise for English Catholicism and Acton's enthusiasm ran high. The Catholic population had increased dramatically to some 700,000 as a result of heavy Irish immigration supplemented by converts from the Oxford Movement. The restoration of the English hierarchy in 1850 was Rome's recognition of the new stature of the English Catholic community. Newman gave exquisite expression to the mood of optimism in his famous sermon 'The Second Spring'.

From 1857 to 1864 Acton and Richard Simpson, a brilliant and outspoken convert, supported by an increasingly cautious Newman, strove to establish a strong liberal Catholic movement in England. Its object was to work towards a reconciliation between Catholicism and the best secular thought of the day. Complete freedom of enquiry was claimed as essential if the work was to proceed successfully. In the controversial Catholic review, *The Rambler*, and its scholarly successor, *The Home and Foreign Review*, Acton published articles and reviews on a wide variety of current and historical topics. His aim was to formulate for his readers a Catholic approach to learning and politics. 'Perhaps in no organ of criticism in this country', commented Matthew Arnold on *The Home and Foreign Review*, 'was there so much knowledge, so much play of mind.'[1] Yet, this high-class review received little support. It disturbed too many long-accepted opinions. Many Anglicans considered it an organ of German rationalism. Catholic bishops were terrified by it. Even Newman, who earlier had his own article in *The Rambler*, 'On Consulting the Faithful in Matters of Doctrine', delated to Rome as heretical, grew afraid of contributing to it lest he be thought disloyal to the Church.

Alternating between despondency and occasional enthusiasm Acton and Simpson continued their efforts despite almost constant criticism and no substantial support from any quarter. The early autumn of 1863 was a period of renewed hope. Two important Catholic congresses were held at Malines and Munich. At the Belgium congress Comte de Montalembert eloquently defended toleration and separation of Church and State as the only working principles for Catholic statesmen. In Munich, a group of Catholic scholars, led by Dr. Ignatius von Döllinger, asserted complete freedom of enquiry as a right of Catholic intellectuals and denied the authority of Roman Congregations to control their investigations. Acton reported on both Congresses in *The Home and Foreign Review*. He suggested that a new age was dawning for progressive Catholics. Catholic Europe was at last coming to terms with modern culture!

Acton's period of hope was short-lived, Rome had no intention of embracing modernity. Before 1863 had run its course it indicated that it was completely opposed to liberal Catholic movements of any sort. The havoc caused to the traditional Church establishment in Italy by the *Risorgimento* movement convinced Pio Nono and his advisers that liberalism in any form was a threat to the existence of the Church. Security lay in stressing traditional approaches. Montalembert was pointedly reminded that his notions on toleration and separation of Church and State were identical to those put forth by Lamennais in the 1830's and condemned by Pope Gregory XVI. In a brief addressed to the Archbishop of Munich, the Pope informed German Catholic scholars that they were bound by directives from the Holy See in their theological and philosophical investigations. Finally, in December, the *Syllabus of Errors* appeared. In stark uncompromising terms the principles underlying liberal Catholicism were condemned. To the plain reader it appeared that liberty itself stood proscribed.

Acton saw no alternative to ending *The Home and Foreign Review*. He could not accept the principles dictated by the Papacy and he was not prepared to continue a Catholic review in open opposition to Rome and an insecure English hierarchy. Ironically, at the very time Acton was imposing silence on himself, Newman, in his masterly *Apologia Pro Vita Sua*, was feverishly responding to Kingsley's charge that Catholic clergy were indifferent to truth for its own sake. From 1864 to 1868 Acton undertook an extensive search of European archives for materials on the development of authority in the Church. More and more he moved towards the conclusion that the abuse of arbitrary power was the over-riding evil from which the Catholic Church had to be rescued if it was to be true to its origins.

When it became known that Vatican authorities were contemplating calling a general Church Council to address the many urgent problems confronting the Church, Acton turned to a study of the Council of Trent. Archives in Rome and Vienna were searched for relevant materials. Acton initially viewed the prospect of an Ecumenical Council with optimism. The Church would have its first opportunity since the Reformation 'to reform, remodel, and adapt the work of Trent'.[2] At Trent, he observed, the Church, to protect herself against the reformers, threw herself into the hands of the State. The Inquisition was sharpened. The Index was established to control literature. Absolutism was promoted in Catholic countries and revolution in Protestant ones. The Council of Trent legislated 'for actual war, separation, exclusion, ignorance'.[3] It impressed on the Church the stamp of an intolerant age, and perpetuated by its decrees the spirit of an austere immorality. But the battles of the Reformation were now over. Mixed religions were accepted, toleration was a fact, literature was no longer effectively controlled, freedom of enquiry was assumed as a right by scholars, politics were freed from control by confessional interests. The very things which the Council of Trent opposed were now capable of becoming the allies, 'the unfailing support of the Church.'[4]

By the time the Vatican Council was convened in December, 1869, it was clear that the advocates of liberal reform would have a difficult time. In several important Catholic journals of opinion, including the semi-official *Civiltà Cattolica*, the proposal was advanced that the central authority of the Church should be reaffirmed by defining the infallibility of the Pope as official Catholic doctrine. Acton viewed the proposal with alarm. If acted upon it would put an abrupt end to hopes that a conciliatory approach to modern political and intellectual movements would be promoted by the Council. Acton went to Rome in November, and in the early months of the Council played a prominent role in attempting to rally bishops to oppose a definition of papal infallibility and to support a programme of reform. His detailed reports to Döllinger on the progress of the closed Council sessions were the principal source for the celebrated *Letters from Rome* appearing regularly in the *Augsberg Gazette* under a pseudonym. He continued another correspondence with William Gladstone with the object of gaining political support to pressure Rome against the definition of papal infallibility.

When it became evident that the dominant group at the Council were opposed to any kind of liberal reform Acton left Rome. He was convinced that the opponents to reform had seized on the doctrine of infallibility simply to create a protective shield against the unsettling movements of thought current in the nineteenth century. Reluctant or unable to meet the challenges of a new age they sought security in an absolute final tribunal. They feared particularly the historical tendency to make fluid what was thought to have been settled and re-evaluate what was believed to have been beyond question.

In the years immediately following the Council Acton hoped that those who had stood out for reform might unite into an effective opposition. But one by one the minority bishops submitted to the Vatican decrees. They consoled themselves with conciliatory statements that minimized the significance of the decrees. Acton himself was caught in a highly unsatisfactory personal dilemma. His own historical approach made it increasingly difficult for him to give unqualified adherence to the decrees; yet, he was not prepared to state that he did not accept them. He wrote to Döllinger, who had been excommunicated for refusing assent: 'I should have to see things much more clearly than I do as to give up the Church which it was you that taught me to know and to love in her greatness'.[5]

Acton's final attempt to make a public statement on behalf of Catholicism indicates how torn he was between an instinctual loyalty to the Church and a form of historical thinking which made official statements such as those promulgated by the Vatican Council difficult to accept without tortuous qualification. In November, 1874, William Gladstone resurrected an ancient argument and belatedly attacked the Vatican decrees on the grounds that they made it impossible for a Catholic who followed them to be a loyal subject of the Crown. Acton, in a letter to the *Times*, responded by arguing in effect that all sorts of impossible and immoral things had been decreed by Popes in the past and this had never prevented English Catholics from continuing as loyal citizens. Why then, he could ask, should their loyalty be currently questioned? Acton was perplexed when plain readers interpreted his letter as a rejection of the Vatican decrees. In particular he found it difficult to understand why Catholics should expect of him any presumption in favour of papal acts. As he complained to Newman: 'I sometimes ask myself whether there is not here a point of fundamental difference which makes my efforts vain to understand the position of other Catholics'.[6]

Acton once identified George Eliot's generation as one 'distracted between the intense need of believing and the difficulty of belief'.[7] The characterization might aptly be applied to himself. Emotionally he was deeply attached to traditional forms of worship and modes of religious expression proceeding from a world view that held less and less relevance for him. A private note suggests deep inner tensions: 'a man of original mind, having begun in a religion not his own choice, finds that it is not entirely his own. He annihilates, he leaves out part, he lives in some illusion, for a time — permanently he compromises'.[8]

It seems clear that Acton intellectually came gradually to adopt a secular view of history, i.e., meaning in history is discovered only within the temporal historical process itself, and freedom (autonomy) is man's inalienable birthright. Since to the religious believer God acts in a providential way his activity somehow has to be evidenced in history and thus amenable to rational investigation. The problem of the relationship of God to human history emerged as the central one for Acton as it did for most nineteenth century religious thinkers who seriously addressed the questions raised by German philosophers since the time of Kant. A Newman could partially escape the problem, his theory of development notwithstanding, by turning his back on German idealism altogether. (Why, he once asked, should one read such writers as Fichte, Schelling and Hegel for oneself, 'for notoriously they have come to no conclusion'.) [9]

Acton's growing sense of separation from the traditional Catholic community points to two world views in conflict. The traditional view proceeded from patristic and medieval roots. In this view the ultimate meaning of history was radically non-secular, with fulfilment located beyond historic time. The purpose of Christian asceticism and striving was the acquisition of personal holiness as a condition for eternal salvation. The visible Church was seen as a hierarchically structured organization with an authority and a wisdom proceeding directly to its leaders from a transcendent God. The focus of authority within the Church was the Pope, who, when acting as Christ's vicegerent, was infallible and not subject to human criticism.

The other view, with roots in the Renaissance and the Enlightenment, was essentially modern and anthropocentric. It saw Christian existence as secular, i.e. time-bound, with ultimate meaning and fulfilment located in historic time. God was found at the centre of worldly historic activity rather than in the transcendental reaches of a totally other reality. In this secular view the work of the Christian was to transform historical existence rather than to reflect passively upon it. The final goal was self-realization. To achieve this goal, freedom of determination by one's own mind and will was a necessary condition. To the adherents of this anthropocentric view the approach chosen by Vatican I would be seen as archaic and irrelevant.

For Acton religion remained 'the first of human concerns'.[10] Religion dealt with the relation of God to man in historic time and was thus the basis of all morality, private and public. The purpose of the Incarnation was to make possible the realization of liberty, 'that condition in which men are not prevented by men from obeying their duty to God'.[11] To the true believer God must be seen as pursuing his work among men. To question this was to doubt God's providential rule. Acton's pursuit as an historian was to trace the workings of God in history. He attempted to explain his quest to Döllinger:

> . . . there is a grand unity in the history of ideas; of conscience, of morality, and of the means of securing it. I venture to say that the secret of the philosophy of History lies there: It is the only point of view from which one discovers a constant progress, the only one therefore which justifies the ways of God to man.[12]

Progress became for Acton the law of history. 'My theory,' one of his notes reads, 'is that divine gov.[ernment] is not justified without progress. There is no raison d'etre for the world.'[13] To argue that the ways of God were mysterious and beyond man's ken was to favour infidelity. In surveying the progress of history Acton came to attach enormous significance to the religious developments of the seventeenth and eighteenth centuries, particularly those leading to a more refined notion of conscience. G. P. Gooch hardly exaggerated when he commented, 'He [Acton] boldly declares the emancipation of conscience from authority to be the main content of modern history'.[14]

If history was seen as 'the true demonstration of religion'[15] then the role of the historian took on a sacred character. His work was a moral work. His judgments were moral judgments and had 'as much to do with hopes of heaven as public or private conduct'.[16] The historian was in effect the guardian 'of the conscience of mankind'.[17] The degree of moral asceticism demanded of the historian by Acton is suggested in an elliptical note:

> Life is not worth living if one can do nothing for one's country, for religious truth and the relief of pain. Yet a

historian must be indep.[endent] of his pract.[ical] object.
It takes a very exalted view of history to renounce all that.[18]

To consider the work of the historian as an autonomous
enterprise directed simply towards a rational reconstruction
of the past, a commonly held view, was for Acton a blas-
phemous proposition. History, he once wrote to Bishop
Creighton, must be 'an arbiter of controversy, a guide of the
wanderer, the upholder of that moral standard which the
powers of earth, and religion itself, tend constantly to
depress'.[19] One of his notes reads: 'Let not our religion, our
politics, our philosophy react upon our history, but let
history influence them'.[20] In Acton's mind the essential
duty of the historian was to stand as the moral judge of
mankind.

The late Sir Herbert Butterfield, in one of his earliest —
and one of his wisest — works, *The Whig Interpretation of
History*, devoted a chapter to the question of moral judgments in history. He identified Acton as the one in whom
'the whig historian reached his highest consciousness'.[21] One
sees Butterfield's point but it can be misleading to characterize Acton as fundamentally a whig historian. Acton's highly
moral approach to history was not that of a Macaulay, for
example, who believed he saw all around him concrete
evidence of the cultural superiority of the Anglo-Saxon race
to any that ever the world saw. Acton as early as 1869 had
come to regard historical whiggism as an outdated concept.
'The problems coming now are beyond its reach,' he commented to Richard Simpson.[22] The flaw in Acton's approach
— if it is a flaw — is not that he saw God smiling unduly on
Anglo-Saxons. He was much closer to a Ranke who feared
lest the evidence of history showed no sign of God at all. For
Acton the alternative to accepting some form or theory of
progress was radical unbelief. Only in their painful strugg-
lings towards personal freedom could he detect signs of the
divine spirit at work among men. Acton's continued protest
was that a profoundly religious impulse was so consistently
thwarted by political and religious leaders who were more

concerned with power than liberty. He once observed:

> Long before we reach our own generation, we see that the same issues are always present, that the same fundamental qualities of thought and character are permanently dividing men, that the struggle for concentration of power, and for the limitation and division of power, is the mainspring of history.[23]

Professor Butterfield, in his criticisms of Acton's moral approach, considered the problem of sinfulness as not really a problem for the historian at all. The truth is, he wrote, 'that the historian, whose art is a descriptive one, does not move in this world of moral ideas'.[24] Most working historians would probably support Butterfield's position but it is doubtful if Acton would have been moved by his arguments. To take from the historian his function as moral judge would eliminate, in Acton's view, the most significant element in his work, and society would be the poorer for it. He considered the historian who refused to stand in judgment on the moral rightness or wrongness of historical actions as surrendering to a pragmatism which was threatening the moral basis of civilization.

Acton was particularly alarmed by the pragmatism which marked the development of British politics in recent centuries and he called upon historians to reverse the trend. Since politics was concerned with those arrangements which enabled men to live freely it should be seen as a moral activity: 'Politics as sacred as religion'.[25] But the accepted wisdom argued that the rules of morality applied primarily to private life. 'The great bulk of cultured men in our day,' Acton despondently observed,

> do not believe that politics are a branch of Moral Science. They think that politics teach what is likely to do good or harm, not what is right and wrong, innocent or sinful . . . [They will say] you must do your duty, in private life, and wherever the plain rules of morality or the applicable laws extend, regardless of consequences. But they would not admit a like obligation in politics.[26]

Another of his notes reads: 'The emergencies of practical politics have introduced a false morality, and it is the mission of history to expose it.'[27] Again the historian emerges primarily as a defender of morality.

By 1880 Acton had drifted into isolation from the English Catholic community. There seemed no one who had sympathy for his ethical position. A private note reveals his profound discouragement:

> The probability of doing good by writings so isolated and repulsive . . . is so small that I have no right to sacrifice to it my own tranquillity and my duty of educating my children. My time can be better employed than in waging a hopeless war. And the more my life has been thrown away, the more necessary to turn now and employ better what remains.[28]

Attempting to find a focus for his life he variously raised with Gladstone the possibility of his receiving some kind of a political appointment — a cabinet post, or perhaps a diplomatic assignment. But these aspirations were prompted more by a deep frustration at the core of his life than by any genuine desire to pursue a career in practical politics. Almost as a distraction he threw himself more into English social life. His wide range of acquaintances and broad culture made him a sought after person. He became a well known figure at London clubs — the Athenaeum, Grillions, the Literary Society, the Breakfast Club. Academic recognition in England came to him in 1888 when Cambridge conferred on him an honorary Doctor of Laws, to be followed in the next year by a Doctor of Civil Laws from Oxford. All Souls' granted him an honorary fellowship in 1890.

In 1894 he finally received a public appointment in which he could make use of the vast historical learning he had absorbed. Lord Roseberry, the Prime Minister, nominated him as Regius Professor of Modern History at Cambridge. At last, it seemed, he was located in a congenial environment with work to suit his talents.

Acton's Inaugural Lecture on the Study of History was

delivered in Cambridge on June 11th, 1895. It was an impressive effort, although its dense elliptical style combined with a highly moralistic emphasis must have confounded many of its listeners. Familiar positions emerged: religion is the first of human concerns; progress is a visible sign of Christ's action in history; achieved liberty is the one ethical result demonstrated by advancing civilization; history, as the story of mankind's pursuit of freedom, is the true demonstration of religion; it is incumbent upon the historian to see his role as not only the moral judge of mankind but also as a kind of moral executioner. The historian, he exhorted his audience, must 'suffer no man and no cause to escape the undying penalty which history has the power to inflict on wrong'.[29]

In his Inaugural Lecture, as in so many of his private notes and letters, Acton assigned a prophetic role to the historian — prophetic in the sense of standing in judgment — and it is perhaps as a moral prophet that we can best see him. When gripped by his daemon he is an Amos or a Jeremiah, consumed by moral fervour, passing solemn judgment on an unrepentant and stone-hearted people. His judgments are severe and magisterial for he speaks not out of his own sympathies but for the Lord of history. Like the true prophet he stands in isolation — 'I find that I am alone. I do not see that this is decisive because I cannot obey any conscience but my own.'[30] — for his vantage point is not that of other men. As a prophet his vision embraces a new purified kingdom open to sinful men if they will but repent and change their ways: 'End with the Kingdom of God which is liberty'.[31]

In March, 1896, the Syndics of Cambridge University Press requested him to undertake the direction of a history of the world, a project later limited to a modern history beginning with the Renaissance. He threw himself into the work of selecting and organizing a team of historians to carry out the project. But as the editors of his Cambridge *Lectures* related: 'He was without the driving force needed to keep in line a heterogeneous body of specialists' and before the work

was well under way his health broke down.[32] His editorial
work on top of his normal university duties tasked his ener-
gies to the limit 'and at the last exhausted them.'[33] Only the
first volume of the acclaimed *Cambridge Modern History*
appeared before his death in 1902.

In retrospect it is fitting that the historian of progress
should have ended his career at Cambridge. Denied entry to
Cambridge as a young man on account of his religion, he
came to be remembered as one of its most distinguished professors. Yet one must receive with some reservation the
account of the editors of his *Lectures* on his 'delight at finding
himself a Cambridge man'.[34] It is clear from his private notes
that a nagging sense of isolation continued. Another distinguished Cambridge historian with immense sympathy for
Acton was close to the mark when he wrote:

> By his contradictions, by his unresolved tensions, and by
> the conflicts on the rim of his intellectual world, the giant
> who could be so charming, so assuredly pontifical, is in
> reality a wounded hero, a hurt lion, with painful inner
> scars.[35]

In the end Acton must be classified as a moral prophet
more than a descriptive historian. Yet it can be fairly argued
that his contribution to a deeper understanding of human
society exceeded that of a dozen more immaculate historians.
His prophetic warnings against new absolutisms hovering
over mankind ring responsive notes for twentieth century
readers. His passion for freedom proceeded from a religious
nature steeped in Christian tradition. It might be argued
that he was unduly influenced by nineteenth century
writers and would have remained on firmer ground had he
rooted himself more consciously in traditional Christian
thought. However, this was an option that was becoming
increasingly difficult for many reflective Christian scholars
of Acton's generation. Whether the movement towards the
secularization of western thought is to be judged a creative
or destructive religious force remains the leading question
confronting contemporary Christian thinkers. Acton's con-

tribution to a resolution of the question cannot be ignored. His flaws, like his talents, were monumental, but when critics have done their worst he remains one of the most stimulating of western historians.

Acton's short-term influence on the development of English Catholicism was minimal. His early efforts to contribute positively to the life of the Catholic community had ended in comparative failure — a failure at the bottom of much of the frustration so evident in his life. In his latter years he drew away from direct involvement in issues affecting Catholicism but continued a devout Catholic in his private life. In the long-term, as a scholar of international reputation, he did more than any modern Englishman, save Newman, to keep alive a spirit of intellectual enquiry as a mark of English Catholicism.

NOTES

1 Matthew Arnold, *Essays in Criticism* (London, 1928), p. 20.
2 Cambridge University Library Add. Mss. 5542.
3 *Ibid.*
4 *Ibid.*
5 Cited in H. A. MacDougall, *The Acton-Newman Relations* (New York, 1962), p. 135.
6 *Ibid.*, p. 136.
7 Acton, *Historical Essays and Studies* (London, 1907), p. 303.
8 C.U.L. Add. Mss. 5019.
9 Cited in T. Kenny, *The Political Thought of John Henry Newman* (London, 1957), p. 33.
10 Acton, *Essays on Freedom and Power* (London, 1956), p. 32.
11 Add. Mss. 4969.
12 MacDougall, *op. cit.*, p. 169.
13 Add. Mss. 5641.
14 G. P. Gooch, *History and Historian in the Nineteenth Century* (London, 1955), p. 362.
15 Acton, *Essays on Freedom and Power, op. cit.*, p. 36.
16 *Ibid.*, p. 32.
17 Acton, *Historical Essays, op. cit.*, p. 383.
18 Add. Mss. 5018.
19 Acton, *Essays on Freedom and Power, op. cit.*, p. 336.
20 Add. Mss. 5015.
21 Herbert Butterfield, *The Whig Interpretation of History* (London, 1951), p. 109.
22 *The Correspondence of Acton and Simpson* (Cambridge, 1975), iii, p. 284.
23 Add. Mss. 5011.
24 Butterfield, *op. cit.*, p. 120.
25 Add. Mss. 5017.
26 Acton, *Letters to Mary Gladstone* (London, 1913), p. 180.
27 Add. Mss. 5011.

28 Add. Mss. 5504
29 Acton, *Essays on Freedom and Power, op. cit.*, p. 48.
30 Cited in H. A. MacDougall, *Lord Acton on Papal Power* (London, 1973), p. 35.
31 Add. Mss. 5504.
32 Acton, *Lectures on Modern History* (London, 1921), p. xviii.
33 *Ibid.*, p. xix.
34 *Ibid.*, p. x.
35 H. Butterfield, *Lord Acton*, Historical Association Pamphlet (London, 1948),
    p. 23.

3

Modernism, aggiornamento and the night battle

Nicholas Lash

Modernism and the Night Battle

'CONTROVERSY, at least in this age', said Newman in 1839, 'does not lie between the hosts of heaven, Michael and his Angels on the one side, and the powers of evil on the other; but it is a sort of night battle, where each fights for himself, and friend and foe stand together'.[1] Perhaps it is ever so. Nevertheless, the temptation is strong, in present controversy and in our interpretation of the past, to clarify complexity by dividing the wheat from the cockle, the light from the dark, 'us' from 'them'. Accounts of the 'Modernist crisis' have notoriously suffered from this tendency. This is particularly unfortunate in view of the fact that the contemporary crisis of Catholic Christianity cannot be understood, I believe, without reference to the confused events of seventy years ago. I accept Alec Vidler's warning that it is too soon to deal historically with the question of the comparisons that may or may not be drawn between 'what so-called progressive, radical or avant-garde Roman Catholic theologians have been saying in recent years and what the modernists said during the first decade of the century'.[2] Nevertheless, it does seem already possible to suggest, provisionally and tentatively, a way of viewing the Modernist crisis which, on the one hand, avoids some of the more obvious weaknesses of earlier interpretations and, on the other hand, throws at least some indirect light on our contemporary situation.

'That the modernist controversy must be held to have been a resounding catastrophe for all concerned seems to me incontestable'.[3] In this essay, I propose to contest that judgement by one of the best-informed recent commentators of the controversy. I propose to argue that, from many points of view, the controversy marked the painful and often tragic beginning of a significant success, of a rich and fruitful renaissance of Catholic life, thought and spirituality, which came near to fruition in the nineteen-sixties. However, I shall also suggest that this renaissance came too late; that, partly as a result, it contained the seeds of its own dissolution; and that therein lies a clue to the disillusionment and confusion which is undoubtedly one of the more striking and disturbing aspects of the mood of contemporary Catholicism.

A Variety of Modernisms

As early as 1909, Tyrrell complained that 'The term "Modernism" is rapidly growing ambiguous. It was first applied, with hostile intent, to that group of Roman Catholics whose position was more or less travestied in the notorious Encyclical *Pascendi*. Next it was appropriated, rather reluctantly, by that same group, to stand, not for the travesty, but for the truth of their position'.[4] The ambiguity of which Tyrrell spoke has continued to bedevil studies of the Modernist crisis. It stems from the fact that the term 'Modernism' refers 'at the same time to a theoretical position that is condemned and to a concrete movement of thought'.[5] None of the leading participants in the 'concrete movement of thought', even those (such as Tyrrell) who were willing, albeit reluctantly, to 'appropriate' the term, endorsed every feature of the 'theoretical position' condemned in the encyclical. In that sense, there were no 'Modernists' or, as has often been said, as many 'Modernisms' as there were 'Modernists'. On the other hand, every one of the leading participants in the movement had held (and, in most cases, continued to hold) at least some views which seemed to be touched, more or less directly, by the condemnation. For all concerned, but perhaps especially for the more conservative, for those most deeply respectful of ecclesiastical authority, there were agonies undergone and a steep price paid.

The failure to distinguish between a 'theoretical system' and a 'concrete movement of thought'; the urgent practical need to salvage reputations and avoid condemnation and harrassment; these are amongst the considerations which help to explain the recurring attempts to draw hard and fast lines between 'Modernists' and the rest of mankind and, in so doing, to restrict the use of the term to the comparatively small group who not only incurred personal censure but who died outside the Catholic communion. Thus, for example, Bishop Butler's description of von Hügel as 'a devout Catholic who was *the friend of* Modernists'[6] is rightly criticized by Alec Vidler as being misleading. We shall return to von Hügel. For the moment, it is sufficient to notice that few historians today would seriously question Vidler's judgement that the Baron was 'the chief engineer of the modernist movement'.[7]

After the initial confusion, in a climate of mutual fear, arrogance, intolerance and repression, the myths began to grow and prosper. In particular, there emerged the complementary versions of what one might call the 'John Wayne's Arizona' view of the Modernist crisis. According to both versions, the controversy did indeed lie between 'the hosts of heaven, Michael and his Angels on the one side, and the powers of evil on the other'. According to one account, the most dangerous subversive movement in the history of modern Christianity was nipped in the bud by the prompt and courageous action of a simple and saintly Pope. There are traces of this myth in Rivière's scholarly and influential study, towards the end of which he describes how Modernism, 'mortally wounded by the acts of Pius X', was then finished off 'by the subsequent action of ecclesiastical authority'.[8] Michael has slain the dragon.

On the other account, a few brave and isolated thinkers, woven together into something like a coherent force by the indefatigable letter-writing and infectious enthusiasm of von Hügel (the incompetence of whose political interventions is admitted even by his staunchest supporters) sought to drag the Catholic Church kicking and screaming into the twentieth century, only to meet with uncompromising rejection by a papacy drunk on the power of an obscurantist authoritarianism made newly possible by the definition of papal infallibility in 1870. This view has had many adherents — from Dean Inge (who had little sympathy for the Modernists, regarding them as foolhardy rather than courageous) to Father Lawrence Barmann. There is a whiff of it in Vidler's judgement, expressed in a letter to Loisy in 1931, that what 'differentiates Anglicanism from Roman Catholicism is the former's rejection of the papal absolutism which was the rock on which modernism inevitably foundered'.[9]

Any attempt to cut these myths down to size runs up against several difficulties. (Such 'demythologisation' need not entail underestimating the extent to which some views of individual 'Modernists' were incompatible with Christian belief, the pastoral irresponsibility of some of their supporters, or the damage done to Catholic life and thought by the paranoia of St. Pius X's thought-police). In the first place, nearly all the major studies that have so far appeared have been more or less self-consciously apologetic in nature. Thus, Loisy's *Mémoires* are an apologia for Loisy; Rivière's book is an apologia for Mgr. Batiffol and the school of Toulouse; Vidler's two books are an apologia for Loisy although, in the more recent of the two, he admits that he finds Loisy a more puzzling character than he had once thought him to be; Marlé's dossier of the correspondence between Blondel, Loisy, von Hügel and others is an apologia for Blondel and his friends; Barmann's book, although it purports·to be about von Hügel, is in fact an apologia for Loisy and Tyrrell; even Poulat's magnificent study suffers from the tendency to give the impression that the crisis was an almost entirely French affair.[10]

In the second place, almost all the studies mentioned tend to concentrate on the theoretical (doctrinal, philosophical, methodological) dimension of the controversy. They insufficiently situate it in the broader cultural, social and political context in which European Catholicism found itself at the turn of the century.

In the third place, by tending to isolate those aspects of the reform movement which came into headlong collision with ecclesiastical authority, most studies present the controversy as if it were the expression of a struggle with only two sides, between only two schools, two climates of thought and belief. But it is just this tendency which has made it so difficult, for example, to see the careers of Blondel and von Hügel in perspective.

In the fourth place, by thus isolating certain features of the reform movement, the impression is given that this movement failed. Thus Loome, whose judgement that the controversy was 'a resounding catastrophe for all concerned' I have already quoted, says that 'In this drama there were few villains on either side, but victims beyond number on both'.[11] (And notice, again the assumption that there were two, and only two, 'sides' to the controversy).

Three Men — and Three Questions

Bernard Reardon has defined 'Modernism' as 'the attempt to synthesize the basic truths of religion and the methods and assumptions of modern thought, using the latter as necessary and proper criteria'.[12] That definition may be thought excessively imprecise. Yet, in so far as it seeks to capture the 'ethos' of the 'concrete movement of thought', rather than to pick out the salient features of the 'theoretical system' condemned by *Pascendi*, it is not too misleading as a description of a widespread mood in late nineteenth century Catholicism, a mood shared by spirits as different as Loisy and Blondel, Tyrrell and Wilfrid Ward, von Hügel and Buonaiuti. Nevertheless, such a definition misleads inasmuch as it fails to indicate the senses in which some of the leading figures in the attempt thus to 'synthesize' or reconcile the 'basic truths of religion' with the 'methods and assumptions of modern thought' were, in their concerns, temperaments and, above all, in their vision of Christianity, profoundly conservative figures. Before briefly illustrating this with reference to Ward, von Hügel and Blondel, it may be worth spelling out some of the methodological implications of the paradox at which I have just hinted.

In times of rapid change, of social and cultural crisis, the most creative contribution may sometimes be made by those few individuals who are enabled to see through the crisis and to prospect its fruitful resolution precisely in the measure that, instead of accepting the presuppositions that determine the battle-lines of today, they seek in another — and therefore an inevitably earlier — cultural context the parameters for the vision which they hope to express. There is an unavoidably tragic element in such men's achievement because, in so far as the 'prophet' is obliged to draw on resources from the past in order creatively to enrich the present, the solutions that he proposes will be, in some measure, 'conservative' in a pejorative sense and, as such, inappropriate.

It is undoubtedly important to ask of men such as Ward, von Hügel and Blondel: Did they seek the synthesis or reconciliation to which Reardon refers? But it is also important to ask: Where did they turn, historically, for their 'model' of a reformed Catholicism, and in what respects was that model likely to prove unserviceable in the new situation?

Wilfrid Ward as 'Modernist'

Wilfrid Ward was neither an original thinker, nor one of enduring influence. He has, nevertheless, been unduly neglected in studies of the Modernist crisis. Not only did he edit the *Dublin Review* during the crucial decade from 1906 to his death in 1916, but he had entered more deeply and sympathetically into Newman's mind than had any of his contemporaries. If, shortly before his death, he described the reformers (including himself) as 'men who strove for provisional freedom in scientific discussion with a view to modifying certain traditional opinions and interpretations of dogma',[13] his language some years earlier had been distinctly less guarded. In June 1900 he had written: 'The work of the adaptation of theology to the exigencies of the times has already been effectively begun; though it may need a time of freedom from agitation and from the repression which follows for its development'.[14] The article from which that passage is taken, an article which had equally hard things to say about both the 'extreme left' and the 'extreme right', was a plea to those in authority to listen to the 'wise' lest, by becoming repressive and out of touch, authority drove the 'wise' into opposition. Not for the first or last time, those in authority ignored the plea. The 'wise', it should be noted, included at this date both Loisy and Tyrrell. The following year, while stressing the differences between Newman's views and those of Auguste Sabatier, he nevertheless referred to the 'extraordinary resemblance between the French writer's treatment of the philosophy of Dogma and the treatment of the same question fifty years earlier by Cardinal Newman'.[15]

In 1903, the year which he later noted as marking the beginning of his divergence from Tyrrell, he published a collection of essays which breathes the optimistic, evolutionary atmosphere that is one of the dominant strands in late nineteenth century thought — a strand especially uncongenial to the authors of *Pascendi*. In the first of these essays, he agrees with A. J. Balfour that it is not the undoubted 'immense increase in our "stock of knowledge" ' which has been the 'really characteristic feature' of the century just ended, but rather the acquisition of a new 'mental framework' or 'point of view'.[16] From this point of view, nineteenth century man, as he views 'the development of man himself, individual and social, religious, artistic, political, philosophical, scientific . . . applies to each department the complete scientific method of observation, induction, hypothesis, deduction, verification'.[17] After this introduction, it comes as little surprise to find Ward endorsing Renan's description of the nineteenth century paradigm-shift as ' "the substitution of the category of evolution for the category of being" ';[18] or to hear him praising Caird, Darwin, Hegel, Loisy and Wellhausen. 'Evolution is, in the view of most of its exponents, essentially optimistic. And it has good reason to be'.[19] These are accents that will be less frequently heard in the Catholic Church after 1907 or, in Europe as a whole, after 1914. Subsequent events will erode the optimism, induce a more critical assessment of evolutionary progress. They will not, however, undermine Ward's conviction concerning the need for change. In 1908, we find him complaining to the Duke of Norfolk: '[Cardinal Mercier] thinks the Roman theology quite impossible: yet though he is hand and glove with the Pope he clearly does not give him the least inkling of this view'.[20] And in 1911, in a Memorandum intended for Cardinal Rampolla: 'I happen to be in contact with many earnest thinkers who feel deeply that the infidel movement can only be stemmed by the reconciliation of Christian faith with what is sound in modern thought and science and research . . . To effect this reconciliation successfully free discussion is necessary'.[21]

In 1901 Canon William Barry wrote to him: 'No Bishop, no Council, can put under ban the scientific method; and what we want is study, acquaintance with the facts as far as it is possible, instead of a journalism that only brings down the lightning'.[22] The man of whom his wife wrote after his death that, for him, the Modernist crisis was not 'a sectarian controversy, but the vast question of the religious future of the human race',[23] would still willingly have endorsed Barry's sentiments fifteen years later.

Perhaps I have sufficiently indicated the extent to which this most orthodox and conservative of English Catholics saw the necessity of 'the attempt to synthesize the basic truths of religion and the methods and assumptions of modern thought'. It is now time to turn to my second question: Where did he turn, historically, for his 'model' of a reformed Catholicism?

Wilfrid Ward as 'Traditionalist'

Wilfrid Ward was a conservative in at least three senses. Politically, he stood well to the right of the Tory party: 'Less and less as years passed did he believe in rule by the whim of the democracy'.[24] Culturally, he was a 'gradualist' with a horror of all forms of revolution. Writing to Bernard Holland a few months before his death, he said of von Hügel: 'I do not know whom I admire more, but our relations have been most curious, as, on the combined theological and political matters which divide Catholics (I mean perhaps rather the politics of theology) we have never agreed'.[25] The admiration for one whom he described, at about the same period, as 'a man of extraordinary gifts and acquirements and of equally remarkable personality and character',[26] was undoubtedly genuine. But that reference to 'the politics of theology' aptly indicates the gulf that separated his passion for order, and fear of radical upheaval, from the Baron's infectious and often disembodied enthusiasm. Nevertheless, within the limits of his conservatism, his life-long aim was to contribute to the production of 'an intellectual atmosphere in which faith was possible'[27] and, in an essay first published in 1895, which his daughter regarded as 'one of the most important he ever wrote',[28] he argued that the time had now come for Catholicism to emerge from the 'state of siege' into which it had been driven after the Reformation, and creatively to re-engage with the other forces that had shaped and were shaping European culture. Whereas the critics of Catholicism regarded the 'rigidity of Rome' as a permanent characteristic, a characteristic which rendered both Christian reunion and the cultural re-engagement of Catholicism quite impossible, that 'rigidity' was, for Ward, a transient tactical necessity, 'the indispensable means of adapting itself to a critical situation'.[29]

In addition to the two aspects of Ward's conservatism already mentioned, the 'political' and the 'cultural', there is a third to which I earlier referred as an inevitable characteristic of the 'prophetic' thinker: namely, his search in the past for the 'model' in terms of which he spells out, in the

59

present, what needs to be done for the future. The sixteenth century may have marked the beginning of that 'state of siege' from which the reformers now sought to liberate Catholic life and thought, but it was not to the sixteenth century that Ward turned for his 'model', but rather to the thirteenth. It was there that he saw embodied the vision of 'the essential largeness of the capacities of Catholicism viewed historically'.[30] For three centuries the 'theological principle' has been 'cramped'. The contemporary need is for 'the exercise of this faith and of this vigorous thought gradually to do the real work, and to adapt our theology in detail to the twentieth-century culture as Albertus Magnus and St. Thomas Aquinas adapted it to the then almost equally novel conditions of the thirteenth'.[31] Thirteen years later, not long before he died, Ward referred to Aquinas as one who had 'found the *Via Media* between condemning the new learning of the day and being carried away by the excesses of its devotees'.[32] That passage carries overtones of the crisis of the previous decade, but the 'model' is still in use.

Von Hügel as 'Modernist'

In turning now to von Hügel, I shall focus my observations on Thomas Loome's study of 'The Enigma of Baron Friedrich von Hügel — as Modernist'.[33] In that study, Loome pitilessly exposed certain weaknesses in the work of those, such as Barmann and Vidler, who have argued not simply for the central role which the Baron played in the Modernist movement (for this centrality is no longer seriously in question) but, more specifically, for the view that he is to be seen as having been a ' "modernist" from beginning to end' (p. 24). As we proceed, the measure of my agreement with and indebtedness to Loome will become clear. But I also have a number of serious reservations about his study, which may be worth indicating at the outset.

Loome rightly deplores the partisan nature of so much writing on the Modernist crisis. His own objectivity, however, is not beyond question. He views with disapproval, even contempt, both 'Modernism' and those who would attempt 'benignly' to interpret it. Modestly leaving to others 'the declension of Rome's sins' (p. 211), the part played by the ecclesiastical authorities and by those who acted on their behalf is, at worst, attributed to 'incompetence' and 'ineptness' (p. 212). More censorious language is reserved for the 'Modernists': they counted amongst their number 'unsavoury clerics' (p. 213); most of them were 'flawed from the start, often profoundly so' (p. 214); they lacked 'moral and religious stability' (loc. cit.); their activities are referred to as a 'frenzied race down the gadarene slopes' (p. 216). Weakness of character and lack of moral fibre are thus given considerable emphasis as partial explanations of the collapse of the 'movement'. Similarly, von Hügel's involvement is attributed, in large measure, to his *naiveté*, even blindness' (pp. 215–216) as a judge of character: he was the dupe of 'Loisy's duplicity' (p. 221).

Loome's final solution to the 'enigma' of Baron von Hügel as 'Modernist' is to see his Modernist period as 'a period of self-deception and of betrayal by others, a *temporary deviation* from the Friedrich von Hügel of both his earlier and later periods and impossible to reconcile with either' (p. 230, my stress). The impression is thus given that the Modernist crisis marks a brief, tragic and fundamentally unimportant aberration in the histories alike of von Hügel and of Catholic Christianity. The 'ultimate significance of the modernist controversy itself' is reduced to that of 'a relatively small part in the life of a man like von Hügel and but a brief episode in the life of the Church' (p. 19). The argument seems to be that, because the crisis was short-lived, therefore it was of only trivial significance. Quite apart from the fact that the duration of an episode is hardly relevant to the question of its significance (our Lord's public ministry was but a 'brief episode'!), such an assessment gives the impression that neither the Catholic renaissance of the twentieth century, nor the often appallingly difficult circumstances in which that renaissance was achieved, were intimately connected with the Modernist controversy.

The 'decisive factor that brought on the débâcle' (p. 214) was, apparently, neither the low moral and spiritual calibre of the 'Modernists', nor the repressive activity of ecclesiastical authority, but 'the religious views which came to characterize so many of' the Modernists (loc. cit.). There follows a superficial account of 'positivism' and 'immanentism', reinforcing one's suspicion that Loome has failed to grasp the complexity, seriousness and urgency of the conceptual and methodological issues at the heart of the controversy, issues which — if the history of ideas is to be taken at all seriously — cannot possibly be reduced to a set of discriminable theoretical disgreements within a common world of perception and discourse. It is, perhaps, significant that Loome ignores the question of von Hügel's relationship, during the years when the 'night battle' was at its height, with Tyrrell, Blondel and Laberthonnière, and that, having told us that the writings of Troeltsch and Eucken on the Modernist controversy 'are of exceptional interest and will be discussed later in this essay' (p. 32), he fails to do so.

'Any benign view of "Modernism" must rest in large part on a benign view of Alfred Loisy' (pp. 217–218). Is a 'benign' view of Loisy one which seeks to exonerate him from the charge of duplicity, or one which acknowledges the quality of much of his exegetical work?[34] The ambiguity of Loome's comment is symptomatic: he never clearly indicates whether he believes that the term 'Modernism' is to be understood primarily in historical or in theoretical terms. That is to say: does the 'enigma' of Baron von Hügel consist in a puzzle as to why he should have become so closely involved in the activities of 'that group of Roman Catholics whose position was travestied in the notorious Encyclical *Pascendi*'? Or does it consist in a puzzle as to why it was that so orthodox, so Ultramontane a Catholic should have held a number of views which seem to stand well within the 'theoretical system of thought' condemned by the encyclical? Loome's study contains a number of valuable clues to both these questions. Unfortunately, he is so concerned to exonerate von Hügel from the charge of 'Modernism',[35] and so insensitive to the complexity of the issues at stake, that he fails to distinguish between them.

It is hardly surprising that the areas of agreement and disagreement between the various participants in the Catholic reform movement at the turn of the century should only slowly have become apparent as the issues clarified. To attempt, retrospectively, in the light of *Pascendi*, to isolate some of the reformers and to ascribe to them alone the title of 'Modernist', and to their activities alone the term 'Modernist movement', is to perpetuate those ambiguities which have for so long bedevilled accounts of the 'Modernist crisis'. What is needed is a distinction between two senses of 'Modernism': one which would cover the reforming movement as a whole, and thus help to explain what it was that for a time held together men whose attitudes and beliefs were in many ways fundamentally opposed; another which would have a more limited reference to the 'theoretical system' condemned by *Pascendi* and to those within the wider movement, such as Tyrrell and Loisy, whose views most closely corresponded to the encyclical's description of 'Modernism'. Von Hügel later attempted to draw just such a distinction, and Loome's failure to perceive its legitimacy is significant.

The distinction occurs in a letter of 1918, to Maude Petre. Loome acknowledges the importance of this letter, but his commentary on it helps to explain why it is that he is able to dismiss as a 'brief episode', as 'that débâcle known to history as "the modernist movement"' (p. 211), a series of events described by René Marlé as 'the gravest crisis to have shaken Christian thought since the Reformation'.[36] In his letter, von Hügel distinguished between 'two Modernisms'. The first he described as 'a permanent, never quite finished, always sooner or later, more or less, rebeginning set of attempts to express the old Faith and its permanent truths and helps — to interpret it according to what appears the best and the most abiding elements in the philosophy and the scholarship and science of the later and latest times'.[37] The 'other "Modernism" is a strictly circumscribed affair, one that is really over and done — the series or groups of specific attempts, good, bad, indifferent, or variously mixed, that were made towards similar expressions or interpretations, during the Pontificate of Pius X'.[38] Since it is of this second 'Modernism' that Miss Petre's forthcoming book will presumably treat, therefore the Baron declines her request for the names of his publications since 1914.

According to Loome, von Hügel's first definition of 'Modernism' is 'highly idiosyncratic . . . one in fact wholly foreign to theological literature'; it will not be found in 'any of the great theological dictionaries. If this, after all, is "Modernism", all serious theological endeavour must be given the name'.[39] It will not have escaped the reader that the definition which Loome finds so surprising is strikingly similar to that which we earlier quoted from Bernard Reardon. What von Hügel was doing was not 'inventing a "Modernism" about which he could only say good things',[40] but accurately describing the aims of the Catholic reformers, from Loisy to Blondel or Wilfrid Ward, from Tyrrell to himself; aims which may legitimately be distinguished from the form of particular attempts at their achievement. If such a definition is absent from 'the great theological dictionaries', this is perhaps because they usually contain more theoretical descriptions, derived from *Pascendi*.[41]

That Christian theology should ever seek to interpret 'the old Faith . . . according to what appears the best and most abiding elements in the philosophy and the scholarship and science of the later and latest times' may today be regarded as self-evident. Catholic theology had, however, as Ward saw, signally failed to make that attempt since, in the sixteenth century, it had withdrawn into its 'state of siege'. Moreover, the extent to which the sustaining of such an attempt entailed a theology in continual process of change and adaptation (von Hügel's 'permanent . . . more or less, rebeginning set of attempts') was perceived with unprecedented force in the nineteenth century and, in the measure that it was perceived, it met with suspicion, hostility and forceful rejection. It is difficult to interpret 'benignly' Loome's abstraction of von Hügel's description from these historical considerations, an abstraction that enables him to say that, if this is what 'Modernism' means then 'Friedrich von Hügel was a "modernist". So also were Augustine and Aquinas, Fénelon and Mabillon. So are we all' (p. 208).

Another way of characterising von Hügel's distinction would be to remember that an acknowledgement of the legitimacy of the questions which the reformers raised, and of the strategic objectives which they pursued ('Modernism One') does not entail a wholesale acknowledgement either of the metaphysical frameworks within which they cast that pursuit, or of the specific solutions which, in the first decade of the century, they proposed ('Modernism Two'). It is only after the publication of *Pascendi* that it becomes possible to say whether or not any particular individual's views were, or were not, 'Modernist' in any of the senses in which the encyclical uses the term. And even after the encyclical's appearance, retrospectively to draw a line between individuals and groups and to say that the activities of only these individuals, or of those groups, constituted the 'Modernist movement' is to distort the scope and significance of that movement the centrality of von Hügel's role in which was quite compatible with his earlier and later aims and convictions. Movements do not have hard edges: would Loome regard activities such as, for example, the correspondence between von Hügel, Blondel and Laberthonnière as falling inside or outside the Modernist 'movement'?

To sum up. It seems to me self-evident that the answer to my first question is: Yes, von Hügel sought the synthesis or reconciliation to which Reardon refers. Loome would not disagree. But, whereas he regards it as 'idiosyncratic' and almost an abuse of language (cf. p. 208) to see the prosecution of this search, at the turn of the century, as in any nontrivial sense a sufficient condition for describing the participants in the Catholic reform movement as 'Modernist', I do not.

Von Hügel as 'Traditionalist'

When we turn to my second question: Where did von Hügel turn, historically, for his 'model' of a reformed

Catholicism? Loome's study becomes indispensable. He devoted the second of his three articles to 'that period in von Hügel's life about which least has been known: his formative years during the 1870's, 1880's and early 1890's' (p. 204). He rightly saw that, in order to understand the strengths and weaknesses of von Hügel's achievement, 'The decisive question concerns the Baron's "pre-modernist" period, the first forty or more years of his life . . . What were the roots from which he grew, the traditions in which he stood and of which he understood himself as heir and continuator?' (p. 123). Both the 'Ultramontanism' and the 'Liberal Catholicism' of his own day were equally distasteful to him, and for the same reason. From being aspects of an integrated, balanced Catholic life, thought and spirituality, they had lost their centrality and become 'parties', warring factions. Von Hügel reached back, far behind the polarities of the late nineteenth century and found, in the 'post-tridentine Church of the late seventeenth century' (p. 126), a forgotten tradition of wholeness, exemplified, above all, in such men as Fénelon and Mabillon. These men provided him with the 'model' for that vision of reformed Catholicism for which he would work, and suffer, for the remainder of his life. 'For von Hügel to have reached back to this tradition and to have found in it his roots represented not unqualified rejection, but fundamental criticism of the categories of his age . . . His achievement was not in seizing a place in the middle, far from the clamour of conflicting parties, but in defining centrality in a way that might permit him to embrace that which was wholesome while rejecting that which had been debased in both traditions' (p. 126), Ultramontane and Liberal.

I have quoted that passage at some length, because it strikingly illustrates the thesis which I earlier sketched concerning the manner in which, at a period of cultural crisis, the great reformer is able to prospect a resolution of the crisis by rejecting the presuppositions that determine the battle-lines of today, and seeking in an earlier cultural context the parameters for the expression of his vision.

66

Thus von Hügel's 'championing of Fénelon was not quaint antiquarianism, but a considered response to the illness of his age' (p. 128). As Loome points out, we need to remember that when von Hügel, writing in 1893, speaks of himself as having ever been 'an Ultramontane, in the old and definite sense of the word',[42] it is the Ultramontanism of Fénelon that he has in mind. It was 'In 1885 [that] the Baron turned for the first time to Fénelon'.[43] When, eight years later, the second volume of Wilfrid Ward's biography of his father appeared, the fascinating analysis which it contained of the Ultramontanism of the 'gentle and sympathetic Fénelon' occurred in a chapter 'for which the Baron provided both essential information and, more important, the major line of argument'.[44]

Loome is surely right in insisting on the paradigmatic role exercised, in von Hügel's thought, by Fénelon and the post-tridentine Church of the late seventeenth century. However, it seems to me that his account of the sources to which von Hügel turned for his model of a reformed Catholicism demands slight, but significant, adjustment. In seeking that forgotten tradition of 'wholeness' which he sought to re-habilitate, von Hügel turned not simply to the seventeenth century expressions of that tradition (before its course was brutally interrupted by the condemnation of Quietism) but also to an earlier expression, in the pre-Reformation Catholicism of the Renaissance. Loome is so concerned to show that, throughout his life, von Hügel remained 'almost belligerently Roman Catholic',[45] and therefore not a 'Modernist', that he insufficiently emphasizes the passion of the Baron's ecumenical concern, and the extent to which, to the end of his life, he often felt more at home — as a Catholic — with some of his Protestant colleagues than with some Catholics whose work he nevertheless profoundly admired. As late as 1921 we find him writing: '*par un des tours paradoxaux si nombreux de la vie, je me trouve, moi, catholique convaincu, profondément aidé à bien m'épanouir, précisément en ce catholicisme de mon ame, par le luthérien Troeltsch et le calviniste*

Kemp Smith, plus ou moins contre les catholiques Blondel et Laber-thonniére.'[46] It needs continually to be borne in mind that, at the height of the Modernist crisis, the Baron was working on *The Mystical Element of Religion.* It is not insignificant that, as Barmann pointed out, the period of von Hügel's friendship with Tyrrell 'coincided with the gradual growth of the Baron's book',[47] of which Tyrrell read the manuscript in 1906, and which was published in 1908. In the Preface, von Hügel explained what it was that had drawn him to the Renaissance in general, and to St. Catherine of Genoa in particular: 'those early modern times presented me with men of the same general instincts and outlook as my own, but environed by the priceless boon and starting-point of a still undivided Western Christendom'.[48]

In the final section of this essay I shall attempt to answer the third of my questions: In what respects were the 'models' to which these men turned likely to prove unserviceable in the new situation at the turn of the century? Without anticipating that answer, there is one aspect of the weakness in von Hügel's achievement, an aspect discussed by Loome, which may be mentioned at this point. Had von Hügel been born a few years earlier, he would have personally experienced, as an adult, the 'tumultuous years surrounding the Vatican Council'.[49] Had he done so, he might have been both more sympathetic to men such as Döllinger, and less unrealistically optimistic that the deep antagonisms internally dividing Catholicism could readily be healed. As it was, lacking personal experience of the earlier conflict, seeking a 'religious ideal [that] was embodied almost exclusively in a Catholicism which had long ceased to exist', he gravely misjudged 'the *de facto* Catholicism in which he endeavoured to realise his ideal' (loc. cit.). There were lessons that had to be painfully learnt.

Blondel as 'Modernist'

Inasmuch as one of the aims of this essay is to question the view that the Modernist controversy was a conflict between two 'sides' or 'parties' — 'heretics' and 'orthodox', 'Modernists' and 'Roman Catholics' — some mention of Blondel is more or less inevitable. His philosophical position was wholly alien to that cast of mind, for which he coined the term 'extrinsicist',[50] which continued to dominate 'officially respectable' Catholic thought for half a century. As a result, he remained a highly suspect figure: when, after the second World War, Garrigou-Lagrange attempted to discredit the work of the Jesuits at Lyon-Fourviere, he did so by exaggerating the influence of Blondel on that school and seeking thereby to reduce their work simply to 'Modernism'.[51] In fact, Blondel remained passionately, even obsessively, committed to 'orthodoxy', and escaped censure. (It could be argued, however, that fear of official disapproval, and the impact on him of the censure incurred by his friend and collaborator Laberthonnière, had a less than wholly beneficial effect on the later development of his thought: who, for example, any longer reads the revised version of *L'Action*?). Von Hügel was immensely impressed by *L'Action* when he first read it in 1895 and tried, unsuccessfully, to interest Wilfrid Ward in the thought of the man whom he described as 'simply a genius of the first rank, little as he looks it'.[52] If, a decade later, the Baron found himself siding with Loisy against Blondel, this alignment can certainly not be attributed simply to the blindness of his friendship for Loisy. It was grounded in profound differences of methodological and epistemological perspective. It is, moreover, interesting to notice that, as we have already seen, a degree of intellectual estrangement survived into a period when von Hügel, too, was concentrating his attention on problems in the philosophy of religion, a concentration which, for von Hügel as for Blondel, was characterized by a profound conviction that, in the last resort, truth is '*given*, not *found*.'[53] 'Man's deepest want is, in reality, for a God infinitely more than such a mere assuager of even all man's wants'.[54] Thus von Hügel in 1918; it might equally well have been written by one who had said, twenty-five years earlier: 'vouloir l'infini, non, ce n'est pas un point de départ, mais un point d'arrivée pour la recherche scientifique.

Mais est-ce un point de départ et un principe pour l'activité spontanee de la vie, voila la question'.[55]

Some mention of Blondel in this essay was also demanded by the fact that his influence on subsequent Catholic thought far outstripped that of either Ward or von Hügel. Jesuits such as Bouillard, de Chardin, de Lubac, de Montcheuil, Maréchal, Rahner; Dominicans such as Chenu and Congar: these are but a few of the outstanding Catholic thinkers of a later generation to have been influenced, in varying degrees, by the thought of the only leading participant in the Modernist controversy for whom the claim can seriously be made that he was an original thinker of European stature, and who has been described as 'probably the most important French philosopher since Descartes'.[56] If, nevertheless, my comments on him are very brief, this is for two reasons. In the first place, I have preferred to concentrate on English participants in the controversy, because the emphasis in this collection of essays is on English Catholicism. In the second place, the 'case' that I would wish to argue for Blondel has already been argued by one far better qualified than myself to do so: Alec Dru.

So far as the first of my three questions is concerned, there is surely no doubt but that the man who, in 1932, spoke of 'having attempted, as a believer, a philosopher's effort',[57] sought to reconcile the basic truths of religion and the methods and assumptions of modern thought. At the height of the controversy, in 1907, he wrote: 'The present crisis, perhaps unprecedented in depth and extent — for it is simultaneously scientific, metaphysical, moral, social and political — is not a dissolution (for the spirit of faith does not die) nor even an evolution (for the spirit of faith does not change), it is a *purification* of the religious sense and an *integration* of Catholic truth. A purification, because what succumbs or dissolves in the present struggles, the decaying institutions, the petrified forms, are either dying or dead . . . It is useless for party to be aligned against party: those who, in order to defend the Church, immure themselves in a fortress of resistance only hasten the spread of change'.[58]

Blondel as 'Traditionalist'

Secondly, where did Blondel turn, historically, for his 'model' of a reformed Catholicism? For Blondel, as for Wilfrid Ward and von Hügel, the conflict in the Church which exploded in the first decade of this century was 'the culmination of centuries of aridity'.[59] Blondel's programme entailed a 'return to tradition . . . not the "tradition" of the empty scholasticism of the nineteenth century, but to the tradition which it obscured'.[60] We are reminded of von Hügel's return to a forgotten tradition of wholeness, and of Ward's vision of 'the essential largeness of the capacities of Catholicism viewed historically',[61] before the 'state of siege' set in. For Blondel, as for von Hügel, the 'obscuring' of this authentic tradition occurred decisively with the condemnation of Quietism. The Quietist controversy marked 'the origin of the divorce between Catholicism and living thought, genuine art and honest scholarship which Blondel and his generation (who rediscovered the spiritual tradition) were the first to recognize, understand and reverse'.[62]

The Catholic Renaissance: Success or Failure?

I have been suggesting that, in order to appreciate the significance of the Modernist controversy for the contemporary crisis of Catholic Christianity, it is necessary, firstly, to dispel the illusion that it was a straightforward collision between two positions: 'Modernist' and 'orthodox'; secondly, to see the controversy against a broad historical backdrop, and not to view it simply in the context of the late nineteenth century; thirdly, to question the judgement that it was simply a 'resounding catastrophe for all concerned'. To study the writings and correspondence of such men as Ward, von Hügel and Blondel is to recover a sense of the controversy as a 'night battle', before *Pascendi* and its aftermath tempted students of the crisis to draw sharp lines, and so distort its bewildering complexity. Secondly, to view the crisis as these men viewed it is to see it as the beginning of an attempt to re-engage Catholic life, thought and spirituality with the forces shaping contemporary culture after a prolonged period of absence from, or, at most, negative presence in, that culture. But, thirdly, to what extent was that attempt successful? According to Dru, the Modernist controversy marked 'the dénouement of a crisis which had been endemic for two centuries and had reached its acutest phase in the nineteenth century. This is not to deny the crisis, but to recognise that it was at the same time a rebirth of Catholicism: the source of a movement for reform which has received official expression in the Second Vatican Council'.[63]

To men who had worked and suffered, often with heroic patience, during the dark decades that followed the condemnation of Modernism, it must have seemed as if that vision of a reformed Catholicism, critically engaged with the world in which the Gospel is to be proclaimed and embodied, had indeed at last received 'official expression'. From being the private preserve of a suspect minority, this vision could now enter into and profoundly influence the imagination, structure and conceptuality of the Catholic community as a whole. It is thus hardly surprising if, a decade later, some of these same men should view with sadness, even bitterness, the confusion and disarray that has led one of their number, Louis Bouyer, to complain that 'what we see looks less like the hoped-for regeneration of Catholicism than its accelerated decomposition'.[64] What went wrong?

At the beginning of this essay I suggested that the renaissance came too late and that, partly as a result, it contained the seeds of its own dissolution. In order briefly to fill out this suggestion, I would now like to consider three distinct, but interconnected factors that have contributed to bring about our contemporary confusion. In so doing, I shall indirectly answer my third question: in what respects were the 'models' of a reformed Catholicism employed by men such as Ward, von Hügel and Blondel likely to prove unserviceable in the new situation?

In the first place, the condemnation of Modernism fatally delayed the flowering of the renaissance. For several decades the Catholic Church remained in a 'state of siege', fully alerted to the danger of attacks as much from within as without, while the prosecution of the vision of Blondel and von Hügel remained the dangerous vocation of a suspect minority. As a result, the 'official expression' of the reform movement, in the promulgation of the Constitutions and Decrees of the second Vatican Council, met with wide-spread bewilderment and incomprehension. If the conciliar documents pointed the way, however hesitantly, towards an eventual 'transformation of structures', they presupposed for their understanding a 'transformation of consciousness' which was too often lacking, both before and after the Council. Moreover, fundamental shifts in the 'structures of feeling' of European, American and Third World cultures, shifts of which the conciliar documents were largely innocent, could not be expected to wait upon the re-engagement of Catholicism with those 'secular' worlds which it had for so long either ignored or viewed with baleful suspicion. As a result, even when the conciliar message did begin to 'get through' to the Catholic community as a whole, it seemed not to speak to the felt concerns and expectations of increasing numbers of people. Thus to the initial bewilderment on the part of many Catholics there were soon added apathy and disillusionment with 'official' Catholicism on the part of many others. In order briefly to indicate the sort of fundamental shifts that I have in mind, it may be helpful to make use of Bernard Lonergan's distinction between 'classical' and 'modern' culture.

According to Lonergan, who believes that the shift from a 'classical' to a 'modern' concept of culture 'necessitates a complete restructuring of Catholic theology',[65] classical culture 'conceived itself normatively and universally',[66] whereas modern culture is conceived empirically: 'It is the set of meanings and values that informs a way of life'.[67] When culture is conceived normatively, it is possible to establish, at least in principle, a set of ideal standards against which particular achievements of meaning and value may be assessed. The worlds of meaning and value have, as it were, a 'centre'. When culture is conceived empirically, however, there is no such set of ideal standards against which particular achievements of meaning and value may be measured. The worlds of meaning and value become 'decentred'. It does not follow that mankind is irrevocably condemned to an insurmountable and anarchic relativism. To individuals, and groups, that may often seem the easy way out. But, that way, 'chaos is come again'. It does follow, however, that questions concerning the possibility of communication, of agreement, of the genuine achievement of truth and value are experienced, with new urgency, in the context of a set of largely ineradicable cultural, racial, class, conceptual and ideological pluralisms. From this point of view Vatican II's vision of a more or less homogeneous programme of reform (for all the lip-service paid to the desirability of a variety of styles of liturgical life and spirituality) is flawed by a residual classicism.[68] I would tentatively suggest that the heuristic structures, inspired by the more or less culturally homogeneous world of seventeenth century Catholicism, within which Blondel and von Hügel pursued their vision of a recovery of Catholic 'wholeness' or 'integration' was, similarly, residually classicist.

The classical conception of culture is, inevitably, elitist: 'On classicist assumptions there is just one culture. That one culture is not attained by the simple faithful, the people, the natives, the barbarians'.[69] If the partial postponement of the Catholic renaissance is one factor which helps to explain our current confusion, and the 'decentring' of the worlds of meaning and value is a second, there is a third which can perhaps best be described as the 'political' factor.

As early as 1883 Blondel wrote: 'There are three human ways of serving the supernatural: either by making room for it in the intellectual order . . . or by making room for it in social and political action . . . or by calling upon it to re-animate the generosity of feelings, the dry or withering heart'.[70] Blondel's social concern is evident, in his opposition to the *Action Française* and his 'permanent horror of the bourgeois philosophy preached by the authorities of Catholicism'.[71] His opposition to 'political Catholicism' may have expressed his hostility to the mistaken identification of the quest for God's kingdom with the pursuit of short-term human goals (an identification which generated the sterile sectarianisms of nineteenth-century Catholicism, 'Ultramontane' and 'Liberal' alike), but was not the form of that hostility perhaps such as inadvertently to have deflected Catholic attention from the increasingly urgent question of the social and political implications of Christian belief?

In von Hügel's case, some such limitation of vision, or restriction of horizon, is clearly discernible. He 'abhorred "political Catholicism" in any form'.[72] Whelan speaks of the 'narrowness of [his] social and political consciousness'.[73] The Baron's 'reflections on the substantive justice of Marxist criticism of industrial society clearly indicate that he knows that the classical approach [to the problem of individual poverty] . . . is not enough, and that something far more organised, massive and public is required'.[74] But he seems not to have suspected that 'a new political reality, perhaps of actually revolutionary proportions' might be demanded 'in terms of his own . . . understanding of man as autonomous secularity'.[75] In Ward's case the interdependence between cultural 'classicism' and a conservative, elitist political stance is quite explicit: the man who saw papal power 'as a breakwater against the running flood of Anarchism and Socialism'[76] believed that, 'In the secular polity as in the ecclesiastical . . . the initiative should lie with the wise men of thought, not with the rulers or the masses'.[77]

Aggiornamento and the Night Battle

The word chosen by John XXIII to characterize that phase of the Catholic renaissance which culminated in the second Vatican Council was 'aggiornamento'.[78] If Catholic thought needed to be brought 'up-to-date', it must have fallen behind the times. When did it begin to do so? After listening to Ward, von Hügel and Blondel, Bernard Lonergan's answer to that question comes as no surprise: it began to do so at 'the end of the seventeenth century . . . When modern science began, when the Enlightenment began, then the theologians began to reassure one another about their certainties'.[79] Perhaps we can say that the twentieth-century Catholic renaissance (from the Modernist crisis to the second Vatican Council) marked an heroic, and in no small measure successful attempt to bring Catholicism 'up-to-date' with the world that came to birth between the seventeenth and nineteenth centuries. It did so, however, just as that world was beginning to disintegrate and disappear under the pressure of new forces, new problems, new patterns of association and frameworks of experience. Hence the exhilaration, swiftly followed by disarray, to which I referred in the previous section.

Both Blondel and von Hügel were passionately committed to the priority of the concrete, in all its irreducible complexity. They abhorred, as alien to the heart and spirit of Catholic Christianity, all withdrawal into abstraction: whether the theoretical abstraction that mistakes some one dimension of language and experience for the multi-dimensional whole, or the practical abstraction that prefers the security of sect or party to the costly 'friction' (that very 'hugelian' word) of Christian discipleship. The Christian who, today, would attempt, in obedience to the 'logic of action', to hold together in mutual tension the 'institutional', 'intellectual' and experiential (or 'mystical') 'elements of religion', is likely to discover, in the next phase of the 'night battle', 'the need, the cost, the glory of this element of incarnation and of death in life, of life through death'.[80]

Twenty years ago, Friedrich Heer observed that 'There has always been a struggle between "above" and "below" in Europe's inner history. The "upper" culture of Christianity, educated humanism and rationalism has struggled against a "lower" culture of the masses . . . During the nineteenth century which really means the era that ended for Europe in 1945 this struggle entered a new phase. For the first time, movements from below broke the surface of the upper culture'.[81] Heer's image captures, I believe, something of the social and epistemological significance of that 'decentration' which is entailed in the shift from 'classical' to 'modern'

culture. If the cultural revolution into which we are enter-
ing, not simply in Europe but across the world, is as fundamental as this image would suggest, it is hardly surprising
that we should find ourselves deprived of familiar landmarks,
of conceptual and institutional securities. But perhaps the
darkness of the 'night battle' is, after all, but one aspect of
the darkness of Gethsemane, of the experience of Him who
taught us, 'once for all, the true attitude towards suffering'.[82]
Which, for a Christian, would be grounds for hope, not for
despair.

NOTES

1 J. H. Newman, *Fifteen Sermons Preached Before the University of Oxford* (London,
   1871), p. 201.
2 A. R. Vidler, *A Variety of Catholic Modernists* (Cambridge, 1970), p. 13.
3 T. M. Loome, 'The Enigma of Baron Friedrich von Hügel — as Modernist', *Downside Review*, xci (1973), p. 210.
4 G. Tyrrell, *Christianity at the Crossroads* (London, 1913), p. 3.
5 R. D. Haight, 'The Unfolding of Modernism in France: Blondel, Laberthonnière, Le Roy', *Theological Studies*, xxxv (1974), p. 633.
6 Cited Vidler, *Variety*, p. 112 (Vidler's stress).
7 Ibid., p. 113.
8 J. Rivière, *Le Modernisme dans l'Eglise* (Paris, 1929), p. 463.
9 Vidler, *Variety*, p. 3.
10 A. F. Loisy, *Mémoires Pour Servir à l'Histoire Religieuse de Notre Temps*, 3 vols.
   (Paris, 1930–1931); Rivière, op. cit.; A. R. Vidler, *The Modernist Movement
   in the Roman Church* (Cambridge, 1934), and *Variety*; R. Marlé, ed., *Au
   Coeur de la Crise Moderniste* (Paris, 1960); L. F. Barmann, *Baron Friedrich von
   Hügel and the Modernist Crisis in England* (Cambridge, 1972); E. Poulat,
   Histoire, Dogme et Critique dans la Crise Moderniste (Tournai, 1962).
11 Loome, 'Enigma', p. 212.
12 B. M. G. Reardon, ed., *Roman Catholic Modernism* (London, 1970), p. 9.
13 Cited M. Ward, *The Wilfrid Wards and the Transition. I. The Nineteenth
   Century* (London, 1934), pp. 160–161. (*Transition*)
14 W. Ward, 'Liberalism and Intransigeance', *The Nineteenth Century*, xlvii
   (1900), p. 971.
15 W. Ward, 'Newman and Sabatier', *The Fortnightly Review*, lxxv (1901),
   p. 808.
16 W. Ward, 'The Time-Spirit of the Nineteenth Century', *Problems and
   Persons* (London, 1903), p. 4.
17 Ibid., p. 7.
18 Loc. cit.
19 Ibid., p. 54.
20 Cited M. Ward, *The Wilfrid Wards and the Transition. II. Insurrection versus
   Resurrection* (London, 1937), p. 317. (*Insurrection*)
21 Ibid., p. 323. Here, as so often in his writings, he is drawing on Newman's
   lecture on 'Christianity and Scientific Investigation', *Idea of a University
   Defined and Illustrated* (London, 1875), pp. 456–479.
22 Ibid., p. 137.

23 J. Ward, 'Introductory Study', *Last Lectures by Wilfrid Ward* (London, 1918), p. xl.
24 Ibid., p. 1.
25 Cited M. Ward, *Insurrection*, p. 479.
26 Cited M. Ward, *Transition*, p. 161.
27 J. Ward, op. cit., p. xxii.
28 M. Ward, *Transition*, p. 195.
29 W. Ward, 'The Rigidity of Rome', *Problems and Persons*, p. 69.
30 W. Ward, *Problems and Persons*, p. xix.
31 Ibid., p. xx.
32 Cited M. Ward, *Transition*, p. 184.
33 *Downside Review*, xci (1973), pp. 13–34, 123–140, 204–230.
34 Loome 'would claim' for Lagrange 'unqualified superiority' as an exegete (p. 216), but he provides no evidence as to whether or not he is competent to pronounce this judgement.
35 'There is a ghost to be laid to rest: "Friedrich von Hügel — modernist" ' (p. 206).
36 Marlé, op. cit., p. 9.
37 B. Holland, ed., *Selected Letters of Baron Friedrich von Hügel* (London, 1931), p. 248.
38 Loc. cit.
39 Loome, p. 208.
40 Loc. cit.
41 Actually, 'Modernism' is defined in Cross as 'A movement within the RC Church which aimed at bringing the tradition of Catholic belief into closer relation with the modern outlook in philosophy, the historical and other sciences and social ideas' (p. 910), but perhaps Loome does not regard *The Oxford Dictionary of the Christian Church* as a 'great theological dictionary'.
42 W. Ward, *William George Ward and the Catholic Revival* (London, 1893), p. 371; cf. Loome, pp. 123–125.
43 Loome, p. 126.
44 Loome, p. 25; cf. Ward, op. cit., p. 116.
45 Loome, p. 229.
46 *Selected Letters*, p. 334.
47 Barmann, op. cit., p. 144.
48 F. von Hügel, *The Mystical Element of Religion as Studied in Saint Catherine of Genoa and her Friends* (London, 1961), Vol. I, p. xxi.
49 Loome, p. 138.
50 Cf. Marlé, op. cit., p. 159; A. Dru and I. Trethowan, *Maurice Blondel: The Letter on Apologetics and History and Dogma* (London, 1964), p. 225.
51 Cf. M. Schoof, *Breakthrough: Beginnings of the New Catholic Theology*, tr. N. D. Smith (Dublin, 1970), p. 109.
52 Cited M. Ward, *Transition*, p. 375.
53 *Selected Letters*, p. 284.
54 F. von Hügel, *Essays and Addresses on the Philosophy of Religion, First Series* (London, 1931), p. 277.
55 M. Blondel, *L'Action (1893)* (Paris, 1973), p. 489.
56 Katherine Gilbert, *Maurice Blondel's Philosophy of Action*, cited B. M. G. Reardon, *Liberalism and Tradition: Aspects of Catholic Thought in Nineteenth-Century France* (Cambridge, 1975), p. 224.
57 Cited H. Bouillard, *Blondel and Christianity*, tr. J. M. Somerville (Washington, 1970), p. 165.
58 Cited Dru, *Maurice Blondel*, p. 32.
59 A. Dru, 'Modernism and the Present Position of the Church', *Downside Review*, lxxxii (1964), p. 105.
60 Ibid., p. 108.
61 W. Ward, *Problems and Persons*, p. xix.

62 Dru, *Maurice Blondel*, p. 24.
63 Dru, 'Modernism', p. 110.
64 L. Bouyer, *The Decomposition of Catholicism*, tr. C. U. Quinn (Chicago, 1968), p. 3.
65 B. J. F. Lonergan, *A Second Collection* (London, 1974), p. 161.
66 Ibid., p. 92.
67 B. J. F. Lonergan, *Method in Theology* (London, 1972), p. xi. Lonergan's interpretation of the shift is intended to be descriptive rather than evaluative. It would be as naive indiscriminately to celebrate so complex, pervasive and ambivalent a process as it would indiscriminately to regret it.
68 Cf. Lonergan, *Method*, pp. 301–302. Fergus Kerr has said that 'there can be no way forward in Christian theology which does not break completely with [the] continuingly potent myth of "European humanity" and its inborn privilege of Reason (*Geist, logos*)', 'Beyond Lonergan's Method: A Response to William Mathews', *New Blackfriars*, lvii (1976), p. 66; cf. K. Rahner, *Theological Investigations*, *XI*, tr. D. Bourke (London, 1974), p. 234. In a number of recent essays, Rahner has explored the implications of the contemporary 'insurmountability' of cultural, and hence philosophical and theological pluralism. Cf. also N. L. A. Lash, 'Understanding the Stranger', *Irish Theological Quarterly*, xli (1974), pp. 91–103.
69 Lonergan, *Method*, p. 326.
70 Cited Dru, *Maurice Blondel*, p. 37.
71 Dru, op. cit., pp. 39–40.
72 Loome, p. 128.
73 J. P. Whelan, *The Spirituality of Friedrich von Hügel* (London, 1971), p. 221.
74 Ibid., p. 222.
75 Loc. cit.
76 W. Ward, *Problems and Persons*, p. 66.
77 J. Ward, *Last Lectures*, p. 1.
78 It is possible that the concept of 'aggiornamento' was born, in the young Fr Roncalli's mind, at the height of the Modernist crisis, under the influence — mediated by Loisy's writings and Roncalli's friendship with Buonaiuti — of Newman's *Essay on Development:* cf. F. M. Willam, *Vom Jungen Angelo Roncalli (1903–1907) zum Papst Johannes XXIII (1958–1963)* (Innsbruck, 1967).
79 Lonergan, *Second Collection*, p. 55.
80 F. von Hügel, *Essays and Addresses on the Philosophy of Religion, Second Series* (London, 1930), p. 88.
81 F. Heer, *The Intellectual History of Europe*, tr. J. Steinberg (London, 1966), p. 1.
82 Von Hügel, *The Mystical Element*, vol. I, p. 26.

4

Cardinal Bourne and the Malines Conversations

R. J. Lahey

THE unfettering of the Roman Catholic church from the shackles of the anti-Modernist period was a long and often painful process. Nowhere, perhaps, were the difficulties more apparent than in the English situation of the 1920s. The suppression of Modernism under Pius X had all but destroyed also the fragile roots of an indigenous, liberal, English Catholic theology, and even now there were no real signs of its revival. Its only great living representative, the lay theologian Friedrich von Hügel, was reduced to publishing as a 'philosopher of religion'. Those clerics who wrote on religious matters had, as individuals, still less scholarly independence, and lacked even a national institution of learning which might provide them, collectively, with some measure of autonomy and mutual support. Not only were they circumspect, but they confined themselves to scholarly concerns which were relatively innocuous. Of works of piety there were plenty, as also new editions of the standard Catholic authors of the past (especially the mystics), and some attention was turned to less controversial historical topics. But there was no real attempt to reconstruct a theological base to meet the needs of a new day. That the biblical treatises published showed little influence of the historical-critical method was hardly surprising, but what was crucial was the near total lack of serious studies, liberal or traditional, of doctrinal or moral subjects. Even the post-Modernist Thomistic revival then in evidence elsewhere had no true English parallel. (It is not without significance that the English Dominican translations of the *Summa Theologica* and the *Contra Gentiles* included neither notes nor commentary.) What did, in fact, predominate was a theological orientation of a different type, overwhelmingly apologetical, and directed as much to the suasion of those outside the Roman communion as to the enlightenment of those within it.

This emphasis reflected the institutional stance of English Catholicism. The practical strategy of the church in 1921 may be said, broadly speaking, to have been threefold: the strengthening and expansion of its own structures, the securing of an increased measure of recognition in English national life, and the attraction of new members to its ranks by conversion, primarily from the Church of England. These goals, in fact, were interrelated, and perhaps the most important among them was the last. The church was by now far removed from the penal days and the struggle to prevent leakage of membership. During the latter part of the nineteenth century and the first decades of the twentieth it gained large numbers of converts (by 1920, almost 13,000 a year). Its authorities had every reason to hope that this trend would increase. The growth of Anglo-Catholic sentiments within the Established Church and the papal denial of the validity of Anglican orders in 1896 both had great effect in the past. Now, it was thought, the internal divisions within Anglicanism over doctrinal differences would once more swell the ranks of converts. The Catholic press, led by the *Tablet* and the *Universe*, played upon these themes. Anglican divisions were contrasted with apparent Roman unity. The Catholic Truth Society, the Catholic Evidence Guild, and several other like organizations were constant in their efforts to promote books, tracts, and lectures directed towards conversions. Never before, said the manifesto of the C.E.G., had the time been more opportune 'for a widespread and *organized effort to bring the Catholic Faith to the masses of the English-speaking world.*' It was not simply, however, or perhaps even primarily, for the increase of numbers and prestige that such efforts were mounted. Most Roman Catholics genuinely saw in conversions the only practical means of advancing the unity of Christendom.

Few Catholics anywhere regarded the newly flourishing church union movement as having any real relevance to their communion. Nor, in fact, were they given much encouragement to do so. Even the Lambeth Appeal of 1920 made only very tentative overtures towards Rome, and it was obvious that its main thrusts lay in the directions of nonconformity and Orthodoxy. More important was the fact that Catholics considered the church union movement to be founded on the premise of doctrinal give-and-take, a concept they utterly rejected. As the *Tablet* told its readers, among Christian bodies, 'no compromise is possible, no agreement can be reached, except by the conversion of one group to the views of another.' Corporate reunion, which implied the existence of an alternative route to unity, was a notion at best illusory, and at worst, as that journal put it, 'unsound and un-Catholic.'

So negative an attitude, however, was not universal among Roman Catholics. For one, Cardinal Mercier, the Archbishop of Mechelen (Malines) in Belgium, had been considering the matter since he had been approached in 1919 about possible Catholic participation in the proposed Faith and Order Movement. This he did not deem consistent with his church's principles. Still, by September, 1920, just after the Lambeth Conference, he had begun to entertain seriously the idea of inviting to Malines groups of Anglican and Orthodox theologians for informal discussions on doctrinal matters. He had even raised the point with Pope Benedict XV (but had received no clear authorization for his plan), when a French priest, Father Fernand Portal, C.M., drew his attention to some aspects of the Lambeth Appeal as it affected Anglican-Roman Catholic relations. Portal had been

associated with the Anglican Lord Halifax in the attempt
to secure papal recognition of Anglican orders, but this had
led only to Leo XIII's 'absolutely null and utterly void'
declaration of 1896. The French priest now perceived that
the climate had changed, and that the offer by the Lambeth
Conference to receive, in the interests of unity, some form of
recognition or commission of orders, made the papal statement no longer an insurmountable hurdle. Portal emphasiz-
ed that the crucial thing was to bring the two sides into
conference. Initially, Mercier was noncommittal. Portal and
Halifax, however, heard rumours of his earlier plans for
such meetings, and when they pressed their views in person
he agreed to receive a group of Anglicans for informal discussions. Mercier did ask why there had been no prior contact with the Catholic hierarchy in England, but he was
satisfied by Halifax's generalization that the unreceptive
attitude of English Roman Catholics towards reunion
precluded any steps in that direction.

Halifax might well have been correct in assuming that a
similar approach made in England would have been un-
productive. For one thing, the involvement of Halifax
himself and Portal would not have been welcomed. The
elderly peer was, no doubt, widely respected. On the other
hand, English Roman Catholics had seen him as their ad-
versary in the Anglican orders controversy and saw him
still, as an Anglo-Catholic, as linked with a party of Anglicans trying to claim for themselves what rightly belonged
only to Rome. Portal was compromised by his own involvement in the Anglican orders question and especially by his
editorship during that time of the *Revue Anglo-Romaine*, a
periodical highly suspect by English Catholics. As a foreign-
er, too, he was liable to the criticism by English Catholics
that he had no real understanding of religious affairs in their
country.

Although he anticipated negative reaction from that
quarter, Halifax did decide, at the prompting of his friend
Stephen Gaselee of the Foreign Office, at least to inform
Cardinal Bourne, as leader of the Roman Catholic church in

England, of what was intended. In fact, his reception by the Archbishop of Westminster agreeably surprised him. Bourne spoke warmly of Cardinal Mercier, an old friend from his student days at Louvain, and Halifax unexpectedly found him 'altogether sympathetic'.[1]

It was against this backdrop that the first of the Malines Conversations[2] began a week later, on December 6th, 1921, as an informal and unofficial discussion on reunion between three Anglicans (Halifax took with him two clergymen, Walter Howard Frere of the Mirfield community and Armitage Robinson, the Dean of Wells) and three Roman Catholics (Mercier, his Vicar-General, Ernest van Roey, and Portal). That meeting, and those which followed, were both friendly and inconclusive. The Conversations continued, in fits and starts, over the next five years, grinding to a halt in October, 1926. By that time Bourne's sympathy had entirely disappeared, and harsh words had been exchanged between him and Mercier.

What was the Cardinal's position over these years? Was it, as is so often maintained, one of unrelenting antagonism to Malines? Did he, in fact, spearhead Catholic opposition to the Conversations both in England and in Rome? In light of the strong negative reaction so general among English Catholics, it was almost inevitable that such assertions were made, both then and afterwards. They were not illogical; they were, however, distortions of the truth.

Bourne's real attitude was far different. His own words throughout the period, both private and public, testify to an open-mindedness towards Malines entirely at variance with the picture usually painted. Opposed he was, certainly, to some features of the way in which the Conversations were conducted. It is also true that he doubted their ability to effect any permanent results. But Bourne was a churchman too fond of moderation not to have a genuine willingness to explore the new associations with the Church of England which these meetings appeared to offer. He saw no harm in talking.

The inherent disadvantage of any moderate position is

that it is open to attack on both flanks. Bourne's stand has been misconstrued not only by Lord Halifax, who later wrote of 'the machinations of Cardinal Bourne and the English Roman Catholics,'[3] but even by the Cardinal's own biographer, Ernest Oldmeadow, who tended to project onto his subject some of his own strong opposition to the Conversations. In this case, the biographer was hardly at arm's length. As editor of the *Tablet*, Oldmeadow himself was involved in the events. A convert to Catholicism from Nonconformity, he had little taste for Malines, which he saw as only offering encouragement to Anglo-Catholicism, and his views could not help but permeate the pages of his paper. No doubt the *Tablet*, then as always, complied with any clear request of Cardinal Bourne, its principal trustee. Still, in this instance it would be quite wrong simply to identify the position of the Archbishop of Westminster with the stance taken in the pages of that paper.

In re-assessing Bourne's role, it is only proper to observe that a certain confusion seems to have surrounded Malines, sometimes even in the minds of those involved. Oldmeadow, for example, suggested that Halifax was less than frank in his initial interview with Bourne, mentioning that the Cardinal later told him that Halifax had failed to describe 'his transactions with the Archbishops of Canterbury and York or the existence of advanced plans.'[4] But this was to transpose a later state of affairs to an earlier period. Before the first conversation, the only involvement of Archbishop Davidson of Canterbury had been to give Halifax a personal letter of introduction to Mercier and privately to warn the Dean of Wells, a friend, to tread cautiously. Advanced plans simply failed to exist; even after the first conversation there was no real design for a *series* of meetings. What Bourne had been given and had welcomed was a fair statement of the situation as it stood — that Cardinal Mercier had agreed to receive at Malines a group of Anglicans for private and unofficial discussions. At the time, nothing more was envisaged.

What is not always appreciated is the essential difference

in character between the first and subsequent conversations. Only loosely did they form a real series, for while the first was an entirely private affair, the remainder were held with the full knowledge and consent of both the Archbishop of Canterbury and the Holy See. How this happened was a complicated affair,[5] with which Bourne had little to do. It was really the election of a new Pope which brought about the change. Within a day of his elevation to office, Pius XI had given to Mercier his clear and unreserved approval for what had been done already and for the continuation of these efforts. At the same time, but independently of Mercier, contact was established between Cardinal Gasparri, the Vatican's Secretary of State, and G. K. A. Bell, the Archbishop of Canterbury's chaplain, through the intermediary of two Jesuits, Father Michel d'Herbigny of Rome's Gregorian University and Father Leslie Walker of Campion Hall, Oxford. Gasparri, a contributor to the old *Revue Anglo-Romaine* and a member of the Papal commission on Anglican orders (his vote was that they were at least doubtfully valid), wholeheartedly supported the opening of discussions with the Church of England. Like Portal, he seems to have been encouraged by the Lambeth Appeal's acceptance of possible commission or recognition for Anglican orders. For their part, the Archbishops of Canterbury and York, who, of course, were completely informed of Bell's role, made it clear through him that they would be prepared to authorize such meetings if a corresponding endorsement were given by Rome. By the end of February, 1923, Mercier was authorized to tell the Anglicans that 'the Holy See approves and encourages your conversations,' and in return the Archbishop of Canterbury had given his own permission for them.

Cardinal Bourne was later to claim, and with considerable justice, that he was kept 'absolutely in the dark' about Malines. However, this was not entirely true. He was certainly notified in advance of the first conversation; afterwards he received from Halifax some information at least as to what had transpired there. There are indications that

Halifax visited the Cardinal for this purpose even before Christmas, 1921. Certainly he paid a later call, clearly recorded by Bourne himself ('to place me *au courant* of the situation'), in November, 1922.[6]

Mercier himself wrote to Bourne at this stage. When the Belgian cardinal received permission to communicate Roman approval to the Anglican side, he also took that opportunity to notify the Archbishop of Westminster of the same. Mercier provided an account of the antecedents of this step, and he did not fail to solicit from his English colleague 'such advice and suggestions as you would be pleased to give me.' To this communication, Bourne replied in a most friendly manner and made it clear that though he was not sanguine about them, he had no fundamental objections to the proceedings. 'I think that these informal conferences may well be encouraged,' he answered, 'though in my opinion it will be *a very long time* before anything definite can emerge from them.' He was less than enthusiastic about the involvement of Halifax, whom he thought 'vague and inconsequent,' and he cautioned Mercier that although Anglo-Catholics might accept the actual existence of a central authority he doubted they would do so as '*an essential part of the Divine Constitution of the Church.*' Bourne, however, did not use the occasion to tender any advice.[7]

Thereafter it is true that Cardinal Bourne was not kept even generally informed about an affair which was so obviously his concern. On Mercier's part, this was probably due more to neglect than to mistrust. Even Halifax, whose feelings about Bourne were as mixed as were Bourne's about him, raised the question after the third conversation (November, 1923) of whether another visit to the Cardinal might not be in order. 'He is always very kind to me,' wrote the peer, 'although I don't suppose he is really very sympathetic — but I think that if I could talk to him quite openly and as it were *sub sigillo* it might be useful.'[8] Mercier welcomed the suggestion and entirely approved, but it appears that Halifax never followed through on his plan. The end result was that at no time during the course of the meetings was the leading

English Catholic prelate given any authentic information as to their content.

The other major complaint concerning the conduct of the Conversations later made by Bourne was that they included no person 'to represent the standpoint of the Latin Church in England.'[9] This was indeed unfortunate, but again it was not due to any deliberate intent on Mercier's part. Walker's nomination as a delegate was actively considered in the period following formal approval of the Conversations by Rome and Lambeth. Portal opposed it, fearing that, as a Jesuit, Walker's ties with Rome were too close, but even Halifax thought differently, writing (though not to Portal), 'he is friendly, and may be utilized.' In fact, it was thought that Bourne, who had spoken of Walker to Halifax, might take the opportunity of Mercier's call for suggestions to put forth the Jesuit's name. However, Bourne, as we have seen, made no requests at all. In the end, it was decided not to add to the original groups before the second conversation, but the need to widen the circle of participants was thereafter evident. Eventually there emerged a consensus on the Anglican side that Bishop Gore should take part, and with him Archbishop Davidson named B. J. Kidd, Warden of Keble College, Oxford. It was quickly accepted that Monsignor Pierre Batiffol of the Institut Catholique in Paris was Gore's logical counterpart, but this still left another Roman Catholic to be chosen. Portal had been advancing the name of Hippolyte Hemmer, also a French priest, but Mercier (and even Halifax) seemed more inclined towards Father Bede Jarrett, the English Dominican Provincial. The Cardinal felt that this move would both create a link with Bourne and offset English Catholic criticism of the reunion movement. At the end of September, 1923, Mercier decided definitely to invite Jarrett, but the invitation was never sent. No sooner was the decision made, than Halifax did an abrupt about-face and sought reconsideration; the peer had just received from Jarrett a letter which he thought too negative.[10] Thus Hemmer became the second new delegate, and an important opportunity to reconcile English Catholic opinion was lost.

By then, the damage was near irrevocable, for the hitherto private affair was on the verge of becoming the centre of a great public debate.

The Conversations had never been publicly acknowledged, but the secret was increasingly difficult to keep. The Archbishop of Canterbury thought this a dangerous state of affairs, and on Christmas Eve, 1923, he attempted to head off possible criticism by issuing an open letter to the Metropolitans of the Anglican Communion. This was generally a very cautious account of the provenance of the Conversations, but Davidson felt obliged to mention the Vatican's cognizance of the matter. At Mercier's insistence, since the Cardinal had no mandate to make the Vatican's approval public, and did not feel, in any case, that this should be done from Lambeth, the passage in question was deliberately vague. Still, to English Roman Catholics the knowledge came as a complete surprise. Oldmeadow wrote to Monsignor James Moyes, Bourne's theologian, for guidance in treating the matter in the *Tablet*. Referring to a press report, he declared: 'I shall be astonished if it should turn out that the Vatican has recognized these Malines discussions in the sense which the *Guardian* attempts to convey.'[11] When the *Tablet* appeared the next day, it attempted to play down this aspect and went so far as to include a statement that nothing of substance was involved. If so, it said, 'more would have to have been heard by the Cardinal Archbishop of Westminster, who has only unofficial and fragmentary accounts of the chats at Malines.'

The next issue of the paper took the same line, even in an article by Moyes himself. He admitted that the Holy See no doubt had some unofficial knowledge of the matter, but Moyes quoted with apparent approval a *Times'* report denying any official cognizance or any encouragement on the Vatican's part. He added also a statement from the same report which affirmed that any Vatican-approved discussions would have employed English Catholics and would have been held in Rome. Despite the proximity of its author to the Cardinal, it is difficult to imagine that Bourne had any connection with this piece. That it appeared as it did was probably due to the fact that Bourne was seriously ill at the time. In any event, there was some backtracking in the next week's issue, when a report from Rome finally acknowledged that the Holy See's approval must have been involved.

This torrent of contradictory assertions necessitated some clarification from Mercier, and on January 18th, 1924, he directed a letter on the subject to his clergy. Much of it was a low-keyed account of the origins of the meetings, but it included the crucial statement: 'it was enough to know that I was acting in agreement with the supreme Authority, blessed and encouraged by it.' Father Sordet, who was with Cardinal Bourne in Rome at the time, described the latter as 'utterly delighted' by Mercier's pastoral. Bourne even sent Sordet to obtain an explanation for the omission of the words referring to the Holy See from the text as reprinted in the *Osservatore Romano*, for he thought that these would still 'the malicious insinuations' of the press. He made a point of asking Sordet to report on the affair to Mercier.[12]

In England, Oldmeadow, who thought the pastoral 'a prolix and futile document,' prepared to give it only a minimum of attention in the *Tablet*, and to 'let this Pastoral sink into the sand under its own weight.' (At Mercier's request, however, he had agreed to print the full text.) But Bourne, perhaps thinking of the *Osservatore*, wrote from Rome to instruct the editor to accord the letter 'the most sympathetic and cordial treatment, and quote largely from it.' He drew special attention to the omitted sentence, which he called the most important in the document. Refuting the position taken so recently by the *Tablet*, he told Oldmeadow that these words revealed 'the fact, known to me in confidence all along, that the conversations were held with the knowledge, approbation, and encouragement of the Holy See.'[13] The Cardinal's instructions were hardly those of an opponent of Malines.

Bourne's genuine support for the conversations was made even more evident in his own Lenten Pastoral for 1924, on 'The Union of Christendom.' While he disavowed any notion of compromise in matters doctrinal, he declared his real and personal commitment to the cause at stake. Further, he entirely repudiated the suggestion that English Catholics as a group were hostile to *rapprochement*. 'How little do the writers or utterers of such things realize what we feel,' wrote the Cardinal, 'with regard to the restoration of England to the unity of Christendom — how there is no sacrifice of place or position that we are not prepared to make in order to attain so great an end.' He did not hesitate, either, to make a more direct reference to Malines in the most positive terms:

> It is to us a matter of rejoicing that members of the Establishment, to whatever school of thought they may belong, should seek from representative Catholics whether they be in France, or in Belgium, or here at home or in any other country, a more complete understanding of what the Catholic Church really teaches. Such contact, with the help and guidance of the Holy Spirit, must be productive of good, even though no actual result may be immediately attained.[14]

Mercier was most appreciative of his brother cardinal's gesture of solidarity. His note of congratulation said that although he had been hurt by accounts in the English Catholic press, he was 'charmed and comforted' by Bourne's pastoral, and especially by its loyal and forthright tone. He assured his colleague in return that his own intention was but to follow his conscience and to serve the Church. There is no record of a reply from Bourne, but it is obvious he did not then feel the need to express any misgivings.

About this time, too, Bourne imposed upon the *Tablet* a silence with regard to comment on the proceedings.[15] Indeed, between early 1924 and October, 1925, that paper gave the Conversations only passing reference. It stated later that its policy was to refuse 'to discuss or even chronicle these Conversations, save in connection with formal statements by responsible persons.'

Bourne's policy appeared to be one of benevolent non-interference. However, there was by no means universal support for this among English Catholic leaders. H. W. Dean, for example, the editor of the *Universe*, felt, as did Oldmeadow at the *Tablet*, that the effect of Mercier's pastoral would be 'most unfortunate.' Moreover, he described it as 'an attack upon the English Catholic body,' and he asked Cardinal Bourne whether something could not be done in Rome about the Conversations. Dean also raised the matter of the effects of Malines upon conversions to Catholicism, describing the talks as disheartening to the clergy and public engaged in that work.[16] Among the hierarchy, too, Malines almost certainly had its opponents. Of the United Kingdom bishops, only Cardinal Logue of Armagh and Bishop Casartelli of Salford addressed messages of any warmth to Mercier upon publication of his pastoral. Archbishop Keating of Liverpool did have some good words for the Conversations in the public press. But it was significant that while several of the bishops imitated Westminster in directing their Lenten pastorals for 1924 to the theme of Christian unity, they did so in markedly cooler terms than their Cardinal and studiously avoided any complimentary reference to Malines.

The two most powerful adversaries of the Conversations, however, were Bourne's English colleagues in the Sacred College of Cardinals, Francis Aidan Gasquet and Raphael Merry del Val. This was not unexpected. Mercier once admonished Gasparri not to allow 'the trio' (almost certainly Merry del Val and De Lai, and possibly either Billot or Gasquet) to reinstate the '*gendarme*' tactics of the past. Obviously fearing a renewal of *intégrisme*, and at the same time thinking of the Conversations, he stressed that 'respect for the truth' had always to be tempered by 'the fire of charity.'[17] It was unlikely that Gasparri needed warning; his policies were as unacceptable to the conservative group as were Mercier's. However, the near election of Gasparri to the papacy in 1922 and the ultimate choice of a man who until a few months before had been his subordinate and protégé, left the Secretary of State in a position of considerable strength and muted his opponents. Public opposition to the Conversations in Roman circles during 1922-24, then, if it existed at all, would have been entirely without effect, for both the Pope and Gasparri remained firm and even enthusiastic in their support of Mercier's actions.

Privately, Merry del Val felt particularly frustrated that he could take no decisive action. Although Secretary of the Holy Office, he was all too well aware of the erosion of the once substantial authority he commanded in anti-Modernist days, when he had occupied that very office now held by Gasparri. In February, 1925, in a letter to Moyes, he made clear his personal feelings. His own raising of the issue in Rome he regarded as futile. 'Any attempt to rectify or counteract the mischief,' he grumbled, 'seems to be resented.' His dislike for the Secretary of State was obviously intense. With reference to the Anglican Orders period, he called Gasparri 'as much at sea in these questions now as he was then, but his position today makes his attitude more mischievous, for he does what he likes.' Merry del Val seemed to feel that only Bourne could take decisive action, in that Bourne's office entitled him to make a direct approach to the Pope. He thought that Bourne should 'speak plainly.' There is no doubt what Merry del Val meant by this, for he continued: 'If he [Bourne] only says what is, of course, true, that anything that can lead Anglicans to the Church or to the conversion of England, must be welcomed by all Catholics, he will be misunderstood as encouraging what is being done.' The Roman Cardinal repeated the charge of 'the many conversions stopped.'[18] Though addressed to Moyes, Merry del Val's remarks were more likely intended for the ears of his superior. If Bourne did become aware of his fellow Cardinal's letter or views, however, he seems to have chosen to ignore them.

Merry del Val told Moyes that Gasquet, too, was 'very distressed.' Unlike his colleague, however, Gasquet ventured even to make a direct approach to the Pope, whom he saw in late October, 1925. Nevertheless, his interview brought him little comfort. 'Although I spoke very plainly,' he recorded in his diary, 'he still approved of the fact that conversations—*private*—could do no harm.' The standard argument against them impressed the Pope not at all. 'He did not put any value on the alleged falling off of conversions,' wrote Gasquet; the Pope told him that even if people were waiting, that just showed that they were not yet prepared to take the step. The one assurance given by the Pope was that no compromise was possible concerning Eucharistic doctrine or Anglican orders.[19]

Even as the Pope approved the Conversations, events in England were bringing to a head Catholic opposition to them. The critics had a field day. Although the content of the Conversations was supposedly secret, there were numerous reports, even in print, purporting to give information about what had gone on. One of the first, in late 1924, was an article by Robert Gordon George (Robert Sencourt) in which the author not only intimated inside knowledge of the meetings (which he probably did not possess), but had even suggested that his English Catholic brethren were entirely unreasonable on the question of reunion by contrast with the French and Belgians. Indiscreetly, too, Halifax made a speech to the Anglo-Catholic Congress in July, 1925, which contained statements about the Roman Catholic position on the papacy and the preservation of the prerogatives of Canterbury in any future reunion. It was widely supposed that his views reflected the tenor of the Malines discussions. There soon followed assertions in the Anglican church press about the difference between the 'ultramontane' stand of English Catholics and the 'moderate' views of their continental counterparts. As the last straw, there appeared in the *Times* a report (never denied by the speaker) of an address given by Portal, allegedly including the incredible assertion that at Malines an agreement had been reached on the principles of the Council of Trent, the one remaining obstacle to unity being the papacy.

This battle of words was joined by the controversial Jesuit, Father Francis Woodlock. Woodlock had already incurred the ire of both Mercier and Halifax for what they regarded as tendentious and unconciliatory remarks about the Church of England. But when the *Church Times*, after Halifax's speech, made uncomplimentary comments contrasting the Jesuit's position with that said to be Mercier's, it was Woodlock's anger that was unbridled. He not only sent a rejoinder to the *Church Times*, but also forwarded a request to Mercier's secretary that the Cardinal repudiate the various Anglican assertions. Mercier entirely ignored the letter. But Merry del Val saw the *Church Times* leader as an opportunity to press his own views once more. He wrote to Woodlock: 'Surely Cardinal Bourne and the English Bishops will take the occasion to make a clear statement and sweep away this false doctrine. I fancy Cardinal Gasquet would be ready to do so and he can do so with the assurance that the true doctrine will be upheld here [i.e., at the Holy Office].'[20] In his reply, however, Woodlock took the view that even statements from such high quarters would have little effect. They, too, would be dismissed as reactionary. Perhaps, though, support from so powerful a source emboldened the Jesuit priest, for following the report of Portal's speech, he addressed a momentous letter to the *Tablet*.

On the surface, most of Woodlock's letter was directed against his Anglican critics. However, there were references to Mercier by name, respectful enough but hardly positive, including a statement about the 'unfortunate result of Cardinal Mercier's silence.' As to the Conversations themselves, Woodlock's kindest remark was that they were 'well intentioned.' He did not bother to conceal his displeasure with them. 'The chief result of the Malines conversations up to date,' the Jesuit asserted, 'has been to discredit the teaching of English theologians.' Despite the *Tablet*'s policy of not printing comment on Malines, Woodlock's letter appeared in the issue of October 10, 1925.[21]

Mercier was angered by the letter, which he saw as an attempt by Woodlock to sabotage the Conversations. He wrote a sharp and sarcastic rebuke to its author and sent a copy to the *Tablet* with a demand that it be published. Oldmeadow, who was unrepentant over having used the letter from Woodlock, professed to feel that to print Mercier's riposte would provoke a scandal. Nevertheless, in the circumstances, he had little alternative but to refer the matter to Cardinal Bourne, to whom he mentioned that Woodlock had the support of Merry del Val and Gasquet. He gave it as his own opinion that publication of Mercier's reply would lower the dignity of the Sacred College.

Mercier's letter marked a turning point in Bourne's attitude to Malines and led to a sharp and bitter exchange between the two old friends.[22] It is evident that by this time the leaks and purported leaks and the accusations of intransigence and ultramontanism levelled against the English Catholics had greatly influenced Bourne's opinions. Above all else — for this was the one specific instance mentioned in the Cardinal's correspondence — Portal's speech appears to have infuriated him, no doubt because Portal, a party to the discussions, seemed to divulge supposedly privileged information. Bourne himself answered Mercier's letter to the *Tablet*, but it was obvious from his reply that it was not the Woodlock affair which really troubled him. After affirming that he thought publication would do personal harm to Mercier, he immediately got on to the wider issues. He referred to the damage done to the Catholic Church in England by 'Anglican exploitation' of the Conversations, and although he absolved Mercier himself of blame, he complained of the indiscretions of other participants.

All this but prefaced Bourne's airing of his own great personal grievance, that Mercier had treated him 'as if I did not exist.' It was only proper, he wrote, that Mercier should have stipulated from the outset that there be no secrets from him. Feeling for Mercier had restrained him from raising the matter before, but now his exclusion left him powerless 'either to correct or control freelances like F. Woodlock who has many sympathizers both here and in Rome.' Forthright as it was, however, nothing in Bourne's letter was a censure of the Conversations themselves. His was rather a protest that the leader of the Catholic Church in

England was deprived of information about them to which he had a right.

Oldmeadow followed Bourne's reply by a personal visit to Malines to seek to resolve the differences between the Belgian prelate and the *Tablet*, but even by his own admission this only 'aggravated' matters.[23] It was immediately after this visit that Mercier, obviously hurt himself, replied to Bourne in terms both impassioned and perhaps ill-considered. He referred to the campaign of 'disparagement and insinuations' waged by Woodlock, to the antagonism towards the Conversations of English Catholics, and even to the 'national and religious struggle' between 'hostile groups' in England. If conferences with the Anglicans had not been held outside England, said Mercier, they would not have taken place at all. He defended his policy of silence about the talks on the grounds that any other course would only give rise to 'passionate discussions in the press.'

Bourne had constantly repudiated similar charges made by others; he could hardly fail to do so now that they were voiced by Mercier himself. His first draft of a reply was long and angry. This, however, was discarded in favour of a curt but calmer letter which was content to insinuate Mercier's lack of familiarity with the English religious situation and to refer to the 'insulting character' of Mercier's remark about the need for secrecy.

Mercier's answer was an attempt at reconciliation. He found it incredible, he wrote, that Bourne could have taken as a personal affront his remarks about the press, which had been intended only as a justification of Mercier's silence in the public forum. (This was, of course, the point at issue between him and Woodlock.) However, for the first time, Mercier did try to vindicate his treatment of Bourne. He found unacceptable Bourne's attempt to compare the Archbishop of Westminster's standing in the matter with that of Canterbury. In Mercier's view, a true analogy could be drawn only between the Anglican Primate and the Holy See, who, as principals, were alone entitled to full information. Mercier thereupon went on to suggest the real reason why there had not been a closer relationship between Westminster and Malines:

> Right up to the present time, Your Eminence has given us no evidence of sympathy, not a word of encouragement. If I am wrong, so much the better, and I will gladly accept and publicly acknowledge my mistake, but I had always and I have still the impression that Your Eminence regards our 'conversations' with displeasure; that, as he sees it, Roman Catholics' every effort ought to be directed towards individual conversions, and that to such conversions our meetings at Malines are more hinderance than help. This impression I had emerged the more distinctly at the time of my stay at Rome last Pentecost.[24]

If these remarks do less than justice to Bourne's attitude, they only serve to illustrate the gulf of misunderstanding which had developed between the two men. In the same letter, however, Mercier did withdraw his insistence on publication in the *Tablet* of his communication to Woodlock and his demand for an apology from that paper.

Within a few weeks, this bitter exchange was a thing forgotten. Mercier lay on his death-bed, and affectionate messages again passed between him and his old friend. He died on January 23, 1926, the cause of Christian unity his preoccupation to the last.

Nevertheless, Bourne had already taken a decisive step. Their angry correspondence had prompted him to approach the Pope himself concerning the Conversations. Only the headings he used for this audience survive, but these make it clear that the Cardinal now had serious reservations about the direction of events. Of course, his leading complaint concerned the disregard for the English hierarchy, but he appears to have felt also that doctrinally a dangerous course was being followed. The two points he singled out were Anglican orders and papal infallibility: 'If orders [are] recognized and teaching authority placed into [the] Episcopate,' he told the Pontiff, the Anglicans 'will have gained all that they wish.'[25] Unfortunately, there is no record of the

Pope's reply, and whether Pius was now ready to reconsider the views he had expressed to Gasquet only two months before is uncertain.

Neither Bourne's audience with the Pope, however, nor Cardinal Mercier's death brought an immediate end to the Conversations. A fifth conversation had been previously planned for January, 1926, to compile a report of progress to date, and in that sense to consummate a first phase of discussions. Whether and in what form they would be continued thereafter would then be decided by the parties concerned. Not until October did this conference finally take place. It gathered in circumstances more dispirited than could have been envisaged when it was first arranged. Not only Mercier, but Portal too, had been removed from its ranks by death, and it met under the unfamiliar presidency of van Roey, now Mercier's successor in the see of Malines.

It does no injustice to van Roey to say that his commitment to the Conversations had not the intensity and ardour of Mercier's; neither had he succeeded to Mercier's independent stature in the Catholic world. His support for the talks had to be tempered by the realization that there were real problems connected with them. Wisdom obviously dictated that he write to Bourne, and this he did as one of his first decisions as Archbishop. Whether he moved spontaneously or at Rome's prompting is not known, but van Roey was unreserved in his assurance that hereafter he would act only in close contact with the English cardinal and in harmony with his views. He stressed that only one more meeting was firmly projected.[26]

While the events of 1927–28 relative to Malines cannot yet be established definitively, it would appear that in that period van Roey and Bourne came to an understanding that no further talks would be held in Belgium. At the end of January, 1928, van Roey issued an official communiqué to the effect that he saw no possibility of resuming the Conversations. What is remarkable, however, is that even before this Bourne had made an approach to the Archbishop of Canterbury offering to continue similar discussions in

England. In a letter to Davidson of December 6, 1927, he went out of his way to emphasize that he had never opposed the meetings at Malines as such. The Cardinal said that his attitude had been 'misunderstood and indeed misrepresented,' and that great difficulty could have been avoided had he been kept properly informed. Nevertheless, Bourne committed himself to continue what had been begun. 'If it be thought desirable,' he declared, 'I should be prepared to depute two or three competent persons to enter into discussion with others chosen by Your Grace.'

The Cardinal reiterated this offer when he met with Archbishop Davidson on February 16th, 1928. (This was *after* the appearance of the encyclical *Mortalium Animos*, which is often supposed to have ended any possibility of renewed discussions between the two churches.) In the interview, Bourne again denied emphatically suggestions of his hostility towards Malines. He did state that van Roey, whom he had seen, had confirmed that no more talks would take place there. However, he assured Davidson that he stood ready to arrange for talks between Roman Catholics and Anglicans in England.[27] Whether Davidson seriously considered this possibility is unknown, and there is no evidence of a reply to Bourne's proposal. But at this stage the Archbishop was probably reluctant; he 'was not very clear that further conferences would prove of value.'[28] Moreover, he had just witnessed defeat in the Commons of the revised Prayer Book after a debate markedly unsympathetic towards Catholic principles, and he probably thought the time singularly inopportune to reopen talks with Rome's representatives. A fresh beginning was left to some future generation.

As regards Malines, the fact that Halifax could believe, in the words of his biographer, that Bourne was 'one of the villains of the piece,' amply justified the Cardinal's own view that his attitude had been completely misrepresented. There are no grounds to doubt that his support for the Conversations, at least until their final stages, if reserved, was nonetheless real. If he felt offended about his exclusion, he was still prepared to hold his silence for four long years. If from Bourne's reticence Mercier formed the impression that the English Cardinal stood among his opponents, he probably failed to appreciate both the strength of the opposition which Bourne could observe at home and the moderating influence which, in fact, the English Cardinal was exercising on that very opposition. When Bourne did make known his private views, it was not to repudiate the Conversations, but to deplore the fact that the Catholic Church in England had been unjustly treated throughout them.

It is often imagined that in the issue between them Bourne stood for 'conversions' and Mercier for 'reunion.' So stark a contrast simply does not accord with the evidence. Indeed, only once is Bourne on record as raising the matter of conversions in this context. He did so in the draft letter not sent to Mercier, and then only as an explanation for English Catholic opposition to the Conversations and not necessarily as a personal opinion. On the other hand, even Mercier could jot down in his notes for a papal audience that he was arranging meetings 'for the conversion of England' (though he later struck out these words); he could refer elsewhere to 'the eventual organization of a converted Anglican church,' and as late as 1924 he could propose Halifax's personal submission to Rome. To suggest that either of the two Cardinals would put the cause of conversions foremost, however, is to do him an injustice. In fact, both Bourne and Mercier, whatever their differences in emphasis and temperament, appreciated that Rome must have some place in the emergent movement for Christian unity. In their willingness to countenance true dialogue, both were really at the eve of Roman Catholic recognition of the ecclesiality of other Christian bodies. There is no evidence that Mercier, any more than Bourne, conceived of the process of unity as anything but reconciliation with Rome; there is every indication that Bourne, like Mercier, was open to the possibilities of corporate, as well as individual, reconciliation. 'The return of our separated brethren to the unity of that one Church,' Bourne described as his own goal in his Lenten

Pastoral for 1927; the phrase could readily have been Mercier's. As regards reunion, what distinguished the two men above all else was most likely only Mercier's optimism as to the nearness of the goal.

But 'reunion' was only one aspect of Malines. Perhaps the real importance of the Conversations lay not so much in any contribution made to the improvement of relations between the Roman communion and other Christian bodies as in their significance within Roman Catholicism. In retrospect, it can be seen that by 1925 Malines had revived the possibility of a diversity of theological explanations within a common doctrinal framework, a notion excised from Roman Catholicism since the frenzy of anti-Modernism. Bourne's remarks to the Pope typify an uneasiness about the theological implications of Malines. By contrast, to Mercier, who throughout the Conversations seemed almost consciously *anti-intégrist*, the possibility of theological pluralism appeared not at all unwelcome. Ultimately that may have been the greatest difference between them.

Cardinal Bourne thought the Malines Conversations, in the final analysis, 'comparatively of very small importance.'[29] If this were a judgement of their practical contribution to reunion, Bourne was totally correct. In a broader context, however, the Cardinal would have been wide of the mark. With Malines, quite unheralded, a new era had arrived in the life of the Church.

NOTES

1 Halifax Papers (hereafter HP), Malines documents (hereafter M), Halifax to Portal, 29 November, 1921.

2 *The Conversations at Malines, 1921–1925* (London, 1927) is the agreed official report. The actual proceedings are in a volume entitled *The Conversations at Malines, 1921–1925: Official Documents*, ed. Lord Halifax (London, 1930), but this is incomplete and must be read with Walter Frere, *Recollections of Malines* (London, 1935). The biographies of the participants also yield valuable material, especially J. G. Lockhart, *Charles Lindley, Viscount Halifax* (London, 1936), and G. K. A. Bell, *Randall Davidson, Archbishop of Canterbury* (3rd ed.; London, 1952). Ernest Oldmeadow, *Francis, Cardinal Bourne* (2 vols.; London, 1944), is also important, but this contains serious errors and omissions, some of which are discussed hereafter. For more recent secondary literature, one may consult Roger Aubert, 'Les Conversations de Malines: Cardinal Mercier et le Saint-Siège,' *Bulletin de l'Academie royale de Belgique (Classe des Lettres)*, 53 (1967), pp. 87–159, the

same author's 'Cardinal Bourne, Cardinal Mercier and the Malines Conversations,' *One in Christ*, 4 (1968), pp. 372–379, and R. J. Lahey, 'The Origins and Approval of the Malines Conversations,' *Church History*, 43 (1974), pp. 366–384.

3 HP, A2, 278.1, pt. IV, Halifax to the Hon. Edward Wood, 1 February, 1928.

4 Oldmeadow, *Bourne*, II, p. 363, n. 1.

5 See Lahey, *art. cit.*

6 Archives of the Archdiocese of Malines, Conversations de Malines, (hereafter AAM, CM), 1922, AI, Bourne to Mercier, 4 December, 1922. See also HP, A2, 278.1, pt. III, Halifax to the Hon. Edward Wood, 7 December, 1921 (postcript of 11 December).

7 Archives of the Archdiocese of Westminster (hereafter AAW), BO I/78, Mercier to Bourne, 30 November, 1922, and AAM, CM, 1922 B III, Bourne to Mercier, 4 December, 1922. Texts of these letters may be found in Aubert, *One in Christ*, 4 (1968), pp. 375–376.

8 AAM, CM, 1923 AI, Halifax to Mercier, 12 November, 1923; see also HP, M, Mercier to Halifax, 15 November, 1923.

9 Undated autograph memorandum, 'Reunion', AAW, BO III/124/4.

10 See HP, M, Mercier to Halifax, 23 September, 1923, Jarrett to Halifax, 24 September, 1923, and Halifax to Gore, 27 September, 1923.

11 AAW, BO I/78, Oldmeadow to Moyes, 28 December, 1923; see also *The Tablet* 142 (1923), p. 825.

12 AAM, CM, 1924, Pastorale, II, Sordet to Mercier, 7 February, 1924. A translation of the pastoral is given by Frere, *Recollections*, pp. 90–109.

13 AAW, BO III/124/4, Bourne to Oldmeadow, 6 February, 1924; see also Oldmeadow to Moyes, 2 February, 1924.

14 *The Tablet*, 143 (1924), pp. 309–310. See also AAW, BO I/78, Mercier to Bourne, 22 March, 1924.

15 See AAW, BO III/124/4, proof of an article entitled 'A Private Sitting Room,' with an undated marginal note in Oldmeadow's hand: 'This was never published. Cardinal Bourne wrote from Rome asking that further comment on conversations be held up.' See also *The Tablet*, 147 (1926), p. 811.

16 AAW, BO III/124/4, Dean to Bourne, 4 February, 1924. Some English Roman Catholics felt even more strongly. Monsignor H. Barton Brown, a convert clergyman himself, wrote to Mercier: 'Eminence! Do you realize that the forefathers of these men by fire and the sword tried to stamp out Catholicism in this country? ... that now the descendants of the very men who persecuted the English Catholics seek to steal from them the very name for which their Fathers died?' He told Mercier that they had not a single convert clergyman since news of the Conversations had become widespread. AAM, CM, 1924, Pastorale, Catholiques, Brown to Mercier, 12 February, 1924.

17 AAM, CM, 1924, BI, Mercier to Gasparri, 6 January, 1924.

18 AAW, BO III/124/4, Merry del Val to Moyes, 14 February, 1925. Merry del Val also sent to Oldmeadow a copy of a Holy Office decree of 16 September, 1864, against Catholic participation in reunion movements, with a request for its publication in *The Tablet*. Bourne, however, thought this inopportune. The document is still in the Westminster archives.

19 Downside Abbey, Gasquet's diary, 24 October, 1925. According to statistics in the *Catholic Directory*, conversions, which had increased from 1921 to 1923, the year of public acknowledgement of the Conversations, declined from a peak of 12,796 in that year to 12,355 (1924), 11,948 (1925), and 11,714 (1926).

20 AAW, BO III/124/4, Woodlock to Bourne, 29 October, 1925, quoting Merry del Val to Woodlock, 28 July, 1925.

21 Oldmeadow justified publication of the letter in its unedited state on the grounds that Woodlock had resented his refusal to publish previous communications (the two were not on good terms), and that the Anglican charges were serious enough to warrant instant notice. AAW, BO III/124/4, Oldmeadow to Bourne, 28 October, 1925.

22 Nearly complete texts of three of the four letters are given by Oldmeadow, *Bourne*, II, pp. 384 sq.

23 AAM, 1925, BI, Oldmeadow to Dessain, 18 November, 1925.

24 AAW, BO III/124/4, Mercier to Bourne, 7 December, 1925 (translation by the author).

25 *Ibid.*, Bourne's notes for papal audience of 15 December, 1925.

26 *Ibid.*, van Roey to Bourne, 29 March, 1926.

27 Lambeth Palace, Davidson Papers, 188 (Reunion III), Bourne to Davidson, 6 December, 1927, and also memorandum of interview of Archbishop of Canterbury with Cardinal Bourne, 16 February, 1928.

28 Bell, *Davidson*, p. 1302.

29 AAW, BO III/124/4, Bourne's notes for Msgr. Carton de Wiart on Dom Lambert Beauduin (undated).

5

Some reflexions on the
English Catholicism of the late 1930s

Adrian Hastings

No age in the modern history of English Catholicism has, I suspect, fallen into greater oblivion than the later 1930s. There are certain recognisable high points in English Catholic intellectual history, such as the Second Spring and subsequent long ascendancy of Newman and Manning, the years of the Modernist crisis prior to the first world war or, again, the zenith of Belloc, Chesterton and their friends after the war. Certainly, for many years for good or ill, the Chester-Belloc dominated the scene, but GK died in 1936 and Belloc's creative period was long past. Finally, subsequent to the second world war, the scene changes drastically with major institutional and numerical growth, linked to the inauguration of the welfare state, heavy Catholic immigration, an immense schools programme and the emergence on a considerable scale of an educated Catholic middle class.

There were various reasons why the later '30s and their particular atmosphere faded rather fast from the collective consciousness, and yet they possessed a singular brilliance of their own — if a partially tainted brilliance — which it is worth recalling. They witnessed indeed what can fairly be called a little renaissance, if one destined to be swept away fast enough by the winds of world war and state socialism.

The fears and counterfears engendered by the Modernist movement and its repression undoubtedly produced in this country as elsewhere a somewhat arid piece of intellectual history in the twenty years subsequent to *Pascendi* and it was only as the 1930s wore on that, at last, a certain relaxation of institutional tension became apparent coupled with a very considerable infusion of new blood. A number of able young cradle Catholics were joined by a veritable spate of glittering converts; some of these had admittedly been received a good deal earlier but they had initially kept fairly quiet. By the mid-1930s they seem to have acquired the sense of a *droit de cité*, encouraged by the best leadership in the religious orders and the very much improved openings for published work. There developed the very strong sense of a Catholic intellectual community, self-confidently speaking of 'the Catholic Revival', sunning itself in country houses or at Campion Hall, publishing its books with the young Frank Sheed, its articles in the revivified *Tablet* of Douglas Woodruff or the *Catholic Herald* of Michael de la Bedoyere, drawing in new members from the worlds of letters, art and even academia.

English Catholicism continued to suffer in this decade from the social split between a small rather consciously English upper class elite and the urban working class, concentrated in Liverpool and the other larger northern towns, with its strong Irish connections. There was still little sense of cultural or political identity between the two — their subsequent drawing together would depend upon the wider social revolution of the post 1945 years. The renaissance of the '30s remained wholly inside the small mostly upper class 'English' segment, which was of course a major cause of weakness. It was only possible at all because of a fairly steady enlarging of that class which had been going on in connection with a marked professionalisation in the public schools. This was the great age of Downside, Stonyhurst, Ampleforth and their companions, the age of the head masters who were near national figures — Trafford, Paul Nevill, Ignatius Rice. These schools would, of course, continue to grow in subsequent decades but the still greater growth in good grammar schools after 1944 would steadily diminish the overall ecclesiastical significance of the boarding schools. But without them the world of Ronald Knox's Oxford chaplaincy and Woodruff's lay orientated *Tablet* and Frank Sheed's annual list of Maritain and Mounier, D'Arcy, Vann and Sheed himself would hardly be imaginable.

It remained, nevertheless, from the side of its home writers a predominantly amateur world, with many of the characteristics of a gentleman's club. It still participated only marginally in the life of a university. Stalwarts like Francis (Sligger) Urquhart at Oxford and Edward Bullough in Cambridge — two pillars of Catholic life to die in 1934 — had not seen it as their role to provide any very public sort of intellectual leadership, and the small though growing group of Catholic academics that followed them presented an almost equally low profile. What had been done was to prepare the way internally, through the development of a relaxed chaplaincy system and a general diminishing of prejudices, for the vastly enlarged Catholic presence in the universities of the next generation. In the 1930s the most striking sign of such a presence was Martin D'Arcy's new Campion Hall in Brewer Street, something of a Mecca for Converts. 'I slipped along Brewer Street like a homing pigeon' wrote Frank Pakenham speaking of his conversion.[1] D'Arcy was by far the most influential clerical intelligence of the decade. It is likely that since Newman no other priest has exercised so deep and prolonged a personal influence upon the English Catholic intelligentsia, and behind the glittering eye of the living Jesuit was the still more pervasive influence of the dead Jesuit. The 1930s were the decade of the belated triumph of Gerard Manley Hopkins. It opened with the second edition of his poems published in 1930 with the introduction of Charles Williams. That was really the moment at which his unique distinction was recognised by a now admiring world, and new impressions followed year after year. Little as the Society of Jesus had appreciated his poetry in his lifetime, it now possessed an added charism in his reflected glory. Listening to Martin D'Arcy reading *The Wreck of the Deutschland* could be a spiritual experience not easily forgotten. Despite D'Arcy's close links and deep sympathy with the gentlemen apologists who were so much in their zenith in those years, his new Campion Hall was a powerful and intended pointer towards the far greater intellectual professionalism which was soon to come.

D'Arcy himself could qualify without question as a theologian, as could one or two of the men at Blackfriars nearby, but there were remarkably few men of weight, priest or lay, who could honestly be so described in the English church at the time. Such as existed were centred upon the three institutions of Downside, Blackfriars and Campion Hall. These three had all in fact nourished young men of great ability and scholarly capacity who were just beginning to make their mark by the late 1930s — David Knowles, Christopher Butler, Victor White, Gervase Mathew, Frederick Copleston. To them should be added the seculars, David Mathew and Philip Hughes. They constituted a new and highly promising class of professional priest scholar whose weight would be strongly felt in the post-war years. Among priests of the previous generation perhaps only Dom Hugh Connolly had achieved a comparable professionalism within a deliberately restricted academic field. Apart from D'Arcy the distinguished priestly names of the '30s — Ronald Knox, Martindale, Vincent McNabb, Bob Steuart — were neither theologians nor professional scholars. They were 'men of letters', radio priests, preachers of genius, on their way to being gurus, but they had maybe lived too long beneath the Modernist shadow to show any desire to stray far into the silent garden of the queen of the sciences, to which they paid an infinite wary deference.

The Catholic world of the later 1930s was, then, one with few recognised theologians, academics or professional scholars. It was a world, moreover, which had emerged, not from the discipleship of Newman or Acton or even Von Hügel, but rather from the swelling circle of Belloc and

Chesterton — and Belloc far more than Chesterton, perhaps
because Belloc had been a Roman Catholic all the time and
his spirit harmonised a great deal more readily with that
dominant within the Church of this period. It is indeed odd
that a Chester-Belloc unity was ever imagined because,
whatever might have been the impression given to their
non-christian disputants, from within the household two
more different visions can hardly be imagined. If one can
somehow compare a very clerical polarity with a very lay
one, and one within a nineteenth century context with one
of the twentieth century, it is not — I think — entirely
fanciful to see Chesterton as standing somehow within the
religious tradition of Newman, while Belloc wore something
of the mantle of Manning. Again, if the Sheeds were central
to the articulate lay Catholicism of the 1930s, both inheriting
the immediate past and striking out in new directions, Maisie
was undoubtedly the disciple of Chesterton, Frank of
Belloc.[2]

It remains somewhat strange to the present generation
how widely Belloc was accepted as the master and father
figure. His vast literary output over forty years of ceaseless
writing could indeed father almost any form of literature
and a very wide range of political viewpoint.

Hilaire Belloc
Is a case for legislation *ad hoc*.
He seems to think nobody minds
His books being all of different kinds.

The Bentley Clerihew was only too much to the point. If
much of his work was wholly unmemorable, quite enough of
it was very much the reverse, be it mostly from his early
years: one can think of the *Cautionary Verse, the Modern
Traveller, Danton,* or *The Servile State.* The Belloc of the '30s
was not creative in that way, but he still somehow maintained his ascendancy by the vastness of his knowledge and
the forcefulness of his opinions — and not only among
amateurs. It is worth noting that the group of men who
produced the essays for his 72nd birthday included several
professional Oxford historians. That group is indeed worth

listing as suggesting something of the core of the Catholic intellectual world (minus its Jesuit wing) at the end of the 1930s: Douglas Jerrold, Ronald Knox, Douglas Woodruff, Arnold Lunn, C. A. J. Armstrong, Christopher Hollis, Gervase Mathew, David Mathew, J. B. Morton, W. A. Pantin and David Jones.

Certainly the Belloc line had been stamped strongly enough upon a whole admiring generation as the Chesterton 'line' (if one could speak of one) never was. Belloc had almost wholly ignored the New Testament and theology; in turn poet, historian, essayist, fringe politician, he was an apologist almost all the time. The post-Bellocian Catholicism of the 1930s was moulded very strongly in this image. It had nearly always something of an apologetic quality, be it in the writings of the Sheeds, of Alfred Noyes, Arnold Lunn, Edward Watkin, perhaps even Christopher Dawson, though these and their contemporaries were gifted men and their apologetics took many a form, some of it very low keyed. With Knox, perhaps the most brilliant of them all, it could remain four fifths hidden in a self-deflating 'all this waste of time' — not a wholly misguided comment on even so superbly devised a piece as *Let Dons Delight*.

What remains striking is the sheer quality, above all the literary quality, of the published work of this period at its best. What other five years could, from this viewpoint, rival those which saw the publication of Waugh's *Edmund Campion*, David Jones' *In Parenthesis*, Knox's *Let Dons Delight* and Graham Greene's *The Power and the Glory*? But these masterpieces (three of which won the Hawthornden prize) were backed by a very considerable body of work, much of it of some distinction: *The Celtic Peoples and Renaissance Europe* of David Mathew, Christopher Dawson's *Making of Europe*, *Voltaire* of Noyes, Maisie Ward's *Insurrection versus Resurrection*, Rosalind Murray's *The Good Pagan's Failure*, and Tolkien's *The Hobbit*! One could easily continue the list: poetry, fiction, history, apologetics, but only the hint of anything which could really be called theology.

Maisie Ward, who had made the second volume of her

father Wilfrid's biography *Insurrection versus Resurrection* into a wide ranging survey of modernism, ends it with a triumphant epilogue hailing the end of 'the siege period' when it would at last be possible to utilise 'all that was really valuable in the thought of the Modernist period'.[3] Algernon Cecil, reviewing the book in the *Tablet*,[4] noted that it 'is instinct with the sense of a great change in the Catholic outlook', her epilogue 'falls upon the ear like the sound of a reveille warning the faithful that it is now indeed high time to awake out of sleep'. To a reader of forty years later that reveille still heartens even if it does sound a little simplistically triumph-alistic; here as elsewhere one finds that confident belief in 'christian civilisation', 'the Catholic revival', or even 'the counter-revolution'.

There was a good deal of highly stimulating philosophy coming across the channel in those years. It was the age of Mounier and Maritain, many of whose works were cir-culating in English translation by the late 1930s. Maritain was probably the most wholesome major continental in-fluence on English Catholicism at the time, and the most firmly anti-fascist one. His work was a major stimulus for Dawson, Gill, the young Barbara Ward, among others. But he too was careful not to appear a theologian. The 'new theology' of Congar, De Lubac, Danielou and the like hardly reached England before the war, though the less challenging work of Masure and Mersch had done so. In the strict realm of theology as in the theory of church government an ultramontanism of the latest Roman vintage was simply unchallenged among the clergy and swallowed *faute de mieux* by the laity and every fervent convert. Manning and his successors really had done their work very well. The English Church was now ultramontane in its thinking through and through. It is striking but unquestionable that even the ablest of its younger priests, men whose wider culture and historical sense could have brought them to a different theological viewpoint, were unmitigatedly ultra-montane. One can think of David Knowles, David Mathew and Christopher Butler. Only in a few lay people such as

Maisie Ward or Edward Watkin, Donald Attwater, Noyes, Malcolm Hay or Sencourt, is there some hint of a different vision of ecclesiastical order.

The most characteristic contemporary practical expression of the ultramontane system was the development of that organisation which came to be known at the time as 'Catholic Action': a centralised, Rome-inspired, hierarchically-controlled, model for the mobilisation of the laity. To the ultramontane mind it was the appropriate response to the new restlessness of the laity and the new apparent powerlessness of the clergy in the socio-political field, and it was really greatly preferable to any 'Catholic party' because the latter had an at least theoretical and potential independence from clerical control which Catholic Action could never have (the willingness of Ultramontanes to sacrifice the Popular Party in Italy and the Centre Party in Germany was only too clear). Catholic Action was, by definition, lay participation in the hierarchy's work under the hierarchy's control — essentially it was devised as a brilliant but absolutely necessary foundation stone within the twentieth century context for the whole ultramontane edifice, and it was hailed in the 1930s by English ultramontanes as just what the times required. Father Philip Hughes put the whole thing with maximum clarity: 'Catholic Action is the layman's movement, but its success presupposes a laity adequately trained and in some measure specially organised. The chiefs of the movement are, everywhere, the bishops. Never again will the Church have to face the trouble that came of an extra-diocesan, extra-hierarchical Catholic organisation where the effective direction of Catholic activity passed to elected committees of clergy and laity'.[5]

Not surprisingly it did not work very well in England. Despite the *Tablet*'s natural denial that it was 'merely a cunning form of Fascism',[6] that is how it only too easily appeared, particularly in view of the Fascist sympathies of so many of the more vocal British Catholics. But perhaps more important than the somewhat fascist image, was the absence of a suitable ecclesiastical or political environment.

If the Catholic Church in this country was at that time almost irretrievably ultramontane in the theological presuppositions of its clergy, it was not so by any means (and this fact is often completely overlooked) in its wider structures or social attitudes which shared far more in the general pattern of contemporary Britain. From this point of view there was a very striking contrast between British and Dutch Catholicism — the latter had developed an ultramontane inspired society in a way the former had not done despite Manning's hopes. There was neither Catholic university nor daily newspaper, neither political party nor trade union. Elsewhere such institutions provided much of the grounding for the large scale activities of Catholic Action. Moreover the rather sharp cultural and political divide between the small Catholic middle class and relatively large working class inhibited common action except upon the straightest ecclesiastical or moral issue. There was, as a consequence, an airy unreality about the campaign to get Catholic Action going. An imaginative native English development such as the Catholic Evidence Guild was quite clearly something very different, and it steered pretty clear of the social and the political despite a strange appeal from one Sheed & Ward author for 'new apostles' who would be 'in the natural order, the propagandists of Fascism, and, in the supernatural order, the lecturers of the Catholic Evidence Guild'.[7] While 'the young movement of Fascism' would work 'that England may attain the happiness of authority in the Corporate State', the 'young movement of the Catholic Evidence Guild' would work 'that England may attain the happiness of authority in the Corporate Church'.[8] It may seem almost unbelievable today that a Catholic publisher who was very far from a crank could produce such rubbish in October 1937 — still more so as the publishers in question were also the leaders of the Evidence Guild and could hardly publish something about their own cherished organisation if they thought it incredibly dangerous or misleading. Here as elsewhere ultramontanism was proving itself an easy bedfellow with fascism. But in practice the profound residual Cisalpinism of English Catholicism rooted in common sense, supported by the wider national society, and quite unbewitched at the working class level by the myth of 'Corporativism', either politely disengaged itself from Catholic Action altogether or transformed it into something very different from Cardinal Pizzardo's model.

A *cause célèbre* of the workings of the ultramontane system and its limitations may be found in the curious incident of the action of the Holy Office over Alfred Noyes' study of Voltaire, which was published by Sheed & Ward, serialised in the *Tablet* and widely acclaimed by reviewers. The book was then secretly delated to the Holy Office and Cardinal Hinsley was abruptly informed that it would be condemned if it were not withdrawn from publication until its errors had been eliminated. The publishers at once dutifully complied with this and they had, at first, the agreement of the author. What the errors consisted in was neither then nor later officially revealed and the whole business quickly stuck in the author's gullet and a fierce correspondence broke out in the *Times* in August 1938. Noyes decided to republish the book in its original form with another, neutral, publisher and this was seen by some as 'Defiance of the Holy Office', though Hinsley did his best to damp down the acrimonious heat and was able to declare a year later that, after all, no alterations whatsoever would be needed in the book.[9]

Other people had judged differently. The reaction of Noyes to the action of the Holy Office had caused both admiration and dismay. 'It is quite impossible to sympathize with his impatient appeal to the Protestant public' wrote Denis Gwynn of Noyes in the *Dublin Review*.[10] The readers of the *Times* were thus labelled 'Protestant' rather than simply a section of fellow citizens. With a few exceptions Catholics showed an almost complete inability to face up to the deeper issues of the case. At the time they simply had not the tools for mounting a challenge to Roman behaviour precisely on Catholic principles. Instead, if the Holy Office would not point out errors, there were industrious fellow Catholics who set about doing so. They came up with dozens of them. Noyes had described a respected 18th century bishop as an 'old imbecile' — how could the censors be expected to pass so offensive a phrase? He had argued that Voltaire, though by no means a christian, had had a more christian conception of God than some of his ecclesiastical opponents and had also behaved at times in a more christian fashion. 'There is something not only Christian, but Christ-like, in the reply of Voltaire' he had written at one point. Such a comment, Gwynn thought, was 'unjustifiable and offensive' and the sort of thing no proper ecclesiastical censor could be expected to put up with. To be fair Gwynn, while playing the ultramontane game, by no means shared the ultramontane objective: the firm subjection of all and sundry to the Roman curia. On the contrary he was, somewhat deviously, hoping to demonstrate pragmatically that a Roman system of censorship just would not pass with sturdy British authors. The system, as Noyes had clearly shown to the chagrin of some and the secret delight of others, could only be upheld so long as it was not challenged. Once this happened the Ultramontane house of cards started to tumble and something had to be done. While the Church was certainly not ready for its official dismantling, it could do little else on pragmatic grounds than turn a blind eye to its partial disregard by the laity. In practice the latter was unprepared to follow an ultramontane line very far either over 'Catholic Action' or over the control of literature, but in theory it offered little support to Noyes in his appeal as a matter of principle to a deeper 'law of religion and the Church' (The *Times*, 20 August) over and against canonical procedures of censorship and suppression.

Fascist sympathies and ecclesiastical ultramontanism were different attitudes and did not need to combine; nevertheless they were both at home in English Catholicism at the time (as they were in Italian Catholicism), they had a good deal in common and could in fact rather easily reinforce one another. The one derided liberal parliamentary democracy as Protestant in inspiration, degenerate and phoney, and lauded Latin and Mediterranean political experience as more genuinely democratic (of a populist kind), Catholic, and 'counter-revolutionary'. The other wholly subordinated local church to Rome and laity to clergy as a matter of divine law. Both tended to prefer Latin models to Anglo-Saxon ones, and obedience and order to freedom and public debate.

The Spanish Civil War broke out in July 1936 and lasted until March 1939. It proved a decisive catalyst in the parting of contemporary loyalties — far more so than, say, the mounting anti-Jewish campaign in Germany — and it placed almost all vocal English Catholics, clerical and lay, emphatically on Franco's side. Eric Gill and his circle were pretty isolated in their pro-Republican sympathies and even 'left-wing' *Blackfriars* did no more than try to keep an open mind either way.

'No sane and instructed man would hesitate to prefer Fascism to Communism' declared the *Tablet* in an important editorial in February 1939. Even at that late date it appealed to Catholics 'not to join or encourage this anti-Fascist crusade'. A few years earlier David Mathew had observed that 'Politics play little part in the Catholic community as such, except in the circle of the Distributists'.[11] Yet there was a dominant political orthodoxy among vocal English Catholics in the 1930s which is quite unmistakable. Douglas Jerrold was probably its most reliable proponent. On a bedrock of conservatism — the Jesuits and the Benedictines had long seemed to vie with one another as to which could more fittingly be described as 'the Tory party at prayer' — there was a continual harping on the positive values of Fascism, and the mystique of 'the Corporate State'. Here too much was owed to Belloc. Despite a very real radicalism in his youth and a capacity for trenchant political observation which never wholly deserted him, Belloc had settled with the years for the dream of some sort of righteous populist dictatorship. Sneers at liberal democracy and anti-semitic jokes had become part of the stock in trade of the with-it Roman Catholic. Theological ultramontanism was for a while fairly easily harnessed to a cultural and social ultramontanism which at first hailed Mussolini, and continued to hail Franco and Salazar, as the finest expressions of the Catholic political point of view. Only a tiny minority of English Catholics shared Maritain's refusal to support the Nationalist cause in Spain and to see both the Spanish civil war and the wider crisis of Europe in the very simplest terms as a conflict between Christianity and Communism; while the anti-religious atrocities committed by the Republican side were harped on ceaselessly, next to nothing was said about the still more numerous atrocities committed by the Nationalists, and little about the persecution of the Jews elsewhere.

The case of the acute amateur Scottish Catholic historian Malcolm Hay is worth recalling at this point. While his early books (in the 1920s and '30s) were immensely well received by Belloc and English Catholics because they most efficiently punctured various segments of British Protestant historical myth, things were quite different when Hay proceeded to analyse with equal vigour the christian tradition of antisemitism. He at once lost almost all his English Catholic friends. As he wrote in 1950: 'My own personal experience tells me that all my Catholic friends (with three or four exceptions) are infected to some degree. They are therefore unable to take an objective view of the Jewish Christian problems which their ancestors have created. I had a small circle of English Catholic 'friends', including several well-known English Jesuits. All those people dropped me completely . . .'.[12]

Frank Sheed, as we have seen, could in 1937 still publish a book which thought it helpful to consider the Catholic Evidence Guild and the Fascist Movement as parallel forces for righteousness. The same book *Fascism and Providence* which made that suggestion declared of the Nazis, 'The Pope has not pronounced against the Nazis — on the contrary he has a concordat with them, and upwards of a million of the four million Nazis are Catholics, and Catholic Bavaria is their particular stronghold and birthplace. Fascism, in fact,

is of Catholic origin and no English Catholic has a scintilla
of right to condemn the Nazis. Catholics who do, and there
are some few who are busying themselves considerably, may
be found to be fighting against God'.[13] Dom Christopher
Butler, reviewing the book in the *Downside Review*, while
mildly critical of some of the author's positions, commented,
'The English public see the most unlovely features of so-called
"Fascism" out of all proportion to those profounder qualities
which have rallied to it so much of the best elements in
western and central Europe'.[14] Even in June 1938 the
Month, while asserting that Hitler 'now serves under the
banner of AntiChrist' could still continue (p. 483): 'Of the
four great European powers only Italy and Germany have
taken the menace of atheist communism seriously, realizing
that if it gets further foothold in Europe it will make an end
of law and order and of civilized life. It is undoubtedly a pity
that those two states are totalitarian, and themselves inter-
fere unduly with the natural liberties of their subjects, but
in opposing communism they are fighting the battle of the
democracies as well'. It is only too clear that even in 1938,
in the majority judgement of the English Catholic intelligentsia, 'civilised life' was not as such threatened by Nazism
and Fascism but only by Communism.

Nevertheless there was always an alternative voice. If
Vincent McNabb's holy simplicity somehow suggested
within the vocal clergy of the '30s an 'alternative society' to
the establishment world of D'Arcy and Knox, a voice
without a Tory accent, his friends from the old Ditchling
community represented in their different ways an alternative lay voice to country house quasi-fascist sympathies.
The hard clarity, indeed ruthlessness, of Eric Gill's convictions challenged prevailing Catholic social orthodoxies
at almost every point: on sex, on pacifism, on seeking an
anarchic rather than a corporatist model for society, on
anticlericalism, on communism, 'A Christian politic should
always be one which leads in the heavenly direction, looks
to anarchy as its guiding star' he wrote in September 1936.[15]
He was confronting here the whole profound Catholic

presupposition that 'law and order' in Church and state was what Catholics should be most concerned to maintain. His critique of communism could be sharp enough and public enough but he had no doubt that 'between Communism and Fascism I'm all for Communism',[16] thus asserting a position which was anathema for almost all his coreligionists; he was even prepared on occasion to associate with communists and, for doing so, received more than one delicately communicated admonition from Hinsley — though Catholics who associated with Fascists would surely not have been so treated! He was quite impenitent.

Gill's disciple and intimate friend, David Jones, drawing on much the same sources of guidance on the Catholic side — Maritain and Dawson and their Blackfriars friends — slowly forged a less trenchant, more enigmatic, more decisively creative body of writing. Both in watercolour and in words Jones' mastery was somehow in locating a very concrete here and now foreground within a perspective of almost unfathomable, yet still human, depth and mystery. That after all is what the Mass, his central point of reference, is all about. A seer where Gill was a prophet, he wove a vast web which convincingly located the war, the fight against tyranny, the immediate predicament, within the central cultural tradition of Europe expressed by the figure of Arthur in one way, the Latin liturgy in another.

The late 1930s were Gill's last and greatest period both in artistic achievement and in vigour of thought — the time of his superb bas-reliefs 'The Re-creation of Adam' under the opening words of *The Wreck of the Deutschland* 'Thou mastering me God' in the League of Nations Council Hall at Geneva. In such work, as in Jones' *In Parenthesis* or Chesterton's splendid but almost unknown *Ubi Ecclesia*, English Catholicism really was manifesting a sensitive Catholicity fully faithful to the best in its heritage and very different from the corporatist flag-waving which too often passed as sound catholicism in those years.

At the time Gill and Jones must have seemed marginal enough, if not cranky, though they were not without their immediate circle of influence: the pressures and anguish of the time were forcing people in more than one direction. They certainly represented an apparently less typical side of English Catholicism, but then so did Hopkins, so did Von Hügel, so — despite the acclaim he received — did Chesterton. If the English Catholic tradition in modern times can be characterised by a certain rather heavy keeping in step at the centre, it can be characterised too by the number of highly creative figures it has sprouted in its margins. Moreover, though they seemed more or less marginal at the moment, such people have time and time again proved not to be marginal at all on the longer view but rather the unexpected bearers of an authentic spiritual continuity.

While the later 1930s were all in all an important and exciting moment within this tradition — a moment of renewed confidence, even of brilliance, whose literary output was very considerable, and in which a serious challenge to the narrow clericalism and unadventurous thought patterns of the post-Manning and post-Modernist eras was at last beginning to be mounted, it has to be admitted that its achievement has been largely swept into oblivion, and from the seeds sown the harvest was seemingly slight. There were various reasons for this. One, clearly, was the effect of the war and of the major social changes which followed it. Another was the increasingly restrictive attitude of church leadership in the age of Griffin and Godfrey not only in this country but also in Rome. The latter years of Pius XII's reign, symbolised better than anything else by the encyclical *Humani Generis*, were not ones really to encourage Catholics to feel, as Maisie Ward had suggested, that 'the siege period' was now over. But there were as well decisive causes inherent within the very nature of what was achieved in those years of Hinsley and Pius XI. There was the amateurishness of so much of it and its rather narrow, almost cliquish, social base. Still more serious, there was the almost criminal blindness to the evils of Fascism stimulated by an all engrossing opposition to Communism. The fondness for Fascism derived not only from an 'enemies of ones enemies are

ones friends' logic but also from two other sources — a
natural sympathy for Catholic southern Europeans from
Italy to Portugal and decades of Bellocian indoctrination
about the fraudulency of western democracy and the perils
of semitic influence.

When the war came and the country found itself called to
fight for democracy and against fascism, Catholics responded
as well as anyone else — their sympathies had never been
very pro-German anyway. In doing so they had inevitably
to bury much of the sentiments of the prewar years and they
did so remarkably easily. What remained of that thinking
when armageddon was passed once more might seem little
beyond a lobby for Salazar and Franco which lingered on
for decades, coupled with the sort of rather phoney nostalgia
which hangs so heavily over *Brideshead Revisited*. The Catholic intellectual community was about to be reformed on
the basis of Butler's Education Act, and such sentiments
would seem to the new generation of Catholics increasingly
odd and uncongenial.[17]

Beyond the flirting with fascism and the country house
atmosphere there was, however, as I have suggested, a great
deal of more solid value as well as literary brilliance, together with a training of new minds, and all this was not
lost. If some of the figures who appeared central in the '30s
never seemed subsequently able to escape from the mental
limitations of the dominant Catholic model of that period,
others certainly did so, pursuing new courses with both
integrity and creativity. Among clerics one may well think
of Christopher Butler — so much more of a prophet in the
1960s than in the 1930s — among lay people Maisie Ward,
perhaps the most homely and characteristically English
figure of the pre-war renaissance; she would sail confidently
on to welcome the age of the priest-worker, the second
Vatican Council and aspects of *aggiornamento* amazingly
remote from the preoccupations of the 1930s. Then again
they were the years in which David Knowles was writing
what may well have been his finest volume, *The Monastic
Order in England*, which so clearly marked him out as the

ablest English Catholic historian since Acton and destined him soon to be appointed to Acton's old chair — the Regius Professorship at Cambridge. They were the years in which Tolkien was getting down at Oxford to work on an epic of vast imagination, very different in formal structure but not so dissimilar in inspiration from that of David Jones — *The Lord of the Rings*. And they were the years in which Barbara Ward first made her appearance as a social thinker and reformer. From a grounding in Maritain and Dawson she was to go steadily forward as one of the great prophets of our time — a person as difficult as any to fit within the normal stereotype of English Catholicism. Finally, if the most solid intellectual achievement within the English Catholic community in the years after 1945 should be judged to lie in the far greater professionalism of its quieter, more academic proponents — mostly lay and increasingly numerous: Evans-Pritchard, Tolkien, Elizabeth Anscombe, Mary Douglas, Donald Nicholl and dozens of others, it is at least arguable that this would hardly have come about without the gentle encouragement and friendship of such as Gervase Mathew, Victor White and Tom Corbishley — priests whose wide horizons, sense of vocation and intellectual discipline had been acquired in those years of the 1930s when 'the siege period' was suddenly — if perhaps prematurely — felt to be coming to its end.

NOTES

1 Frank Pakenham, *Born to Believe*, Jonathan Cape, 1953, p. 97.
2 Maisie Ward, *Unfinished Business*, Sheed & Ward, 1964 p. 309.
3 Maisie Ward, *Insurrection versus Resurrection*, Sheed & Ward 1937, p. 546.
4 The *Tablet*, 18 December 1937.
5 Philip Hughes, *Dublin Review*, April 1939, p. 216.
6 The *Tablet*, 2 July 1938.
7 Christopher Butler, The *Downside Review*, January 1938, p. 105, reviewing and summarising the argument of J. K. Heydon, *Fascism and Providence*, Sheed & Ward, 1937.
8 J. K. Heydon, *Fascism and Providence*, p. 153.
9 Alfred Noyes, *Two Worlds for Memory*, Sheed & Ward, 1953, p. 273.
10 Denys Gwynn, the *Dublin Review*, October 1938, p. 206.
11 David Mathew, *Catholicism in England*, Sheed & Ward, 1936, p. 261.
12 Alice Hay, *Valiant for Truth, Malcolm Hay of Seaton*, London, 1971, p. 150.

13 J. K. Heydon, *Fascism and Providence*, p. 142.
14 The *Downside Review*, January 1938, p. 105.
15 *Letters of Eric Gill*, edited by Walter Shewring, Jonathan Cape, 1947, p. 362.
16 Robert Speaight, *Eric Gill*, Methuen, 1966, p. 238.
17 See the remarks of John Lynch in the chapter on England in *The Church and the Nations*, ed. A. Hastings, Sheed & Ward, 1959, p. 9.

6

English Roman Catholicism in the 1960s

Bernard Sharratt

I

Roman Catholicism has a power of elimination that many living organisms might envy. Once a position has been abandoned, surprisingly little time is needed for the belief to develop that it was never occupied, and we do need to remind ourselves occasionally that we have come a long way . . .[1]

IN 1958 Eugene Langdale wrote, concerning historians of English Catholicism, that 'for them, the history of Catholicism in the 19th Century seems to be summed up by the struggle alongside O'Connell for Catholic Emancipation, the Oxford Movement, the Earl of Shrewsbury's foundations and Pugin's architecture, Newman's intellectual brilliance, and the great dynasty of Archbishops of Westminster, which began so majestically with Wiseman and Manning', and he noted, correctly, that of the few works concerned with the post 1850 period perhaps the most accessible did not contain even a chapter on the RC church among the working class.[2] It is a mark of one small shift since 1958 that in 1975 there finally appeared a major scholarly study of English Catholicism which at least acknowledged that a more complex kind of social history is required.[3] But the problem of historical method remains acute for the study of Catholicism; various models might be proposed: at a relatively preliminary sociological level, it has been suggested that English Catholicism is best seen in terms of tension and overlap between the 'Hiberno-Catholic' and 'Pure English Catholic' strains or the interaction between 'old Catholic gentry', immigrant-derived working-class and aristocratic/upper-class-convert elements;[4] another approach might be developed by elaborating historically the distinction between the governmental-episcopal, the intellectual-prophetic and the devotional-'mystical' structures of the RC church generally.[5] More secular models might be adapted, drawn perhaps from the study of sub-cultural formations (such as recent work in labour history) or from anthropological perspectives. A brief essay, particularly one focussed on the 1960s, can only be drastically selective, but the chosen angle of presentation is offered with at least an awareness of these historiographical difficulties.

My point of entry is education, since it is possible to employ the concept of 'education' at a variety of levels: to grasp a religious body as primarily an arena of ideas, defined not by economic power or institutional organisation but centrally by beliefs and ideological cohesion; to recognise catholicism in the 1960s, the decade of Vatican II, as predominantly characterised by a process of complex re-education, including the articulation and assimilation of a body of influential texts, the constitutions and decrees of the Council; and, thirdly, to pinpoint the catholic schools system as the sociologically central component of specifically English Catholicism, the major mechanism by which the RC community both maintains its group-identity and aligns itself to the norms of the wider society.[6] The first part of this essay interweaves these three emphases in a schematic reading of the history of 1960s English Catholicism; the second part attempts a further re-patterning to suggest a more specifically theological fourth dimension to the notion of education.

1. *Education, Laity and Theology*

In the mid-1960s the number of baptised Roman Catholics in Great Britain was estimated at about 5M, or nearly 10% of the population; those 'practising' in England and Wales was reckoned at 2.2M. In 1964 a Catholic Teachers' Conference claimed a total of 741,000 pupils in Catholic maintained and independent schools; by 1972 that total was given as 900,000, of whom about 750,000 were in the 2,500 maintained schools, and the Catholic school population was said to have increased by 25% during the decade. Clearly the capital outlay on schools was large, an estimated £150M from 1945 to 1970, of which the Catholic community was responsible for approximately £50M, most of it borrowed, with interest payments running at £2.5M to £3M each year. Archbishop Beck, the hierarchy's spokesman on education, estimated in 1965 that the overall debt would take 20 or 30 years to erase. At diocesan level, the financial centrality of Catholic schools is clear: between 1952 and 1970 the Archdiocese of Birmingham Building Fund spent £21M, of which 99.7% was devoted to schools (buildings, interest, fees, administration); in 1969/70 the Arundel and Brighton Diocese Development Fund spent well over 60% of its total budget on school buildings and interest payments. In the light of this degree of investment, both of personnel and of money, one can speculate that in a situation where, suddenly, there were no Catholic schools to maintain, 'Not only would the church find itself with thousands of activists and vast sums of money with no obvious purpose, it would have to find some other collective identity capable of holding its members together.'[7] The crisis of identity and of priorities hypothetically indicated here is a useful preliminary measure of the actual crises and preoccupations of the 1960s.

Whatever the sociological function of the RC schools system, the consistently declared policy of providing a place for every Catholic child in a Catholic school derived, officially and legally, from Canon 1374 which simply stipulated that policy; but attitudes in this area were also tinged by the tone of Canon 2319 which prescribed excommunication for a Catholic who entered a 'mixed marriage' with the intention of educating the children outside the Catholic faith. The link between these two constitutive moments — education and marriage — suggested a deliberately self-perpetuating process of social enclosure and also focussed some delicate problems for ecumenism during the decade.[8] Yet despite this impressive expenditure, by the mid-6os only 60% of English RC children actually had Catholic school-places to go to, and the effectiveness of those schools was often challenged. In 1966 Cardinal Heenan stated: 'I am not sure how, sociologically, it could be proved that Catholic education is not justified; that must be left to personal opinion.'[9] Various efforts were made to transform personal opinion into research-based knowledge: a psychology-based survey of current pupils revealed considerable internalization of views and values taught at school, mainly of an other-worldly and privatized devotional kind, but various sociological investigations seemed to reveal that, on leaving school, the level of religious practice, even by the minimal criterion of Sunday mass-attendance, was hardly affected by previous education at a Catholic as opposed to a non-Catholic school; other studies showed a distinction in attitudes to the parish as a social organization — that those who remained at a parochial secondary school till 18 often recognised the parish as a social unit (providing a youthclub, dances, social contact etc.) while the religious activities of the church became secondary, merely habitual or non-existent for them, whereas those who attended a non-parochial grammar school often showed higher awareness of the parish as a religious focus but were ignorant of or uninterested in its social functions.[10]

Such findings both provoked and indicated complex consequences. The increasing awareness that in Catholic schools 'religion' might be meaning little more than private feelings, both devotional and sexual-moral, and 'doctrine' sometimes only a pattern of propositions, akin to geometry, stimulated a movement to assimilate at the pedagogical level many of the emphases also being incorporated, in the

early 60s, into the debates and documents of the Vatican
Council. A 'catechetical' awareness began to develop: in
1964 the first lecture-tour in England of Johannes Hofinger,
director of the Manila Pastoral institute, helped to publicize
the then comparatively little-known work of the National
Catechetical Centre, established in London in 1959; in 1965
only about 30 graduates of the Lumen Vitae centre in
Brussels (established 1946, open to international students
since 1957) were at work in England; that same year the
London Centre became a College of Catechetics and by
1967, as 'Corpus Christi College', it was widely-known, with
45 graduates a year and able in addition to provide weekly
lectures to 1,000 people, a summer school, and short courses
at each of 13 Catholic Colleges of Education.[11] A range of
new textbooks and periodicals began to appear, supplement-
ing the once-lonely *Sower*: an English edition of the *On Our
Way* series was undertaken, the American *Bible Today*
became popular, the *Clergy Review* ran a regular feature on
'Teaching the Faith'. The two main groups involved in this
upsurge were lay teachers and nuns, other aspects of whose
lives were also slowly changing.[12] One characteristic series
of the mid-60s marks a number of shifts: *Where We Stand* was
the collective title of a sequence of cheap 60-page books,
which can be compared with the late 1950s *Faith and Fact*
books; both series were planned systematically, but whereas
the earlier series rested on an encyclopaedic arrangement
combining semi-apologetics with an emphasis on 'knowledge'
(church history, other faiths, etc.), the later series was
structured round a biblical and trinitarian theology; the
collective titles indicate the change of mood, the later having
a provisional overtone, a sense of viewpoint rather than fact;
moreover the later series was almost entirely produced by
English writers, unlike the earlier which was largely composed of translations from the French *Je sais; Je crois*
library; and among those English contributors were a few
lay Catholics writing theology.

The lay theologian was a fairly important aspect of
English Catholic life in the 1960s. Whereas Chesterton and

Belloc might provide apologetics, polemic or spiritual reflections and Frank Sheed produce popularizations of neo-Thomism, the 60s lay writers were possibly a new breed. Before the war perhaps only a few hundred Catholics graduated from universities each year; by the mid-60s some 5,000 Catholics were graduating and another 4,000 qualifying at colleges of education every year, so that by the end of the decade at least a considerable body of educated laypeople was present in the Catholic community.[13] Their opinions and attitudes, expressed organizationally in such groups as the Newman Association (with about 3,000 members in mid-decade) or the more diffuse Catholic Renewal Movement, and in letters to the Catholic or national press, in articles and books, and at the local parish level, were one focus of the re-education process of the period. An early sign of this lay theological presence was the semi-private newsletter of Michael de la Bedoyere, *Search*, which in the early 60s raised many of the issues later to become publicly contentious; another was the role played by Neil Middleton and Martin Redfern at Sheed and Ward, in making available English translations in paperback form of such continental theologians as Rahner, Schillebeeckx and Kung, and in providing an outlet not only for English professional theologians (Charles Davis, Herbert McCabe, Nicholas Lash et al.) but also for laymen writing theology from a professional background in other disciplines (Brian Wicker, Terry Eagleton, Adrian Cunningham, Walter Stein, Hugo Meynell, et al.).[14] Other lay-controlled periodicals appeared: *Herder Correspondence* (Jan 1964 to June 1970) described by Cardinal Heenan as 'the poor man's ecclesiastical *Private Eye*',[15] provided detailed investigative journalism on the Council and international Catholic developments; *The Newman*, particularly in its new format from 1968 to 1970, acted as a forum for its members and others; *Slant* (Spring 1964 to Jan 1970), originally an undergraduate venture which tried to argue for a marriage of marxism and christianity, went on to develop an idiosyncratic style of theological thinking;[16] *New Christian* (Sept 1965 to mid-1970) offered a fortnightly comment on more current affairs from an ecumenical and often radical stance. The lay, and clerical, personnel involved in these efforts overlapped considerably and also tended to be active in other influential areas, as in the Downside Symposia, which met frequently from 1952 onwards and produced a series of books on issues that both anticipated and developed conciliar themes, or the December Group, annual from 1958, which gradually became a gathering-point for 'radicals' of a *Slant* or *New Blackfriars* tendency; and a wider circle of lay people became active in parish councils, diocesan and national commissions. These groups of lay activists were distinguished from older — and continuing — forms of lay organization (the Legion of Mary, Catholic Womens Guilds, YCW,) by their sense and assertion of relative independence from clerical or hierarchical control and perhaps by an increasing and sometimes frustrated awareness that they had assimilated and responded to Vatican II more rapidly and enthusiastically than had many of the clergy and episcopacy. Behind that awareness was the accessibility of information about the Council and of the Council's own declarations;[17] as Abbott's *Documents of Vatican II* (1966) became a best-seller, there was a new, authoritative and easily-available norm against which to judge the actions and decisions of those who previously could claim to speak authoritatively without declaring the specific reference-point for that authority.

Given the availability of those texts, which seemed both to be easily intelligible and to have displaced much previous thinking and teaching, and given the presence of an articulate and educated laity, the question of clerical education became — if for no other reasons — a pressing one. Articles multiplied on 'the vocations crisis' and on 'seminary reform', and some reforms were actually made.[18] The traditional major seminary course consisted of two years mainly neo-scholastic philosophy followed by four years of theological study, again largely based on neo-scholastic premises, with Church History, Scripture and Canon Law accompanying these. From about 1963 a small element of 'pastoral work' was

introduced — deacons began venturing outside the en-
closed seminary and visiting local hospitals or helping in
neighbouring parishes — and soon changes in curricula
followed: thus from September 1965 Ushaw re-arranged
its courses to inter-weave philosophy and theology through
the six years and made increased use of seminars rather than
lectures, while students were allowed some flexibility in
arranging their own timetables. At the Westminster diocesan
seminary at Ware, the teaching trio of Charles Davis,
Hubert Richards and Peter de Rosa made more considerable
changes in the content of courses, aligning them with the
biblical and liturgical emphases dominant at the Council; in
1965 Richards and de Rosa were transferred to Corpus
Christi College and Davis to the Jesuit seminary at Heythrop, which was formally elevated the same year into a
Pontifical Athenaeum. Heythrop, 16 miles from Oxford, was
symptomatic of two issues of the time: since all seminaries
but especially those of religious orders tended both to be
generous in staff-student ratios and to have difficulty in
ensuring suitably qualified staff, it was intended that Heythrop should gather under its wing the less viable Religious
seminaries; and it was also hoped that its 'proximity' to
Oxford would encourage some relationship with the university. A concern for accreditation by ordinary academic
bodies was also apparent in the negotiations of Ushaw with
the University of Durham in 1967 and of Upholland with
Liverpool and Manchester; eventually in 1970 Heythrop
moved to London and became a constituent college of the
University of London. More widely, dissatisfaction was
sometimes voiced with the quality of Catholic theology in
England, and the need for contact with and training in
university theology faculties was urged. In 1968 one writer
could declare that 'as a result of recent deaths and other
forms of departure from the ranks, the age group of the
forties contains no-one with an established, or even promising, theological reputation' and that in the last century the
seminaries 'between them have not produced a single theologian with a nation-wide reputation'.[19] Judged by inter-

national and non-Catholic standards both statements were, and remain, true.

The reference to 'departures from the ranks' indicates some related problems. By the end of the decade, the director of 'Bearings', an organization for helping ex-priests, could suggest that 'perhaps 100 or so priests and religious are leaving the ministry each year'; many of those would have difficulty in finding employment due to lack of acknowledged qualifications, despite full-time education up to their mid-twenties.[20] Some of those departures — which included a number of theologians and scholars[21] — were due to ecclesiastical conflict or frustration, others to specific and personal issues and some at least seemed to be based on the decision that their christian vocation could be more fruitfully followed precisely as laymen. It was also argued that the possibility of an active, and relatively independent, lay involvement within a large grouping of concerned laity was a factor in the decline in numbers of seminarians.[22] More-over, in contrast to the absence of major theologians, the English catholic community in the 60s included a number of laypeople eminent in their secular and academic professions; in 1966 John M. Todd could claim: 'Sociology, demography, medicine, psychiatry, delinquency, family and neighbourhood problems, public relations, mass media — in these and many other spheres I could name Catholics near the head of their professions and highly respected. Yet the whole of this world is held at arm's length by our bishops.'[23] That final sentence indicates a felt gulf, but a second and different gap could also be claimed to exist. John Todd spoke as one of the minority of educated laity which Geoffrey Moorhouse, in a 1964 *Guardian* article, saw as enjoying the tacit support of some Regulars but as mainly in latent conflict with the majority of the episcopacy and dio-cesan clergy; 'somewhere in between', he added, 'are the mass of the laity, unaccustomed to anything but dutiful response to orders from above, ill-equipped intellectually to reconcile faith with the other gifts that God has given them, and tragically bewildered by the imminent rift in their

church.'[24] It is a journalist's comment, but it directs attention back to that elusive category, 'the mass of the laity', and
to the wider process of re-education that involved, in a
different sense, 'the mass of the laity'.

2. *Language, Liturgy and Marriage*

On March 20th 1960 Archbishop Heenan of Liverpool
received a reply from the Sacred Congregation of Rites
establishing, in answer to his query, that section 12 of the
Congregation's Instruction of 1958 did exclude the public
recitation of the rosary during Mass in October. 'We have
come a long way . . .' The 1958 Instruction was concerned
with 'encouraging the active participation of the faithful'
in the Mass. It was one of a series of instructions and per-
missions which had included allowing the Easter Vigil to be
held at midnight on Holy Saturday, experimentally for one
year, in 1951, a permission renewed for three years in 1952
and then made permanent; in 1953 evening Masses were
cautiously allowed for the whole church, with the eucharistic
fast reduced, and in 1957 both regulations were extended and
clarified. By 1959, when Vatican II was announced, these
were almost the only changes to have impinged upon the
English laity *en masse*. In the early 60s those who advocated
the use of the vernacular in the Mass were, in England, a
smallish minority, though Dialogue Masses, in Latin, were
becoming acceptable. There was, in other words, very little
preparation before the promulgation, in December 1963, of
the Constitution on the Liturgy: the catechetical movement
and changes in seminary theology had barely begun, while
the laity depended more on press-reports than on parish
instruction or episcopal pastorals for an awareness of the
coming changes. When the hierarchy issued the new 'Rite of
Low Mass for use from November 29th 1964, the response in
some lay quarters was immediate and fearful: Douglas
Woodruff, veteran editor of *The Tablet*, wrote to the *Daily
Telegraph* (17th Nov 1964), 'in *The Tablet* . . . we have not
left our readers in doubt how much we regret what is happen-
ing, seeing it as a regression into nationalism, and a widely

unpopular one'; another correspondent wrote (*Telegraph*, 7th Nov 1964), 'There are many Roman Catholics who do not express their views outwardly, who are filled with sorrow at the passing of Latin in the liturgy and look forward to the coming changes with dismay. The laity as a whole were not clamouring for the vernacular until the idea was driven into them by clever propaganda'; on 30th November 1964 a personal 'ad' in *The Times* announced 'Will anyone wishing to preserve the ancient Latin liturgy in England, and who wishes to join me in an appeal write Box . . .' A petition against the vernacular, signed by perhaps 3,000, was sent to the hierarchy. The later Latin Mass Society was to build upon such responses. When English for some parts of the Mass (Epistle, Gospel, Gloria, Credo, Domine non sum dignus, 'prayers at the foot of the altar') was finally introduced in Advent 1964, a fully Latin Mass was not excluded; a majority of the dioceses made the vernacular obligatory at all Low Masses on Sundays and at weekday evening Masses, and in many dioceses the parish priest could decide to use English also at weekday morning Masses; some dioceses, at least, allowed some Masses entirely in Latin each Sunday. At that stage, only a few dioceses, such as Westminster and Portsmouth, were readily willing to grant permission for Mass to be said facing the people. At a press conference on 12th February 1965 Bishop Dwyer of Leeds was reported as saying that 'eventually' the Mass would be divided into distinct blocs of English and Latin. On 2nd May 1967 an Instruction from Rome finally allowed the whole of the Mass, including the Canon, to be said in English.[25]

Clearly, a detailed chronology of the liturgical and other changes cannot be given here, but the selective account offered above highlights, first, the speed both of the changes and in the expectations about coming changes, and, secondly, the fact that some Catholics saw the introduction of the vernacular as the abandonment of a fundamental position. Certainly by 1970 it would be unthinkable to enter a normal parish on a Sunday and find the congregation engaged in the public recitation of the rosary while a priest and server murmured a Mass, including Epistle and Gospel, in Latin.[26] Yet given that the major liturgical changes were compressed into about four years and that, far from there having been 'clever propaganda' for the changes, the dominant religious education of English Catholics had previously produced an a-liturgical, privatized, inner-devotional spiritual attitude, it is possible to see that there was indeed a fundamental 'danger' in the change from Latin to English. For insofar as contemporary English 'ordinary' language has tended to suffer from a historically recent inflection that provides no adequate common vocabulary for acutely personal experiences, in anguish and in love, or for the complexity of social experience, it has also been disabled in developing an appropriate language for changing modes of spiritual and liturgical experience; indeed, the split between 'the personal' and 'the social' embedded and articulated in everyday language is an aspect of that deep legacy and also chimes with certain central problems in ecclesiology. The Anglican tradition, with the richer resources of an earlier linguistic heritage still resonant in its liturgy and hymns, has perhaps retained a fullness of religious language which — whatever its own current disadvantages — was never available to the same degree within the English Catholic community.[27] The 'danger' of a change from Latin to an English marked by the distinct vocabularies of contemporary discourse and biblical-liturgical research, perhaps lay most dramatically in the fact that, previously, it was not just the language *of* the Mass that was in Latin but also, to a crucial extent, the language *about* the Mass. While the Mass was a mystery in which one took no active part and the Gospel and Epistle were inaudible and unintelligible runes, and while, most importantly, 'transubstantiation' was something that occurred while you bowed your head and a bell tinkled, it was possible for the language of private devotion or a prayerbook to substitute itself for the language of theology; but when the Mass became the 'Eucharist', the 'Lessons' or 'Readings' suddenly said unfamiliar things in English

(Paul's letters and the Old Testament do not make easy reading, let alone listening), and the language about the Eucharist (in 'homilies' rather than 'sermons') became talk not about private devotion or a neo-scholastic conundrum but about apparently familiar experiences like a meal, a meeting or a community, it was suddenly easier and perhaps unavoidable to ask whether one really *understood* what it all *meant*. And since meaning and language cannot be finally separated, the absence of an adequate language would lead to an awareness of unintelligibility of a different order from the unintelligibility of unknown Latin. In theological circles one facet of this problem had emerged, even in England, in the debate about 'remythologization' in the early 1960s, an issue that also haunted the catechetical movement;[28] another aspect was indicated by the brief popularity of various books of prayers and meditiations in 'modern' or 'urban-style' language, such as Michel Quoist's *Prayers of Life*.[29] But in 1964/5 this problem touched on more controversial ground: the Eucharist itself.

Throughout 1964 considerable press coverage was given to the debates in Holland on the meaning of 'transubstantiation'; the debate came nearer home with the response, at least among clergy, to an article on 'The Real Presence' in the *Clergy Review*; and finally on 3rd September 1965 a papal encyclical, entitled *Mysterium Fidei*, reaffirmed a traditionalist interpretation; on 1st December Cardinal Heenan invited Francis Clark S.J. to lecture the English Bishops, assembled in Rome for the Fourth Session, on 'The Real Presence: an appraisal of the recent controversy'. Both the encyclical and Fr. Clark's version of the doctrine caused ripples of relatively muted discontent among some theologians in England and, more specifically, in ecumenically-minded non-Catholics.[30] But neither the controversy nor the encyclical provided a language accessible and intelligible to the non-theologically educated layperson. Its immediate effects in England, perhaps, were to encourage some heresy-hunting by the conservative Catholic Priests' Association, an avoidance of the real difficulties in pulpits, and a self-censorship in pursuing the necessary theological reformulation; but its most long-term effect was almost certainly to re-encourage the kind of attitude articulated, somewhat later, in a historical comment meant to have a contemporary application: 'Within the Church, it [Liberalism] led to excesses far from the reasoned modification of doctrine that it claimed, and to a refusal to understand the beliefs and feelings of a large mass of Catholics, let alone to explain things to them in their own terms.'[31] As a formula for the 1960s this would presume that the 'large mass' had 'their own terms' in which it was possible to 'explain' or 'understand' their 'beliefs'; but the fact that much new theological writing in the 1960s was regarded, by ordinary laity and by some clergy, as 'above the heads' of the 'large mass' not only led to misunderstandings and eventually to a hostile, uncomfortable or simply indifferent atmosphere for serious theological thought, but also revealed retrospectively just how inadequate Catholic education in England had proved to be. Whatever its success in maintaining a Catholic identity sociologically, the massive investment in education seemed still to have left many Catholics 'ill-equipped intellectually to reconcile faith' with some post-conciliar expressions and explorations of that faith.

But if some of the liberals or radicals were guilty of a failure to understand the 'beliefs' of Catholics, others seemed capable of not understanding the 'feelings' of large numbers of Catholics. Since the second major effect of a Catholic education seems to be an unusual emphasis on sexual morality, it was not surprising that for many Catholics the most contentious issue of the 1960s involved a matter of sexual morals. The initial debate on contraception was relatively temperate in tone; when Archbishop Heenan on 7th May 1964 issued a statement on behalf of the English hierarchy maintaining that 'We cannot change God's law' in the matter of birth-control, one typically-restrained reaction was voiced by M. de la Bedoyere, 'The very negative statement of Archbishop Heenan about birth control will cause dismay among the more progressive and informed Catholics'; an Anglican scholar wrote to the *Times* pointing out that the statement

misquoted St. Augustine in a 'special pleading' way to allow
the changes that were already accepted; there was a slight
flurry over an interview with Bernard Haring in the *Guardian*
and a survey claimed that 40 % of Catholic couples in Britain
were using 'outlawed' methods.[32] The same year the special
papal commission was established and when lay experts
became the majority of the reconstituted commission in
early 1965 it seemed possible that the Pope's request for
public silence on the issue might be a straw in the wind of
change. In October 1965 a survey of the private opinions of
Newman Association members indicated a probable majority opposed to the traditional teaching.[33] In 1966 the
strains became more visible: a detailed demolition of
traditionalist arguments was refused an imprimatur and had
to be published under a pseudonym; even a 'liberal' position
like Haring's came under attack for a fundamental inability
to speak the language of 'experience' when dealing with the
actualities of marriage; but at the same time Cardinal
Heenan, in his June Pastoral, could speak significantly of
changes in moral teaching.[34] Early in 1967 reports filtered
through that perhaps 90 % of the Commission were in favour
of change, and in April the secret report, supporting change,
was published; yet as the final decision was delayed and
delayed it became increasingly apparent that the issue might
produce a crisis based on claims of authority rather than the
merit of arguments.[35] When, finally, on 29th June, 1968,
Humanae Vitae was published, the reaction of many prominent
laity and even clergy was openly critical; though delayed
till after an official statement from the hierarchy, a dissenting letter signed by 55 priests, many of them nationally
known, appeared in the *Times* on October 2nd 1968; the
same week the *Tablet* published a dissenting statement signed
by 75 laypeople, most of whom were not only eminent as
doctors, lawyers and academics but were also leading members of Catholic organizations and National and Diocesan
Commissions.[36] The more immediate reactions of diocesan
bishops, during August and September, had significantly
varied. Two days after the encyclical Fr. Paul Weir, of the

Southwark diocese, was quoted in the *Evening Standard* (1st Aug 1968) as saying: 'I have in the past told people that they are entitled to freedom of conscience because the teaching of the church was in doubt. I don't see how I can continue to do that. At the moment I would say that it was also impossible to accept the Pope's decision or to urge it upon others. What the solution is for me I don't yet know.' His Vicar-General immediately suspended him from preaching and hearing confessions and on 12th August his bishop, Archbishop Cowderoy, suspended him from all priestly functions; a pastoral letter on 11th August from the same Archbishop said, in part, 'Some of our poor, simple people have been misled by disobedient priests, who did not heed the command of the Holy Father that the traditional rules be followed until and unless he made a change. They, like other priests, were told not to confuse their people with the specious argument that the law was in doubt, when the Pope said it was not in doubt.' In similar vein, Archbishop Murphy of Cardiff said in his pastoral — presumably without intending any irony — 'If this encyclical has proved anything, it has proved in these matters of interpreting the natural law that all honesty, all compassion, all erudition, all theological acumen is of little account.' In Nottingham Bishop Ellis followed Southwark's example in suspending critical priests. Cardinal Heenan's pastoral of 4th August anticipated the more compassionate tone and attitude of the later joint statement, in emphasising that those married couples unable to cease practising 'unlawful' contraception 'must not abstain from the sacraments'; such a proviso marked the distance travelled since the much-publicized case of Dr. Anne Biezanek in the early 60s.[37] But perhaps the most significant statement came from Archbishop Beck of Liverpool in an interview in the *Catholic Herald* (23rd Aug 1968): 'In a moral crisis of this kind I think the only thing one can tell people is that they must do what they think is right . . . I think everybody has the duty to form his conscience and it's part of my responsibility, and part of the responsibility of the teaching church, to help people to form their own consciences'; in the same interview Archbishop Beck remarked: 'I think we have gone away from the concept of the Church teaching and the Church taught to a realization that these two are organically so closely connected that they must form one — the whole people of God.' The second comment speaks the language of Vatican II, but it is clearly in tension with the narrower concept of 'the teaching church' in the first comment. A similar tension is apparent in the agreed formulations of the letters *ad clerum* sent to each priest by their diocesan bishops in late October 1968, concerning dissent over *Humanae Vitae*: 'The Bishops of England and Wales have no wish to inhibit reasonable discussion . . . Priests are required in preaching, teaching, writing in the press, speaking on radio, television or public platforms, to refrain from opposing the teaching of the Pope in all matters of faith and morals. If a priest is unwilling to give this undertaking the bishop will decide whether he can be allowed without scandal to continue to act in the name of the church.'[38] It is difficult to see how these conditions could not 'inhibit reasonable discussion', but the strain indicated here was deeply symptomatic: the problem of who spoke and acted 'in the name of the church' and the question of the relationship between 'our poor simple people' and other elements in the church's composition underlay both a number of other issues and the formal changes in the institutional structure of English Catholicism during the decade.

3. *Institution, Authority and Conscience*

'In him the Church looks at itself from the outside, and understands from that perspective the depth of its own corruption.' Herbert McCabe quoted these words, from a *Guardian* article (5th Jan 1967) concerning Charles Davis's decision to leave the Catholic church, in his editorial comment in *New Blackfriars* for February 1967, and also quoted some of the reasons given by Davis in an *Observer* article (1st Jan 1967): 'The official church is racked by fear, insecurity and anxiety, with a consequent intolerance and lack of love . . . There is a concern for authority at the expense of truth, and I am constantly saddened by the workings of an impersonal and unfree system.' But after citing some of the more objectionable or foolish actions and statements of ecclesiastical authorities, McCabe argued that 'It is because we believe that the hierarchical institutions of the Roman Catholic Church, with all their decadence, their corruption and their sheer silliness, do in fact link us to areas of Christian truth beyond our own particular experience and ultimately to truths beyond any experience, that we remain and see our Christian lives in terms of remaining, members of this church.'[39] Fr. McCabe was immediately removed from his editorship, on orders from a Roman authority that seemed incapable of understanding either the English language or English sensibilities, and was further, if briefly, suspended from his priestly functions. The resulting movement of protest on the part of many who knew McCabe, read *New Blackfriars* or simply valued the claims of open justice, and the somewhat obscure story of the source of the dismissal itself, highlighted one point which the editorial had made. Charles Davis had written of those who 'remain Roman Catholics only because they live their Christian lives on the fringe of the institutional church and largely ignore it'; disputing this use of 'institutional', McCabe had argued: 'Consider a few institutions: Spode House, the Newman Theology Groups, the Union of Catholic Students, the Young Christian Workers, University Chaplaincies, the Catholic press including even *New Blackfriars*. None of these are exclusively for Catholics but no sociologist would hesitate to describe them as Roman Catholic institutions. It is within institutions such as these that a great many Catholics nourish their Christian lives.' It was largely through the personal contacts and informal connections fostered by such institutions that the protest over McCabe's dismissal was organized, but, more importantly, the relationship between such groupings and 'the overall and relatively impersonal structure of the hierarchy', visible in this incident, not only poses a general problem for the social historian of Catholicism but also, during the 60s, constituted a practical — and ultimately theological — problem for the Catholic community in trying to implement some of the teachings of Vatican II.

Three aspects of this problem can be briefly noted. The Vatican Council had encouraged the setting-up, at parish, diocesan and national levels, of various commissions — on ecumenism, liturgy, education, among others. Given the concentration of expenditure on more traditional priorities, the financing of these commissions posed a problem: thus in 1967, at a time when one diocese was committed to a debt of £4M for a new cathedral and was planning nine new churches for a small new town of 80,000 population, the annual budget of the National Council for the Lay Apostolate was reckoned to be £100.[40] In 1967 it was estimated that £200,000 needed to be raised to ensure the efficient existence of the new commissions; on 7th March, at the hierarchy's request, a small committee, of three laymen, Bishop Worlock and Mgr. Norris, met to plan a fund-raising campaign; the idea emerged of an appeal to be made in each church by laypeople, both for money and for the offer of skills and talents to be put 'at the service of the church'; the scheme was entitled 'The New Pentecost' and was announced at a press conference by Cardinal Heenan on 9th May, the appeal itself to be made on June 2nd, Whit Sunday; adverts in the press also announced the scheme — at an estimated cost of £10,000. Given the very compressed schedule, it was no surprise that the appeal was not very successful. But more importantly, it was presented — both in the Cardinal's press conferences and in letters *ad clerum* — as the initiative of 'the laity'. Yet only three laymen were at all responsible; even those making the local appeals were to be 'chosen' by the parish priest and the text of what they were to say was stipulated beforehand.[41] As an exercise in 'consultation' and in the description of a fund-raising campaign as 'The New Pentecost' the episode indicated that, still, 'the bishops have not really begun to grasp that Vatican II implies a different type of attitude to their lay people'[42] and that the hierarchy had not yet even learned to speak the language of the Council, or the New Testament, in appropriate ways. The actual establishment of some diocesan commissions and councils revealed more of a shift in attitude: for example, the Portsmouth Pastoral Council, which met for the first time in March 1968, had a total membership of 144, of whom all but 19 were elected by deaneries, religious orders and existing organizations, and the majority overall was lay; Liverpool's Pastoral Council was composed of 20 priests, 10 religious and 30 laypeople, elected by a process of nomination from diocesan-wide recommendations. But if the principles of consultation and election were increasingly operative in these areas, in the matter of episcopal appointments themselves such principles were clearly more difficult to establish.[43] It is a comment on the historical amnesia even of 'progressives' that whereas in the 1780s it seemed most likely that an English hierarchy, if formally established, would be chosen by a committee of laymen, in the mid-1960s the most 'liberal' suggestion seemed to be that the laity might be 'consulted' on the choice of their bishops — and even that suggestion had no visible practical effect.[44] At least by the end of the decade, in 1969, Cardinal Heenan could register, in a curious conflation of rhetorics, a new official attitude: 'It is certain that it is no longer possible for central authority to hand down decisions affecting the whole church without full consultation with representatives of all sections of the church. The growth of education has altered the attitude of both clergy and laity. They still want to belong to the one fold of the one Shepherd but they do not want to be treated like sheep . . . Citizens of the City of God, no less than citizens of modern nations, are prepared to submit to authority only if it is seen to be reasonable and responsible.'[45] Four months later, however, the Cardinal forbade any discussion of celibacy at the nationally-elected Conference of Priests at Wood Hall, thereby revealing that a tradition of authority changes most slowly: in 1958, for example, his predecessor Cardinal Godfrey had forbidden the discussion of war and peace at a meeting of the Catholic

Nuclear Disarmament Group.[46] What had, perhaps, weakened slightly was a corresponding tradition of deference to such authority; but even where a selective repudiation of clerical-episcopal control was hesitantly evident, the line tended, crucially, to be drawn — despite popular talk of 'the priesthood of all believers' — at the doors of the liturgical gathering itself; that source of extra-liturgical hegemony remained, in practice, the almost-unquestioned province of the ordained priest.

Some did, indeed, go further, in different ways. If the issues of controlled liturgical reform, ecclesiastical reorganization, lay participation and consultation, episcopal appointments, celibacy and birth-control, seemed to many the dominant concerns, there was also a current that increasingly saw such matters as peripheral, as 'the detailed eccentricities of ecclesiastical ant-heaps.'[47] From occupying a central position within the ecclesiastical institutions, as ordained priest, Council *peritus*, professor of theology at Ware seminary and Heythrop, editor of the *Clergy Review*, and veteran of many official committees, Charles Davis moved, in December 1966, with public suddenness, to being a christian without formal membership of any ecclesiastical organization, a stance of 'creative disaffiliation'; by the early 1970s he could look back and find the internal affairs of the Roman church quaintly irrelevant.[48] Something of that attitude found expression among Catholics and other christians during the decade: from an apparently traditional position, the liturgical reforms of the Council could be seen as a 'preoccupation with questions of cultus' and the issue of the vernacular as fundamentally irrelevant except to bishops and priests professionally concerned with outward forms, while what really mattered, as always, was only the inner spiritual rebirth of the individual;[49] from a more fashionable standpoint, models of the early church or the image of a future 'church of the diaspora' could be evoked, in which the church had no property, no schools or seminaries, no complex organization and few full-time priests;[50] in various modes and mixtures both these attitudes were intermittently embodied, in agapés, in home-made liturgies, in unofficial ecumenical communions, in explorations of old and new forms of meditation and mysticism, among loosely-knit networks of christians who deliberately did 'live their Christian lives on the fringes of the institutional church and largely ignore it.' And, characteristically of the times, some of those of whom the hierarchy was most wary on other issues offered trenchantly effective critiques of such positions.[51]

In another sense, however, there were more fundamental issues than those which concerned the Council. Beneath all the preoccupations of church reform, the basic questions of theology loomed again. Particularly after Bishop Robinson's *Honest to God* in 1963, it became clearer to many christians that 'heated conviction and reforming zeal born of impatience with the ecclesiastical set-up are no substitute for concrete beliefs about God and man when one is face to face with those who do not share one's assumptions.'[52] That recognition was perhaps especially present in the slow growth of dialogue between christians and marxists during the decade, and in the assimilation by some theological thinkers of the fundamental challenge inherited from the 19th century, not the apparent clash of 'science' and 'religion' but the undercutting of 'belief' by the sociology of knowledge, the awareness that all forms of understanding are socially determined and therefore historically relative.[53] In that perspective, issues not only of biblical interpretation and development of doctrine became newly problematical but also the very possibility of theology itself, of any talk about God. By 1973 one theologian could formulate the basic problem the 1960s left unresolved: 'The flight to biblical studies and patrology, or to sociology and poetry, so typical of the opposing wings in the new generation . . . must lead to an impasse in the long run unless we face up to the philosophical problems that all these various disciplines ignore.'[54]

A minor incident in early 1970 drew together many of the threads of the previous turbulent decade. David Konstant, the highly-respected chief adviser on religious education to the Archdiocese of Westminster, and John Cumming, a member of the editorial board of the notorious *Slant*, published a jointly-written school textbook which attractively and intelligently presented the results of much of the new catechetical and theological thinking. It was refused an imprimatur for the Dublin Archdiocese; aware of that refusal, the censor for the Westminster Archdiocese nevertheless granted an imprimatur. Among the passages to which the Dublin censor objected was a sentence which stated that 'conscience' should be seen more as 'a faculty dependent on formation by society and individual inquiry.' The book was called *Beginnings*.[55]

II

Roman Catholicism has a power of elimination that many living organisms might envy . . . However helpful this negative capability may be for promoting peace in the Church, the theologian must face the historical facts of change without attempting to palliate them.

THE question of the relation between history and theology was a characteristic concern of Catholic thinkers in the 1960s, variously posed in terms of 'salvation history', 'development of doctrine', a 'theology of history', or apparent in an interest in Teilhard de Chardin, the process theology derived from Whitehead, or even the 'death of God' school of Altizer and Hamilton. But perhaps only in the fields of biblical study and liturgical research did the precise details of actual history seem to impinge upon more strictly theological writing, since the more overarching question tended to be formulated largely with an emphasis on abstract possibilities or in terms of epochal generalizations and the history of 'ideas'. By the end of the decade, however, the accepted academic practice of a relatively autonomous 'history of ideas' was itself experiencing a crisis of method: new models of the history of scientific theories were proposed, in terms of 'paradigm shifts'; a post-structuralist notion of 'epistemic

shifts' in the deep structure of a period's fundamental intellectual assumptions became briefly fashionable; and the
influence of a newly 'anti-humanist' marxism suggested
both that changes in ideology were logically structured
within an interdependence of concepts (the notion of
'problematic') and that such changes were dependent upon
changed social relations within the fundamental economic
and secondary institutional (educational, legal, familial,
political) apparatuses of a society.[56] By way of conclusion, it
may be worth briefly sketching a wider context and possible
interpretation of 1960s Catholicism in the light of these
accounts of change.

For some purposes, it remains possible broadly to divide
the history of English Catholicism into periods. The pre-
1850 tenor of Catholicism is only just being re-examined, as
is the brief complex moment of Modernism; the 1960s
concentrated more on the 'rediscovery of Newman' as in
tension with his own period, from 1850 to Vatican I, and
then as patron figure for the ending of the restrictive phase
between Vatican I and Vatican II.[57] More specific parallels
were drawn: the abandonment in 1966 of a Roman alle-
giance by Charles Davis, the leading English Catholic
theologian, was sometimes compared in significance to
Newman's conversion to Roman Catholicism in 1845, as the
issues involved in McCabe's dismissal might be seen to
reproduce those in the turmoil over *The Rambler*.[58] Newman's process of conversion produced his *Essay on the
Development of Doctrine*; the publication in the July 1859
Rambler of his *On Consulting the Faithful in Matters of Doctrine*
led to his secret delation to Rome. The two texts are linked
in their theological concern with the relation between the
'consensus fidelium' and episcopal or papal functions, a
problem that first came to critical prominence for Newman
in his historical study, *The Arians of the Fourth Century* (1833).
But that concern is also linked to two other central texts of
Newman, *The Idea of A University* (1852) and *Grammar of
Assent* (1870); one is concerned with the place of theology
as a science among others and with the need for an educated

laity, in the context of establishing a Catholic university in Dublin, the other with the complex convergence of considerations that lead not so much to scientific proof as to a commitment in belief and conscience — an inquiry conducted in the shadow of Vatican I's definition of infallibility. At the centre of the links between these texts and issues is the problem of the 'knowledge' that the 'simple faithful' have of their christianity.

The 1960s saw perhaps the emergence of a different, though related, pattern of links, a re-working of that 'problematic'; again, at the centre were the relations between belief, lay education and theological understanding. The impact of Vatican II in England could be experienced by many of the faithful as an extraordinarily compressed period of 'development of doctrine', at the practical heart of which was the rediscovery of the role of the laity, the laos or whole people of God. In that respect Newman's insistence on the function of the laity received partial endorsement. But the policy of 'consulting the faithful' was actually implemented only at various levels of administration and then only hesitantly and minimally. In this process it was, inevitably, the minority of highly-educated laity which played a predominant role; that minority was, on the whole, university-trained but not in 'theology' as a scientific discipline of knowledge; they therefore only incompletely fulfilled Newman's hopes of the 1850s. Yet in taking their new-found place within the ecclesial community, many insisted upon retaining the values of a secular academic community even in areas more theological than administrative: freedom of research and debate, autonomous organization, forceful articulation of the viewpoints of opposing schools of thought, an awareness of the complexity of language appropriate for adequate thought and sensibility, a recognition of the rigorous standards involved in any appeal to 'reason'. And some tried in various ways to probe beyond the shifts of Vatican II towards a further development of theological thought, from a basis not in the familiar pattern of clerical-scholastic training but from the locus of their own experience and from the resources of their own disciplines, often with significantly different criteria of argument and of method. In particular, Catholic literary critics, working from a sense of literature as the 'centre' of a humane education, evolved a distinctively English mode of theological writing during the 60s, at the core of which was, again, a concern with theological reflection upon the relations of language, experience and thought.

But at the same time two features of the wider intellectual life of the decade impinged upon the task of theological re-education: a developing critique, within the universities themselves, of both the academic assumptions and internal practices of higher education, and a fundamental erosion of the claim of any 'science' to be objectively rational. In the student movement of the late 60s, in England as elsewhere, these issues were linked to wider concerns with the political and economic structure of the society.[59] Political and even economic issues figured intermittently in specifically Catholic preoccupations during the decade, with the publication of papal encyclicals like *Pacem in Terris* and *Populorum Progressio*, Pope Paul's visit to the UN in 1965, and parish-organized petitions against abortion reform; and in many respects the structural tensions and changes within the church reproduced those both in the larger society and within the radical political currents of the time — a questioning of authoritarian or only shallowly democratic modes of organization and a challenging of congealed traditions of thought, behaviour and attitude. But the major intersection between Catholics and politics was of a quite different order. The decade began with a mildly-interested national press discovering the news-value of Pope John, the Council and ecumenism; it ended with daily coverage of a bitter civil war in Northern Ireland, with armed Catholics and armed Protestants killing one another in the name of a cross-tangle of religious loyalties, political allegiances and economic interests. The brutal fact of Ulster again posed, in yet another way, the problem of the relation that actually obtains between the 'belief of the faithful' and a commitment to christanity; in the cruellest fashion ecumenism was a visible part of that problem, but so also, in a more profound and disturbing manner, was the question of the social and ideological determinants of religious 'faith'.[60] The conflict in Ireland seemed to make clear the final message, and warning, of the decade. If theological thought is intimately linked to and has to reflect upon the complexities of historical change and conflict — as Newman's study of Arianism had once indicated — and if christian belief is only fully incarnated in the actual life of the 'whole people of God', then Northern Ireland may eventually demand and stimulate, even in English Catholics, a more searching theological and practical response to the problem of being a serious christian believer than Vatican II did. If that response does not occur, the difficult renewal of the 1960s may finally be seen to have remained largely an instance of the 'detailed eccentricities of ecclesiastical ant-heaps.' Newman put the basic point well enough in 1859, in words that now have a sadly ambiguous application:

> I think certainly that the Ecclesia docens is more happy when she has such enthusiastic partisans about her as are here represented than when she cuts off the faithful from the study of her divine doctrines . . . and requires from them a fides implicita in her word which in the educated classes will terminate in indifference and in the poorer in superstition.

NOTES

1 G. Egner, 'Contraception: Tradition Revisited', *New Blackfriars*, March 1966. I have mainly relied on periodical articles and press material published during the decade itself; this has necessitated a fairly large, though still obviously selective, number of references. I am generally indebted to *Herder Correspondence* which, as a monthly journal of report, was able to offer perceptively compressed accounts of contemporary developments.

2 Cf. E. Langdale, 'Les milieux ouvriers', in D. Mathew, ed. *Catholicisme Anglaise*, Paris 1958, pp. 82–96, esp. p. 83. His target was clearly G. A. Beck, ed. *English Catholicism 1850–1950*, London 1950. The omission has been partly but unsatisfactorily remedied by e.g. K. S. Inglis, *Churches and the Working Classes in Victorian England*, 1963; S. Mayor, *The Churches and the Labour Movement*, 1967; and J. Hickey, *Urban Catholics* 1967.

3 J. Bossy, *The English Catholic Community, 1570–1850*, 1975.

4 Cf. e.g. B. Bergonzi, 'The English Catholics', *Encounter* Jan 1965; G. Scott, *The RCs*, 1967; D. Fisher, 'The Changing attitude towards the Irish in Britain', *Hibernia* March 1965; O. R. Sweeney, 'The Emigrant', *The Furrow*, June 1964.

5 Cf. J. H. Newman, preface to third edition of *Lectures on the Prophetical Office of the Church*, 1877; F. von Hügel, *The Mystical Element of Religion*, 1909.

6 Cf. A. Cunningham, 'Notes on Strategy', *Slant* 30, 1970.

7 Cunningham, art cit. For population figures in this paragraph, cf. *Herder Correspondence*, III, 4, 1966 and III, 7, 1966, Statistical Supplements; E. K. Taylor, 'Ecumenism and Conversion', *Dublin Review*, Spring 1965; for slightly different figures and a detailed breakdown cf. A.E.C.W. Spencer, 'The Demography and Sociography of the Roman Catholic Community of England and Wales', in *The Committed Church*, ed. L. Bright and S. Clements, 1966. For expenditure on schools cf. M. P. Hornsby-Smith, 'A Sociological case for Catholic schools', *The Month*, Oct. 1972. For Beck's estimate, cf. *Tablet*, 15 Jan. 1965.

8 For opposed views on the linked issues of mixed marriages and education, cf. e.g. articles by L. Kovacs and J. McKee in *Clergy Review*, March and July 1964, and L. Orsy in *Gregorianum* 1964, iv. On 18th March 1966 an Instruction from Rome made minimal modifications to mixed marriage regulations; five days later Pope Paul and Archbishop Ramsey of Canterbury had their first official meeting; the Instruction gravely disappointed Archbishop Ramsey, cf. *Church Times* 20 May 1966; for Archbishop Heenan's possible role in this rather gauchely-handled timing cf. D. Fisher, 'Catholics still coasting', *New Christian* 24 Feb. 1966. Ecumenical developments have been largely omitted from this essay, as its focus lies elsewhere, though ecumenism might be analysed as one facet of the problems broached in Pt. II; cf. e.g. M. Miegge, 'Ecumenism and neocapitalism', *Slant* 30, 1970.

9 Cited in *The Case for Catholic Schools*, published by the Union of Catholic Students, 1966, from a teach-in at University College, London, in Feb. 1966. Cf. also A. E. C. W. Spencer, 'How effective are catholic schools?', *Slant* 4, 1965; *Religious Education*, ed. P. Jebb, 1968; *Catholic Education in a Secular Society*, ed. B. Tucker, 1968.

10 Cf. M. Lawlor, *Out of this World: a study of Catholic values*, 1965; L. de Saint Moulin, 'Social Class and Religious Behaviour', *Clergy Review*, Jan 1968; J. Brothers, 'Two Views of the Parish', *The Furrow*, Aug. 1965 and *Church and School*, 1964. For the debate in the 60s on the role of the parish, cf. e.g. C. K. Ward, *Priests and People*, Liverpool 1961; C. Davis ed. *The Parish in the Modern World*, 1964; C. Boxer, 'The Church as a community in the world: 1: the parish experience' and '2: an interpretation', *Slant*, 13, and 14, 1967; L. Pyle, 'Vatican II and the parish' in *Directions*, ed. T. Eagleton, 1968; cf. also the debate between Eagleton and M. Dummett in *New Blackfriars*, Aug., Oct. and Dec. 1965, and pamphlet series, *The Living Parish*.

11 For developments in catechetics cf. e.g. *Herder Correspondence*, II, 5, May 1965; III, 6, June 1966; IV, 3, March 1967.

12 Cf. e.g. *The New Nuns*, ed. Sr. C. Borromeo, 1968; for the wider problem cf. e.g. Sr. Mary Cuthbert, 'Women in the church', letter to *Ampleforth Journal*, Feb. 1966, and Dympna Pyle, 'Glory, jest and riddle: woman in a man's world', *Slant* 15, 1967.

13 Cf. A. E. C. W. Spencer, 'The Crisis of Priestly Vocations in England', Presidential Address to 9th International Conference on Sociology of Religion, Montreal, Summer 1967, printed in *Herder Correspondence* IV, 12, Dec. 1967.

14 The dates may be worth recording of the English translations of: Rahner, *Free Speech in the Church*, 1959, *Nature and Grace* 1963, *Mission and Grace* I, 1963, II, 1964, *Theological Investigations* I 1961, II 1963, etc.; Schillebeeckx, *Christ the Sacrament*, 1963, *Marriage, Secular Reality and Saving Mystery*, 1965, *Mary, Mother of the Redemption*, 1964. *Vatican II: the real achievement*, 1967, *Revelation and Theology* 1967, *Concept of Truth and Theological Renewal* 1968; Kung, *Council and Reunion* 1961, *Justification* 1964, *The Church* 1967, *Infallibility* 1971. The English school produced, e.g.: Davis, *Liturgy and Doctrine*, 1960, *The Study of Theology* 1962, *The Making of a Christian* 1964; McCabe, *The New Creation* 1964, *Law, Love and Language* 1968; Lash, *His Presence in the World* 1968; Wicker, *Culture and Liturgy*, 1963, *Culture and Theology* 1966; Eagleton, *The New Left Church* 1966, *The Body as Language* 1970; Cunningham, *Adam*, 1968; Stein, ed. *Nuclear Weapons and Christian Conscience*, 1961, *Peace on Earth*, 1966; Meynell, *Sense, Nonsense and Christianity*, 1964. *Nature versus Grace* 1965; Rosemary Haughton, *Christian Responsibility* 1964, *On Trying to be Human*, 1966, *The Transformation of Man* 1967.

15 Cf. *Sunday Telegraph* 6 Feb. 1966. For *Herder Correspondence's* assessment of Cardinal Heenan, cf. *HC* II, 11, Nov. 1965.

16 For a sympathetic account of *Slant* cf. B. Wicker, *First the Political Kingdom*, 1967; for unsympathetic accounts cf *Herder Correspondence* V, 1, Jan. 1968; Peter Hebblethwaite, 'Ambivalence in the Catholic Left', *The Tablet* 9 Aug. 1969, and correspondence 23 Aug. 6, 13, 20 Sept. 1969; cf. also the critiques by Donald Nicholl, 'A Layman's Journal', *Clergy Review*, August 1966; B. Sharratt, 'Locating Theology', *Slant* 22, 1968; A Wall, '*Slant* and the Language of Revolution', *New Blackfriars* Nov. 1975.

17 The reporting on the Council by Desmond Fisher, editor of the *Catholic Herald* from March 1962 to early 1966, was of crucial importance here. The circulation figures of the Catholic press in 1966 were: *Universe*, 300,000; *Catholic Herald* 100,000; *Catholic Pictorial* 38,000; *The Tablet*, and *New Christian*, had about 14,000, *Clergy Review* 5,500 and *New Blackfriars* 2,200; cf. *Herder Correspondence* III, 5, May 1966 and letters in III, 7. Add to these the coverage by the national press and the various journalistic books about the Council by Xavier Rynne, Bernard Wall, etc.

18 On vocations cf. e.g. Spencer art cit. note 13 above; the special issue of *Christus Rex*, no. 2, 1967, and articles by J. F. McGrath, 'Where have all the young men gone?', *Clergy Review* June, July, August 1965. In 1965 there were about 5,000 secular priests in England and Wales, or 1 to every 500 practising Catholics, cf. *Catholic Directory* 1965. On seminaries cf. e.g. C. Davis, 'Theology in a seminary confinement', *Downside Review* Oct. 1963, J. F. Randall, 'Seminary community', *Clergy Review* March 1965; C. Ernst, 'Philosophy in the seminary', *New Blackfriars* March 1965; M. de la Bedoyere, 'Freedom for the seminarian', *Search* April 1965; A. Cunningham 'Seminaries' and F. McDonagh 'Education for the priesthood', *Slant* 4 1965; S. Moore, 'Training in the junior seminary', *Clergy Review* Oct. 1965; A seminarian, 'Intellectual freedom in the seminary' *Slant* 8, 1966; D. Hickey, 'Philosophy: the old or the new?' *Clergy Review*, Aug. 1966.

19 M. Winter, 'Catholic Theology in England', *Clergy Review*, June 1968. Cp. N. Lash, 'English Catholic Theology', *The Month*, Oct. 1975.

20 D. Gibson, 'Don't Answer back, Children', *New Christian* 19 March 1970. It is difficult to judge the accuracy of his estimate but no official figures seem to be available.

21 By the mid-1970s the list of theologians who had ceased to practise an ordained ministry included such well-known names as Charles Davis, Hubert Richards, Peter de Rosa, Peter Harris, Nicholas Lash, Peter Hebblethwaite, Joseph Blenkinsopp . . . A list of 25 prominent figures is given in A. Hastings, 'The Priesthood Today: II', *Tablet*, 15 May 1976.

22 Spencer, art cit., note 13.

23 J. M. Todd, 'Making the Council work in England', talk on German radio, printed in *Herder Correspondence* III, 11, Nov. 1966. In other fields he could have added the significant number of philosophers, often Wittgensteinians, who were from a Catholic background: Anscombe, Geach, Kenny, Dummett, Smiley, Cameron, Barrett, etc. Catholics were also prominent in such diverse fields as anthropology and the trade unions. An example of the hierarchy's suspicion of sociology and related disciplines was the continued refusal, throughout the decade, to finance an adequate study of Catholic educational assumptions; the plea was still being made in 1972, cf. Hornsby-Smith, art. cit.

24 G. Moorhouse, 'Catholics at the Crossroads', *Guardian* 29th Oct. 1964.

25 Cf. *Herder Correspondence* II, 4, April 1965, to which I am indebted for the quotations in this paragraph.

26 By the mid-1970s indeed such practices were being severely criticized and even proscribed by a papacy and episcopacy insistent upon a new uniformity; cf. the cases of Fr. Baker of Downham Market in 1975 and of Archbishop Lefebvre in 1977. In 'The reform of the Roman church', *Sunday Times*, 12 Dec. 1965, Hans Kung had expressed the fear that post-Vatican II Catholicism would soon assume the same rigidity as post-Tridentine Catholicism and urged as a priority the fundamental reform of the Curia.

27 For aspects of the argument in this paragraph, cf. e.g. R. Williams, *Culture and Society*, 1958, and *Keywords*, 1976; I. Robinson, *The Survival of English* 1973.

28 Cf. e.g. E. Hill, 'Remythologizing: the key to the Scriptures', *Scripture*, Jan. 1964. On 21 April 1964 the Pontifical Biblical Commission issued an 'Instruction on the Historical Truth of the Gospels'. The English *Jerusalem Bible*, 1966, provoked further debate; its general editor, Alex Jones, had earlier raised the issue of language and theology in his *God's Living Word*, 1963; later treatments revealed the influence of Leavis's literary criticism and Wittgenstein's philosophy, e.g. McCabe, *Law, Love and Language* 1968, Eagleton, *Body as Language* 1970, S. Moore, *God is a New Language* 1967.

29 English translation 1963; cf. his *The Christian Response* 1968, and e.g. D. Rhymes, *Prayer in the Secular City*, 1967, C. Burke, *Treat Me Cool, Lord*, 1968. Compare these with the spiritual reading fare briefly examined in E. O'Brien, 'English Culture and Spirituality', *Concilium* IX, 2, Nov. 1966: Marmion, Vonier, Goodier, Leen etc.

30 Cf. H. McCabe 'The Real Presence', *Clergy Review*, Dec. 1964, and F. Clark, 'The Real Presence', *Unitas* (Rome) summer 1966.

31 R. Griffiths, 'The Catholic Revival: Reaction then and now', *Clergy Review*, Oct. 1972.

32 Cf. *Herder Correspondence* I, 7, July 1964, *Evening Standard* 7th May 1964, *Times* 11th May and *Guardian* 9th May 1964. The hierarchy's statement was probably prompted by an article in *Search*, April 1964, by Archbishop Roberts, in which he rejected the 'rational grounds' for the Roman position as unconvincing. For the official treatment of Roberts, cf C. Davis, 'The Case of Archbishop Roberts', *Clergy Review*, April 1966 — a perhaps significant article for Davis himself.

33 M. Lawlor, 'Birth Control: report on members' attitudes', *The Newman*, Oct. 1965; a 'probable' majority because only 984 (c 30%) of the membership responded and because some Newman Circles tended to be suspicious of the London-based leadership; cf. *Catholic Herald*, March 24th 1967 for later tensions in the Association.

34 G. Egner, *Birth Regulation and Catholic Belief* 1966; cf. N. Middleton, 'Roman Censorship', *New Christian* 17 Nov. 1966; R. Haughton, 'The Renovation of the Old Jerusalem', *New Blackfriars* Sept. 1966, reviewing Haring.

35 Cf. Archbishop Roberts interview, *New Christian* 9th March 1967; R. Nowell, 'An Agonizing Choice', *New Christian* 4th May 1967. For the Report itself see *National Catholic Reporter* (U.S.A.) 19 April 1967 and *Tablet* 22, 29, April, 6 May 1967.

36 *Tablet* 5th Oct. 1968. Between them they held some 55 senior posts in Catholic organizations of a voluntary and official kind.

37 Cf. A. Biezanek, *All Things New*, 1964.

38 Letter *ad clerum* of Thomas Holland, Bishop of Salford, 22nd Oct. 1968; almost identical phrasing occurs in e.g. the *ad clerum* of Charles Grant, Bishop of Northampton, 23rd Oct. 1968. Behind the formulae lies the curious notion of 'keeping quarrels in the family' of the church — a plea emitted by Cardinal Heenan e.g. at a reception for the Newman Association in 1965 and by the Apostolic Delegate during the 'McCabe affair' in 1967; the notion is curious because no way of generally communicating within that 'family' is immune to the attention of the national press.

39 H. McCabe, 'Comment' *New Blackfriars*, Feb. 1967, reprinted in *The McCabe Affair: Evidence and Comment*, ed. S. Clements and M. Lawlor, 1967, which documents the whole incident, and in *Purification of the Church*, S.C.M. Press 1967, which also reprints M. Dummett's 'How Corrupt is the Church?' from *New Blackfriars* Aug. 1965. The reference to 'experience' also had local overtones, cf. the two symposia, *The Experience of Marriage*, 1965, and *The Experience of Priesthood*. For other reactions to Charles Davis's decision, cf. *New Christian* editorial, 29th Dec. 1966, B. C. Butler in *Sunday Telegraph* 29th Jan 1967, N. Middleton in *New Christian* 23rd Feb. 1967, J. Wilkins in *Frontier* Spring 1967, and the later reviews of Davis's *A Question of Conscience*, 1967, by P. Harris, *Tablet*, 18th Nov. 1967, G. Baum, *Frontier* Spring 1968, B. C. Butler, *Clergy Review*, Feb. 1968. Perhaps the most considered response came in the Spode House conference, Sept. 1967, which produced *Authority in a Changing Church*, ed. N. Lash, 1968; cf. *Herder Correspondence* V, 4, April 1968.

40 The building figures were given at the 13th Spode House Visual Arts Week, April, 1966, the budget figure by Spencer, art cit., note 13.

41 Cf. e.g. the *ad clerum* of the Bishop of Leeds, 7th May 1968. For a general account cf. *Herder Correspondence* V, 8, Aug. 1968.

42 Todd, art. cit.

43 Cf. the series 'How Not to Appoint a Bishop', in *Herder Correspondence* VI, 3, March, 6, June, 1969, VII, 1, Jan., 2 Feb., 5, May 1970. For Pastoral Councils cf. *Herder Correspondence* V, 5th May 1968.

44 Cf. Todd, art. cit. D. Fisher, 'In the Long Run', *Frontier*, winter 1966; compare: Bossy, op. cit., ch. 14 and E. Duffy, 'Ecclesiastical Democracy Detected': i: 1779–87; ii: 1787–96', *Recusant History*, X, 1970; cf. also G. D. Sweeney, below, pp. 208–32.

45 *Tablet* 25th Oct. 1969, reporting press conference of 18th Oct. 1969.

46 *Tablet* 28th Feb. 1970; in June 1967 Pope Paul had published his encyclical, *Sacerdotalis Caelibatus*. For Godfrey, cf. A. Downing, 'The Thought Barrier', *Slant* 2, 1964.

47 T. Beaumont, announcing *New Christian* in last issue of *Prism*, Sep. 1965.

48 Cf. interview with Davis, *The Month*, Jan. 1971.

49 Aelred Graham, 'The Pathos of Vatican II', *Encounter*, Dec. 1965.

50 Cf. e.g. J. O'Connell, 'Purification as Decay: the church and the process of modernization', *Clergy Review*, July 1966; E. Hill, 'The post-conciliar Papacy', *New Blackfriars*, Aug. 1966. Cf. also D. Fisher, 'Sjaloom', *Frontier*, Spring 1967.

51 E.g. R. Haughton, 'The Christian Dilemma', *New Christian* 30th Nov. 1967, T. Eagleton, 'Why we are still in the Church', *Slant* 14, 1967.

52 R. Hughes, 'Arguments and Experience', *Prism*, Sept. 1965. Perhaps the most effectively critical review of *Honest to God* was that by H. McCabe, *New Blackfriars*, July/August 1963.

53 Cf. especially G. Vass, 'Last April in Marienbad', *Slant* 18, 19, 20, 1968, and A. Cunningham, 'Cultural Change and the Nature of the Church' in *The Christian Priesthood*, ed. N. Lash and J. Rhymer, 1970. Cp. e.g. B. C. Butler, 'Belief in Science and Reason in Religion', *Downside Review*, Jan. 1966.

54 F. Kerr, 'The "Essence of Christianity": Notes after de Certeau', *New Blackfriars* Dec. 1973. The new English translation of Aquinas, *Summa Theologiae*, 1963–76, emphasised this point.

55 Appropriately, the final report in the last issue of *Herder Correspondence*, VII, 6, June 1970, was concerned with this episode.

56 Cf. T. S. Kuhn, *The Structure of Scientific Revolutions*, 1962; *Criticism and the Growth of Knowledge*, ed. I. Lakatos and A. Musgrave, 1970; M. Foucault, *The Order of Things*, 1970; L. Althusser, *For Marx*, 1969, and 'Ideology and Ideological State Apparatuses' in his *Lenin and Philosophy*, 1971.

57 E.g. J. H. Newman, *On Consulting the Faithful*, ed. J. Coulson 1960; *Newman: A Portrait Restored*, ed. Coulson, 1965; *The Rediscovery of Newman*, ed. Coulson and A. M. Allchin, 1967; Coulson, *Newman and the Common Tradition*, 1970.

58 E.g. J. M. Cameron, 'Problems of the editors of religious journals', *Times*, Feb. 25th 1967; cf. Holmes, above, pp. 16–34.

59 Cf. esp. *Student Power*, ed. R. Blackburn and A. Cockburn, 1969, in particular P. Anderson, 'Components of the national culture', which helps situate both English marxist thought and the centrality of Leavis; cf. also M. Horkheimer, *The Eclipse of Reason*, New York 1947. Compare the urge to encyclopaedic knowledge in the *Faith and Fact* series discussed above.

60 Cf. e.g. P. Gibbon, 'The Dialectic of Religion and Class in Ulster', *New Left Review*, 55, 1969; R. Rose, *Governing without Consensus*, 1971; R. Rose and D. Unwin, 'Social cohesion, political parties and strains in regimes' *Comparative Political Studies*, 2, i, 1970; E. McCann, *War and an Irish Town*, 1974; M. Farrell, *Northern Ireland: The Orange State*, 1976.

PART II

Four Essays
by
Garrett Sweeney

7

The forgotten council

Garrett Sweeney

SUCH widespread interest has been aroused by a recent critical study of infallibility[1] that the importance of some previous historical work on Vatican I may easily be overlooked.[2] This would be unfortunate, for the Fathers of 1870 are desperately in need of assistance from historians. Unlike their successors of Vatican II, they were never in a position to wear their hearts upon their sleeves and verbalize at will. They were inhibited within the confines of dogmatic constitutions and seem commonly to be remembered only by the anathemas and definitions preserved like dead flies in the amber pages of Denzinger. Yet these are but a fraction and a poor reflexion of the living faith to which they bore witness at the Council. And this faith deserves no less attention than the ultimate dogmatic formulations. *Lumen Gentium* gives a reminder that there is an authentic expression of faith whenever the episcopate concurs 'in a single viewpoint'. If so, the whole proceedings of Vatican I in their historical context deserve an attention which has not hitherto been accorded them: speeches, reactions, rejections and approvals — even political manœuvres — may all reveal common viewpoints which may not have received the accolade of dogmatic definition but are nevertheless authentic expressions of faith and necessary to an understanding of those formulae which were finally put to the vote.

Had this attention been given at an earlier date, the Church might have been spared no little woe in the past hundred years. It cannot be said that much respect has been paid since 1870 either to the wording of the Vatican defini- , tions or to what went on in the minds of those who formulated them. It is one of the unexplained mysteries of catechetics that so soon after the Council had refused to predicate infallibility of the Pope, catechisms came out with statements that 'The Pope is infallible'. Newman may have been overdramatic in describing the aftermath of Vatican I as 'the great offence'.[3] But he was not far from the truth.

It seems no less passing strange that much of the current criticism of infallibility should be made in the name of propositions which, in fact, were held by those very same Fathers who constructed the infallibility definition. It is not a discovery of 1970 that 'no one is infallible but God himself';[4] respect for this principle was basic to the terms of the definition one hundred years ago.[5] Similarly with theories of papal inspiration and 'Roman absolutism'; both were rejected by the Fathers of 1870 — who would be surprised to learn, one hundred years later, that they had failed to do so.[6] But all this seems to have passed into oblivion. Much as the non-professional theologian may appreciate the case for a reform in the rôle of the papacy, he may be pardoned if he gets the uninformed impression that this could largely be accomplished in the name of Vatican I, and not by its rejection. The essential is to recover the history of what so speedily became a forgotten Council.

1. The Role of the Papacy in Defining

Perhaps the greatest weakness of *Pastor Aeternus* was that it failed to specify the precise rôle, within the process of faith, of an infallibly-defining Pope. The People of God have such a variety of teaching facilities provided for them that they can become embarrassed by such richness. They can read the written Word of God and communicate the faith to each other; when they are in complete unanimity they can also authenticate their faith as the infallible revelation of God. They can learn also from the doctoral office of theologians and from their bishops — who, in turn, can also authenticate their faith by their unanimity whether dispersed or in council. Add to this the teaching authority of the Holy See, whether speaking with an infallibility which does not depend on the agreement of the Church, or speaking infallibly with its agreement, or just not speaking infallibly at all. To which of these should the faithful first turn? — to their co-faithful in the back streets of Bermondsey? — or to the Apostles' crowning dome? What, in short, is the precise rôle of the papacy in the process of faith? Vatican I gave no formulated answer.

The fear of both Inopportunists and Non-infallibilists at the time of the Council was that the proposed definition would give an overwhelming importance to the papacy and eliminate every other teaching office in the Church. From outside, Döllinger gave utterance to prophecy that 'every other authority will pale beside the living oracle of the Tiber, which speaks with plenary inspiration and can always be appealed to'.[7] From inside, Dupanloup fought the concept that the Pope was himself the whole of the Church;[8] echoed from the New World by Bishop Domenec of Pittsburgh, speaking as the Voice of Catholic America, which 'did not make the Pope a sort of God, impeccable, infallible, holding everything in his own hands':[9] to which must be added — if only to preserve it for some anthology of the inimitable Latin spoken by a convinced Britisher — the remark of Bishop Connolly of Nova Scotia that *iuxta schema, omnes episcopi ecclesiae aequivalent zero.*[10]

In point of fact, these particular fears were to be falsified by the history of the next hundred years. Far from overwhelming every other authority, the papal prerogative remained obstinately dormant: to be aroused (if indeed it was then aroused) only for a brief moment in 1950 for the definition of the Assumption. But this restraint can be interpreted neither as accidental nor as due to papal distrust

163

of its own powers. It must be seen rather as the observance of built-in obligations never indeed defined, but recognized explicitly by the Conciliar Fathers as limiting the action of the papacy to rare and exceptional occasions.

This comes out most clearly from the explanatory discourses of Bishop Gasser of Brixen on behalf of the Deputation of the Faith. He explains the word 'define': it is 'to put an end to wavering [*fluctuationi*] on some doctrinal matter'.[11] At greater length: 'the proper occasion for such definitions comes when in some part of the Church there arise scandals concerning the faith, disagreement and heresy — which local bishops are unable to eliminate either by individual action or by a provincial council. In consequence of this they have no other remedy than to refer the matter to the Holy See'.[12] The explanation is clear enough. The defining rôle of the papacy is restricted to occasions when there is doctrinal dissension, and when God's revelation cannot be identified by means of either the unanimity of the faithful, or that of their Bishops. As Gasser noted in phrases which throw considerable light on the irregular incidence of infallible utterances in the Church's history, it is a 'special privilege' which corresponds to a 'special condition'.[13] It neither supplants the 'sense of faith' of the People of God nor eliminates the teaching office of bishops. There is a place for it only when these have failed. To use a phrase which enjoys current popularity, its rôle is 'subsidiary'.

Gasser's explanations seem to have gained universal acceptance. Mansi records no dissentient *rumor* — not even *submissus*. Can they be accepted as the faith of Catholics? And, if so, why were they not written into the definitions? They were not; and the reason for this self-denying ordinance may also be gathered from the records of debate in the Council Chamber.

At one point, Cardinal Guidi had pressed for a defined statement of the obligations that restricted the papacy when making irreformable pronouncements. In particular, he wished for a formula binding the Pope to consult at least an appropriate section of the episcopate, and to investigate the tradition of other churches. Gasser replied to this suggestion, and his answer contained two points. The logic of the first is somewhat hard to follow. He argued that a canon expressing limiting conditions would imply that the Council consider- ed itself to be above the Pope. In reply to this it might have been argued — but was not — that such a canon would have meant no more than that God is above the Pope: a state- ment to which none of the Fathers could have taken legi- timate exception. The second point had more substance. Gasser noted with some reason that to insert conditions belonging to the moral rather than the dogmatic order would be both useless and confusing. It would be useless because no one could verify whether or not the conditions had been fulfilled. And it would be confusing because without such verification there would be endless subterfuges and un- certainties in accepting any given definition. He ended with a most odd application of John 21:18: 'Therefore Peter must be left to gird [cingat] himself in accordance with the words of our Lord Jesus Christ. For Peter does not grow old as the world does, and his power is always renewed like the eagle's.'[14] In other words, there were undoubtedly obliga- tions that the Pope was bound to observe, but if he did not do so of his own accord, there was no one in the whole wide world who could make him do it.

In hindsight, it can only be regretted that the Council, if it had to define the papal prerogative at all, did not also define the moral obligations which circumscribe its rôle in the process of faith. These obligations appear to be — if the 'single viewpoint' of the Conciliar Fathers is any guide — part of the deposit of revelation. They can be taught in the Church as much as can the defined truths of Vatican I. A complete treatment of the infallibility question should therefore include both the defined prerogative of the papacy and its undefined obligations. To teach one without the other is to create an imbalance which has created needless misunderstanding both inside the Church and outside. But the bishops of 1870 were not notably ecumenical in outlook, and some may have been imperfectly pastoral. Their deliberations were framed with two main objectives in view — to eliminate Gallicanism and to enable the faithful to discriminate between what was, and what was not, a valid papal definition. Had they been more outward-looking and conscious of the needs of those who do not belong to the household of the faith, they might well have added a definition of those obligations which make the Chair of Peter the last, and not the first resort of the Pilgrim Church in its progress towards faith.[15]

Some slight consolation may be found, however, in the very words of *Pastor Aeternus* if read in the light of the conciliar discussions. It has already been noted that to 'define' means 'to put an end to doctrinal dissensions insoluble at any lower level'. And the term 'supreme' as qualifying the Apostolic authority by which the Pope defines, would seem to have the same implication that papal definitions should be only the last resort of a dissentient Church. Even the definition itself, terse though it is, may thus be shown to imply some circumscription of the rôle of the papacy when teaching with whatever infallibility God has communicated to his Church.

2. *Who is Infallible?*

Any careful reading of *Pastor Aeternus* will show that it does not mention 'papal infallibility' or make the statement that 'The Pope is infallible'. It came near to doing so. When the draft of the fourth chapter was circulated to the Fathers, it at first bore the title 'On the infallibility of the Roman Pontiff'. This met with such opposition that the Deputation of the Faith speedily changed it to read 'On the infallible teaching office [*magisterium*] of the Roman Pontiff'.[16]

Was this amendment due to an unexpected shyness on the part of the Council, making them unwilling to say what they really meant? Gasser indeed suggested that there should be some delicacy towards the feelings of the Germans, to whom 'infallibility', when translated, might be mistaken for 'impeccability'.[17] And he also considered that the statement 'The Pope is infallible' was not false, but only 'incomplete'.[18] But the most effective objection came from the Dominican Cardinal Guidi, who said bluntly that infallibility must not 'appear to be some personal or habitual property or prerogative' of the Pope; and that the Church must not lay itself open to the calumny that it 'attributed to a man that which belongs only to God and the truth he has revealed'.[19] As has been noted, his words have been re-echoed one hundred years later by Hans Küng; in close harmony with John XXIII's 'I am not infallible. I am infallible only when I speak *ex cathedra*. But I shall never speak *ex cathedra*.'[20]

Back in England after the Council, that hottest of infallibilists, Manning, was at great pains to explain to his flock why the definition made no mention of the Pope's infallibility: by this omission it 'excludes at once the figment of a personal infallibility';[21] it was 'not a quality in any person'; nor was it 'to know or to make known new truths or to communicate new revelations'.[22] But, at least in this regard, Manning was no more acceptable as a prophet in his own country than was Newman, and there were too many whose first reaction to Vatican I was an Act of Oblivion.

To get the facts still clearer: the structure of the definition must be analysed and note taken of the one and only use of the word 'infallibility' which occurs therein.

The definition is in two parts of unequal length. The first part is explanatory, leading up to and giving reasons for (*ideoque*) the second, which is so formulated as to be a condemnation (in its own terms) of the 4th Gallican Article of 1682: 'therefore the definitions of the said Roman Pontiff are irreformable of themselves, and not by reason of the agreement of the Church'.[23] This conclusion was, in fact, the final target of the definition, bringing with it the discomfiture of whatever Gallicans may have survived to 1870.

The explanatory part of the definition can itself be further broken down. Why are such definitions irreformable? — because, when he makes them (and the conditions under which they are made are carefully defined), 'the Roman Pontiff is in possession of (or "powered by": *pollere = pot valere*) that infallibility with which the Divine Redeemer wished his Church to be provided'. And if the further question is asked: how can one know that at such moments the Church's infallibility is operating in the Pope, the definition gives the answer 'by reason of the divine assistance promised him in the person of Peter'.

Such were the terms, and such the structure of the definition. When the Fathers said that papal definitions were irreformable they meant precisely that and nothing more — the definitions were irreformable, not the Pope infallible; when they said that this irreformability was due to the infallibility which Christ gave to the Church they meant what they said — and not that it was due to something that should be described as 'papal infallibility'.

Somehow or other, between the definitive vote of 18 July 1870 and the communication of the conciliar teaching to the faithful, a gap was jumped — from the irreformability of papal definitions to papal infallibility, and from the infallibility of the Church to that of the Pope. This needs explanation. And the answer seems to be that the human mind, like water, tends to take the easiest way out and follow the line of least resistance. If some reason has to be found why formal definitions from the Holy See can be utterly relied on, while statements from individual laymen or Bishops can not, the easiest way out is to imagine that the papacy is endowed with some sort of divine possession or gift, peculiar and personal to the Pope, raising him head and shoulders above the common run of men, episcopal or mortal.

Neither before, during, nor after 1870 has there been any shortage of minds ready to take the line of least resistance. In England, W. G. Ward credited the Holy Father with 'new inspiration'.[24] France's Louis Veuillot thought it 'much simpler' to hold that definitions were 'whispered directly in the pope's ear by the Holy Ghost'.[25] The Italian Jesuits in *Civiltà Cattolica* went one better with beautiful dreams of God meditating inside the papal head.[26]

Even in the Council itself, there were suggestions that the Holy Father enjoyed some sort of spiritual gift withheld from the rest of the Church. Various formulae were tried out: charisms, gifts, an endowment (*dos*), or a *lux transiens* — a spiritual comet, snuffed out as soon as discerned from the dome of St. Peter's. But the feeling of the Council was overwhelmingly that the source of infallibility was not to be found elsewhere than in the normal process of divine revelation and that, as Bishop Ketteler of Mainz put it, it should not be taught that 'the Roman Pontiff has — as it were in his breast — the tradition [of revealed faith] by virtue of some sort of infusion from on high'.[27] Eventually the Fathers fell back on the statement, rather vague but sufficient, that the irreformability of papal definitions was due to the Church's own infallibility, by reason of the divine assistance promised to Peter.

That, no more and no less, is the faith of Vatican I. There is no point in asking what makes the Pope infallible, for that is not the teaching of the Church; and silly questions will get silly answers. It is, however, very much to the point to ask how it comes about that papal definitions are inerrant and irreformable — and this is a serious question which deserves a serious answer. The answer was given only in embryonic form by the Council of 1870. It needs to be completed from Vatican II.

In brief it is this: there is infallibility all over the place; the Church is full of it. Every genuine act of faith is inerrant, because it proceeds from the action of the Holy Spirit, who is himself infallible. The problem is to identify the genuine act of faith — the act which, amid all the bogus imitations which have plagued the Church since the days of Gnosticism, is really prompted by the Holy Spirit. There are other ways of identifying the genuine article — unanimity of the faithful or unanimity of the episcopate. But when these fail, it is the faith of the Holy See which is the fruit of the Spirit, inerrant, infallible, and irreformable.

Lumen Gentium is explicit. When, with the divine assistance, a Christian accepts the 'Word of God', he 'clings without fail to the faith once delivered to the saints'; the 'body of the faithful as a whole', being 'anointed . . . by the Holy One cannot err in matters of belief'.[28] Any genuine act of faith, in fact, must necessarily be infallible because derived from the assistance of the Holy Ghost, whose infallibility no one as yet has thought fit to call in question. And it should be noted that it is the faith, and its divine author, which is infallible — not the very human believer. This was no new idea. At Vatican I Archbishop Dechamps of Malines had spoken of an 'infallibility of faith belonging to all the members of the Church'.[29] In this sense, the Pope can be no more and no less in possession of infallibility than 'the last member of the laity' — that notional but useful character, invented by Augustine and immortalized by Vatican II.

Given that the Holy Father shares a divinely-assisted faith with all the People of God, his articulation of that faith in a definition must obviously be irreformable. The explanation of that irreformability given by Vatican I — that he is 'in possession of that infallibility with which the Divine Redeemer wished his Church to be provided' — is amply sufficient, and there is no need to postulate transient lights or any other part of the norml equipment of an infallible Pope. But this is not enough for the papacy to fulfil its responsibilities as 'supreme Shepherd and teacher of all the faithful'. A Pope might well be possessed of infallible faith all day and every day — and he can likewise err. To be a teacher, he must not only have the truth, but be known to have it. In secular teaching, it is a commonplace that the profession requires not only knowledge to communicate, but also an authority by which the content of the teaching is known to be true. This authority may derive from a university degree, a certificate or a diploma; in default of these, personal qualities may often make it clear that the man knows what he is talking about; and the teacher of heuristic bent will lead his pupils into the laboratory to discover for themselves the truths he wishes to impart. But in all cases there must be authority and authentication, and this holds good also of the teaching of the faith.

It was Bishop Legat of Trieste who, at the Council, saw most clearly that the point at issue was the authentication of the faith of the Holy See; not how the Pope can have an infallible faith, but how he can be known to have it. Knowledge of revelation came only through the 'Holy Ghost, who, by the illumination of minds and hearts, teaches the whole truth and recalls to the Church of Christ all that the Divine Teacher said to his disciples'. Peter received no special commission to communicate this knowledge: he was told, not to 'teach', but to 'confirm' his brethren.[30] The Petrine office was therefore to provide authentication for the genuine faith that comes from God, amid all the imitations that come from the inventive mind of man. Dechamps had made much the same distinction prior to the Council, contrasting a 'passive' infallibility common to all members of the Church with the 'active' infallibility required for teaching;[31] but his terminology is out of favour in an age which considers it improper to suggest either that the laity are passive or the hierarchy active.

The only question thus left for the Fathers to answer was this: how can the faithful know that the Pope, when terminating doctrinal controversies from the Chair of Peter, is expressing a faith formed with the assistance of the Holy Spirit? To which they replied: 'by reason of the divine assistance promised him in the person of Peter'. This 'divine assistance' is further explained by Vatican II as identical with 'the charism of the infallibility of the Church herself... individually present' in the Pope:[32] a timely warning to those who might be tempted to engage once more in the fruitless search for some spiritual additive given to the papacy but withheld from the rest of the Church. In short, the definition of 1870 does little more than spell out the promises made to Peter. If we want to know why papal definitions are inerrant and irreformable, it is because our Lord said so: when it fell to him to 'confirm' his brethren, Peter's faith would not fail.

The defined faith of Vatican I is clear — and clearer still if read together with the teaching of Vatican II. Every genuine act of faith is infallible, proceeding from the Holy Spirit. If, in accordance with the Johannine injunction, the faithful have to 'test the spirits to see whether they are of God', they will find true faith in the unanimity of the whole Church. Failing this, they must look for unanimity in the episcopate. If this in turn should fail them, let them turn to the Holy See, for Christ has promised that on such occasions the faith of the successor of St. Peter would be a faith formed by the Holy Spirit. This is reasonable, logical and in accordance with the needs of the Church; it is Scriptural withal. There is no need to add to it by postulating papal infallibility or teaching that 'the Pope is infallible'. This at least is owed to the memory of Vatican I.

3. *The Chair of Peter*

Writing in 1930, Abbot Cuthbert Butler concluded his historical study of the 1870 Council by asking 'Was the Vatican Council worth while?'. And he answered the question by saying that the infallibility definition 'closed up the ranks of Catholics and rallied them with united loyalty and enthusiasm round the Chair of Peter as never before. Not even an Innocent at the height of his temporal sway over Christendom wielded an authority so wide-cast, undisputed, beneficent, as do the Popes since the Vatican Council'.[33] One may wonder if he would have written in the same strain after 1968. In default of the investigative techniques beloved of sociologists, it is unwise to pontificate on current attitudes of the faithful; but, if reports of papal allocutions in the *Osservatore Romano* are any guide, it would seem that the Holy See is itself conscious of a diminution of its influence. How far is this the result of misreading the history and teaching of Vatican I? — of ignoring the warnings of Newman and Manning (such unlikely yokefellows in this respect)? There may at least be a suspicion that the faithful have been trained for a hundred years to shop for nothing but Instant Infallibility from a permanently Infallible Pope, and now find that the stock has been sold out and the shelves are bare.

If so, there is urgent need to find some firmer basis for that devotion to the Chair of Peter which appears to be so deeply rooted among the People of God, and which presumably stems from their infallible sense of faith. It has been maintained, not without some show of truth, that the infallibilist movement of 1870 was primarily an expression of this devotion.[34] Paradoxically, it seems to be this same devotion which lies at the root of current criticism of Vatican I. It is impossible to read Hans Küng without being moved by his sincere appreciation of the 'Petrine Service', his deep compassion of a Pope for whom his office has been made into an insupportable burden, and his vision, in the person of Pope John, of what the papacy could be.[35]

Can a recovery of the history of Vatican I help towards a renewal of this devotion to the Chair of Peter? Negatively: yes — in so far as it clears away misconceptions and allows it to be seen that infallible definitions are the least important rôle of a teaching papacy.

History bears out the teaching of Vatican I that such definitions are the last desperate resort of the faithful when all other means of authentification have failed. It is no coincidence that the Petrine prerogative was not invoked throughout the first four centuries of the Church's history, when the *Pax Romana* made possible the gathering of the episcopate in councils. Then came the definitive Letter of Leo I on the Incarnation in 449: it was the age of Attila and of Genseric, and communications were already breaking down. Even so, until the onset of the Reformation and in the course of fifteen centuries, no more than four infallible definitions can be identified.[36] The urgent situation created by Lutheranism was met in 1520 by the *Exsurge Domine* of Leo X — but, as soon as practicable, the work of definition was left to the episcopate gathered at Trent. The seventeenth century brought a positive rash of papal definitions: four within sixty years. These seem difficult to tie in with Vatican I's concept of the Petrine office as a court of final appeal, for they were concerned with the rather abstruse aberrations of Jansen, Molinos, Fénelon and Quesnel — but it must be remembered that this was the hey-day of Gallicanism: not a good moment to convoke any sort of council. Lastly came the condemnation of the Council of Pistoia in 1794 and (if it can indeed be considered a papal definition in the sense of Vatican I) the definition of the Immaculate Conception in 1854.

Each of these occasions was in some way an example of a 'special condition' which, to revert to the words of Gasser at the Council, called for the exercise of a 'special privilege'. But special conditions do not recur as regularly as the changing seasons. They belong to particular moments in the history of the Church and such moments may never occur again. It may well be that the time for papal definitions has now passed, outmoded by Bishops Unanimous — or, if not unanimous, at least able to catch the next transatlantic jet and argue themselves into unanimity. There are some signs of this development already. Neither the declaration on the Immaculate Conception, nor that on the Assumption, were definitions in the Vatican I sense of ending a controversy: their expressed purpose was to honour our Lady; both contain the formula 'in agreement with the wish of the whole Church', and Pius XII adds that he is speaking 'with the almost unanimous agreement' of the whole episcopate. If the whole Church is in agreement, are not these dogmas already authenticated without recourse to the Petrine promises? And it may be noted that a new organ by which the episcopate can voice its unanimity has been provided by the *Motu Proprio* of 15 September 1965, instituting an on-going world-wide Synod.

If papal definitions should disappear from human history there need be no regrets. They belong only to times when the Church is sick, and torn by dissensions that cannot be cured by discussion and agreement. The Petrine prerogative is not a glory of the Church; it is a disagreeable necessity, like the skill of the surgeon. The desire for its use is, as has been remarked,[37] a pathological condition.

Should the practice of papal definition fall into abeyance, the faithful may go back to Vatican I and learn that the Chair of Peter has another rôle which may prove of much greater importance to them. Bishop Zinelli of Treviso gave the Fathers a timely admonition that it was already the accepted faith of the Church that papal pronouncements, made 'with the bishops, whether gathered together or dispersed' are not subject to error.[38] In this sense, the papacy is the voice of the universal Church, gathering together the 'single viewpoint' of the episcopate and the 'universal agreement' of the faithful, ascertaining it and making it known to the whole world from its unique position 'at the centre' of the Church.[39]

But to speak in definitions by no means exhausts the teaching potential of the Holy See. In one respect the formulae of Vatican I leave behind them some regret — in that, searching for some verbal shorthand to limit papal definitions, and largely at the suggestion of Ullathorne,[40] it hit upon the phrase *ex cathedra* as if the sole function of the Chair of Peter were to issue infallible pronouncements. It would be a poor view to restrict the papal teaching office to the chalk-and-talk methods of the class-room: to the didactic method of handing out statements that have to be accepted, memorized and repeated back. A good teacher leads his pupils in a search for truth, and our Lord presumably meant Peter to be a good teacher.

Whatever one's views on doctrinal development, it seems generally agreed that the Pilgrim Church is far from possessing the fullness of faith, let alone vision. As Yves Congar puts it — with due acknowledgement to Aquinas who thought it up first — we live 'in and towards the faith'.[41] A rapidly developing world, exploding both in population and in knowledge, throws up problems which should be answerable from revelation, but to which no authenticated answer can yet be given. The Church is thus in an heuristic situation: in search of truth and in need of a good teacher to guide and lead them. If it can be recognized that to provide this guidance and leadership is also a function of the Chair of Peter, some solution will have been found to the vexed question of what precisely is the value of the 'ordinary' teaching of the papacy. But in this no help can be found in Vatican I, and very little in Vatican II.

Lumen Gentium, in fact, says that the ordinary teaching of the Holy See must be received with 'a religious submission of mind and will',[42] but fails to say what it means by this: thereby creating alarm and despondency. Such teaching is not infallible. It cannot call for the assent of faith. Is it then valueless? Are papal encyclicals (its most frequent expression) no more than letters from some obscure local bishop? This conclusion seems inescapable by those who can conceive of papal teaching as nothing but didactic. But if the Chair of Peter is recognized as possessing also an heuristic rôle, the ordinary teaching of the papacy becomes of cardinal importance.

The process begins, as the German episcopate has suggested,[43] when the Pope speaks out to provide the Church with 'the best certitude available'. To do less than this would be to fail in his duty of protecting the faithful from error in faith and morals. He may be wrong or he may be right. If right, the People of God, with the assistance of the Holy Spirit, will assimilate his teaching, give it internal assent, and finally authenticate it by their unanimity. If wrong, the faithful under the guidance of the Holy Spirit will reject it, and no harm will be done. But the Holy See will have done its duty. No one but the Pope has access to all the faithful throughout the world, can test their 'sense of faith', or ascertain their agreement. In the light of this, papal encyclicals become far more than messages from a local bishop. This interpretation gains credibility from the structure of *Humanae Vitae*. In the concluding paragraphs, Paul VI lays no obligation of assent upon the faithful; instead, he tells the clergy that they have the duty to place (*proponere*) the Church's teaching before the people; they are to do this 'in the certainty that the Holy Spirit, present when the teachers of the Church are expounding true doctrine, enlightens the hearts of the faithful from within and invites them to give their assent'.[44] This may provide a model for the ordinary teaching of the papacy: not an authenticated document of the faith, but a stage — and an indispensable stage — on the Pilgrim Church's road to faith.

In all conscience, the Chair of Peter has an authority and a teaching rôle indispensable enough to win the devotion and loyalty of the faithful without exaggerating the importance of papal definitions or imagining the 'figment of personal infallibility'. Perhaps a fair enough judgement on what has often been taught in the last hundred years might be based on some words spoken four centuries ago by Melchior Cano at the time of the Council of Trent: 'Peter has no need of our lies or our flattery. Those who blindly and indiscriminately defend every decision of the Supreme Pontiff are the very men who do most to undermine the authority of the Holy See instead of supporting it — destroy it instead of strengthening its foundations.'[45] If those foundations can be strengthened by a return to Vatican I, the recovery of that Council's history will have been no otiose or academic exercise.

NOTES

1 Hans Küng, *Infallible? An Enquiry* (Eng. trans.), London, 1971.
2 Thus Gustave Thils, *L'Infaillibilité Pontificale*, Gembloux, 1969: which has the merit of citing copiously from Mansi. With this may be read Dom Cuthbert Butler, *The Vatican Council 1869–70* (ed. Dom Christopher Butler), London, 1962.
3 A. Farrer and Others, *Infallibility in the Church* (An Anglican-Catholic Dialogue), London, 1968, p. 74.
4 Hans Küng, op. cit., p. 197.
5 Thils, op. cit., p. 132.
6 Cp. Hans Küng, op. cit., pp. 201 and 23; with Thils, op. cit., pp. 136 and 191.
7 Janus, *The Pope and Council* (Eng. trans.), London, 1869, p. 48.
8 Thils, op. cit., p. 62.
9 Ibid. p. 114.
10 Ibid. p. 128.
11 Thils, op. cit., p. 150.
12 Ibid. p. 226.
13 Ibid. p. 221.
14 Thils, op. cit., p. 194.
15 For a discussion of possible deeper and murkier motivation among the Infallibilists, *vide* V. Conzemius, art. 'Why was the Primacy of the Pope defined in 1870?' in *Concilium*, April 1971, pp. 75–83. For conclusive evidence of this, however, historians may have to wait the baring of all men's hearts at the Last Trump.
16 Thils, op. cit., p. 212.
17 Ibid. p. 5.
18 Ibid. p. 134.
19 Ibid. p. 132.
20 Hans Küng, op. cit., pp. 197 and 71.

21 Manning, *The True Story of the Vatican Council*, London, 1877, p. 173.
22 Ibid. pp. 182–3.
23 The 4th Gallican Article of 1682 ran as follows: 'In controversies concerning the faith, the Sovereign Pontiff takes a leading rôle. His teaching is the concern of each and every church. But his judgements are not irreformable unless the Church gives its agreement.'
24 Thils, op. cit., p. 130.
25 Ibid. p. 131.
26 Butler, op. cit., p. 61.
27 Thils, op. cit., p. 232.
28 *Lumen Gentium*, §12.
29 Thils, op. cit., p. 86.
30 Thils, op. cit., p. 128.
31 Ibid. p. 86.
32 *Lumen Gentium*, §25.
33 Butler, op. cit., p. 488.
34 V. Conzemius, art. cit., pp. 75 ff. This was also the opinion of Newman, whom he cites to this effect.
35 Hans Küng, op. cit., pp. 12 and 198–203.
36 This identification of papal definitions has been taken from E. Dublanchy, in *Dict. de Théol. Cath.*, Tome VII, cols. 1703–1704, s.v. Infaillibilité du Pape.
37 By Vergote: cited in Yves Congar, art. 'Infaillibilité et indéfectibilité', in *Rev. des Sciences Phil. et Relig.*, October 1970, p. 608.
38 Thils, op. cit., p. 19.
39 The expression is Gasser's; ibid. p. 192.
40 Ibid. p. 201.
41 Yves Congar, art. cit., p. 609.
42 *Lumen Gentium*, §25.
43 Cf. Karl Rahner, art. 'On Non-infallible judgements', *New Blackfriars*, November 1970.
44 *Humanae Vitae*, §§28 and 29.
45 Cited (from Dupanloup) Thils, op. cit., p. 91.

8

The primacy: the small print of Vatican I

Garrett Sweeney

IN 1974 the Vatican II Decree on Ecumenism was already ten years old. It was in this that Paul VI and the Conciliar Fathers made public their belief that some of the doctrines of the Church need re-statement: 'If the influence of events or of the times has led to deficiencies . . . in the formulation of doctrine . . ., these should be appropriately rectified at the proper moment.'[1] The issue in 1973 of *Mysterium Ecclesiae* by the Congregation of the Doctrine of the Faith, showed that the Church was still of the same mind.[2] Among formulations which have suffered from the influence of the times, the definition of the Primacy seems to rate pretty high up in the charts and to be overdue for restatement. The present Pope has himself noted that it is 'undoubtedly the most serious obstacle on the ecumenical road'. While modestly protesting that 'It is not easy for us to plead our own cause', he has indicated a possible line of rectification in words that might easily have come from any spokesman of the minority at Vatican I: 'Should we try once again to present in precise terms what it purports to be: the necessary principle of truth, charity and unity? Should we show once again that it is a pastoral charge of direction, service and brotherhood, which does not challenge the freedom or dignity of anyone who has a legitimate problem in the Church of God, but which rather protects the rights of all and only claims the obedience called for among children of the same family?'.[3]

It can hardly be said that much has been done in recent years in fulfilment of the Pope's request. Most of the best thinking on the Primacy seems to have been done in the years immediately preceding Vatican II, notably by Hans Küng[4] — whose thought appears to lie behind the statement made by the present Pope. Since the Council, and especially after the publication of *Humanae Vitae*, more attention had been directed to Infallibility than to the Primacy. In any case, it takes a long time for professional theology to percolate down to popular catechesis. At a level of writing less academic, the efforts of Cardinal Suenens to restate the dogma in terms of coresponsibility have met with as little favour as Bishop Butler's suggestion that the analogy of the British Constitution might provide a clue.[6] A convincing re-formulation of the Primacy is still to seek.

There are, however, indications that the sands of time are running out and that the Church cannot wait much longer for an authentic 'rectification' of the dogma. Disagreement on the basic nature of the Primacy seems to be behind that constant tension between local churches and the Roman Curia which has characterized the immediate aftermath of Vatican II. Holland is not the only thorn in the flesh. Papal nominations to the episcopate are challenged elsewhere; the traditionally-obedient Church in Spain turns upon the Curia;[7] the draft *Lex ecclesiae fundamentalis*, circulated by Cardinal Felici in 1971, seems to have met with almost universal rejection, few being prepared to accept that authority should be 'conceived as an emphatically centralized form, individualized in the person of the Pope' and leaving no room for 'the essential freedom of local churches and a pluralism of their experiences and charisms'.[8] German Catholics hint darkly that the Roman Church is hell-bent on its own destruction, complain of Curial 'claims for which there can be no warrant in the New Testament or even in Vatican I',[9] and are not helped by an Apostolic Delegate who seems to know better than the Bishop of Limburg how to run his diocese.[10] For good or ill, the Ukrainian Church has been at loggerheads with a Papacy for which it has shed its blood, seeks autonomy and fails to find it.[11] Could there be any more 'proper moment' for a restatement of the Primacy than now?

1. *"The Influence of Events or of the Times"*

The search for a re-formulation might well and profitably be directed in the first instance, not to the findings of modern theologians, but to the thinking of the Minority of Vatican I. This was the one occasion in the history of the Church when bishops came together from all over the world for a discussion of the Primacy. If something went wrong with the definition, it is at least reasonable to suppose that there might be something right in the thought of those who opposed it. Moreover — and the point is of immense importance and an awful warning to those who read dogmatic statements without reference to their historical context — the rejection of amendments proposed by the Minority does not mean that they were erroneous. Zinelli of Treviso, spokesman for the *Deputatio de rebus fidei*, killed the amendments with the greatest courtesy by announcing that many of them were 'excellent and worthy of inclusion in the relevant chapters', and that the only reason why they could not be accepted was that the *Schema* had already received general agreement:[12] a curious argument which leaves one to wonder why amendments were invited at all. If the proposals of the Minority were so excellent, it seems worth while re-examining them and seeing why, under the influence of the times, so many bishops were content to let them perish without trace.

For the sake of clarity, it will be well to recall that the first step towards the final definition was taken on 21 January 1870 with the distribution of a *Schema de Ecclesia*. In response to comments from the Fathers, this was superseded on 9 May by a *Schema de Romano Pontifice*. The most notable change in the treatment of the Primacy was the insertion of a paragraph on the divine institution and rights of the episcopate, now the third paragraph of Chapter III of *Pastor Aeternus*. This revised document was subjected to a lengthy General Discussion in fourteen General Congregations lasting from 14 May to 3 June. Most of this Discussion centred on the Infallibility question, and little was said about the Primacy. A Special Discussion on the Primacy (Chapter III) began on 9 June and continued for five General Congregations until 14 June. Seventy-two amendments emerged from this Discussion, and they were printed out and circulated to the Fathers. A vote on them was taken on 5 July, after Zinelli had painstakingly explained what his Deputation thought of them.

This vote of 5 July deserves close attention. It was the only occasion when the opinion of the whole Council could be sounded on the Primacy as distinct from the question of Infallibility. The method of counting votes was crude. No names were recorded. The Fathers were asked to express their convictions by the simple process of standing up or sitting down, and a quick leg-count showed which way the Holy Ghost was blowing. In this way, throughout a hot July forenoon, almost all the amendments were consigned to the waste-paper basket by *longe major pars*, or by *fere omnes*.

This large Majority is not, however, impossible to identify. Individual votes were recorded on 13 July, when the whole Constitution including both Primacy and Infallibility was presented *en bloc*. As there was a strong tendency for those who supported the Infallibility definition to give support also to that on the Primacy and vice-versa, the 75% who voted orally in favour on the later date were most probably the same who had on the earlier date given the silent *Placet* of their legs.

It is a commonplace of Vatican I history that the voting tended to follow lines of national or cultural division. Italy, Spain, and Latin America by themselves produced 259 *Placets* — enough to be described as *longe major pars* in comparison with the 150 from all over the world which expressed dissatisfaction. The smaller hierarchies of Europe were 100% conformist: Holland, Belgium, Switzerland, Portugal, Greece, and the Balkan provinces of the Ottoman Empire. There was complete unanimity in favour of the whole Constitution from Australia and New Zealand; virtual unanimity from Canada and Ireland — also from areas ruled by missionary Vicars Apostolic, whether in the Far East, Africa, North America or Scotland. Assent was, in short, most marked in countries where there was no serious Christian challenge to Catholicism.

Dissent, by contrast, became more serious in areas which had to face an anti-Catholic polemic, and where the Church had to provide a reasoned apologetic for its beliefs. One-third of the bishops of the United States, and over 40% of those of France, could not take *Pastor Aeternus* as it stood. The Uniat Churches of the Ottoman Empire tipped only slightly in favour of the Majority. The hierarchy of England and Wales tipped slightly in favour of the Minority, and would have tipped right over if it had felt committed enough to stay for the voting.[13] But most of them, before the heat of the summer, had returned to England's pastures green.

Dissatisfaction with the Constitution was most evident in Austria-Hungary and in what was shortly to become the German Empire. Two-thirds of the bishops from Central and Eastern Europe refused an unconditional assent. These vast areas, covering nearly 40% of European Catholicism[14] were grossly under-bishoped as compared with Italy or Spain, and could muster no more than 59 votes at the Council. Those who like futile exercises in arithmetic may calculate that if the Catholic population of Central and Eastern Europe had been represented by bishops in the same proportion as operated in Italy,[15] there would have been about four hundred and fifty of them at the Council, of whom perhaps three hundred would have voted with the Minority, swamping the 197 Italian *Placets*. This is not wholly idle speculation. However wrong Döllinger may have been in challenging the ecumenicity of Vatican I on the grounds that the faithful of Central and Eastern Europe were inadequately represented,[16] it may well be argued that the imbalance of representation was largely responsible for the insufficiency of the final definitions.

Italianism

The formidable Italian vote was evidently the largest single factor in rejecting the amendments proposed by the Minority. Some idea of the mentality which lay behind it may be gathered from the thirteen speeches on the Majority side made by Italian bishops during the General and Special Discussion.[17] From these may be collected a theology of the Papacy to which it is difficult to give a name. It seems inept to describe as 'Neo-ultramontanism' a doctrine which went so far beyond the ultramontanism of Bellarmine. Ratzinger uses the term 'Papalism';[18] but it would be regrettable to attach the papal name to a doctrine now recognized as erroneous. No one, apparently, has suggested 'Italianism', but as its principal spokesmen came from Italy, there is as much reason to give it that name as there is to attach the label of Gallicanism to the system of Pithou and the brothers Dupuy.

One element in this system was a belief in the inerrancy of the Holy See in matters of discipline. Thus Gastaldi of Saluzzo, most eloquent of Italians, who enjoyed himself immensely over twenty columns of Mansi: 'We can be, and must be, sure that our Lord is always standing by his Vicar, with the result that no act or decree of his will impede the sanctification of souls.'[19] Similarly Salzano, a Curial and Bishop of Tanes *in partibus*, attributed a divine quality to the papal governance in that it was always guided by 'a prudence inspired from God' when deciding whether or not to seek counsel from the episcopate.[20] The line between Pope and God became very thin. Natoli of Messina, in what was almost the silliest speech of the whole Council, went to the brink of blasphemy by winding up his peroration with a parody of the first Palm Sunday: 'as soon as the Council has passed the decree, a shout will rise up all over the world: "Hosanna to Pope Pius IX; Hosanna to the Fathers of the Vatican Council; Hosanna three times and four times over to Pius".'[21] Whether the Italians really believed what they were saying is difficult to tell. Courtesy so often took precedence over truth, as perhaps it should, and as Pio Nono found out when the people of Ravenna, who had greeted him as 'second only to God' on his visit in 1857, rejected his sovereignty three years later.[22] The most explicit papolatry of the Council, however, came not from an Italian but from Caixal y Estradé of Urgel. He fished out for public approval some precedents for identifying the Pope with God, of which the most outrageous came from an address to Eugene IV at Florence, delivered on behalf of the Jacobite Ethiopian Patriarch: 'As I speak to you I am dust and ashes in the presence of you who are God on earth. For you are God on earth and Christ and his Vicar.'[23]

Some of the Italians attributed to the Pope powers which are not normally given to mortal man. Lenti, Bishop of Sutri and Nepi but also a Curial, exasperated by the contradictory accounts given by three pairs of prelates from three different countries as to the effect which the Infallibility definition would have, took comfort from his belief in papal omniscience: 'from the watchtower of his Chair, he looks out over the whole world, and knows very well what is the condition of the Universal Church at the present time'.[24] Another Curial, Cardoni of Edessa *in partibus*, himself gave no utterance during the debate, but was taken to task by Haynald of Kalocsa for putting into print a belief that by some alchemy the Holy Father could transmute a local synod (*conciliabulum*) into an Ecumenical Council.[25] All this added up to a 'personal' theory of the Primacy, parallel to the theory of 'personal' Infallibility which the Council was later to reject. If the Pope's person were endowed with the ability to know the business of bishops better than they knew it themselves, and if he were inerrant in matters of discipline, it was folly to leave any decisions to ignorant and errant bishops.

Another characteristic of Italianist thought at this time was the rejection of the *sensus fidelium*, now recognized by Vatican II as an authentic source of infallible truth, as a *locus theologicus*.[26] This was laid down clearly by Cardinal Patrizi, Secretary of the Holy Roman Inquisition, who put the laity firmly in its place with his speech at the opening of the General Discussion: 'Who can be unaware that matters belonging to the supernatural order, and full of hazards, which ought to be dealt with and discussed only by prelates of the Church within the innermost sanctuary, have been the subject of debate by — of all people — the laity: presumptuously, without authority, stupidly, and with great damage to right-thinking men.'[27] So also Gastaldi, dealing rapidly with the Minority argument that the Constitution would be offensive to both the Catholic laity and to their separated brethren: 'Among *loci theologici* I have found Scripture, Tradition, the decrees of Councils and of Popes; but never public opinion.'[28] It was a bad time, anyway, for public opinion whether in Church or State. The tide of liberalism had ebbed steadily since the uprisings of 1848. This was especially true of the last days of the Temporal Power and while the Secretariat of State was in the hands of Antonelli, who is reported to have said that 'newspapers should limit themselves to announcing the functions in the Papal chapels and giving interesting news of Chinese insurrections.'[29]

If no recognition as a *locus theologicus* was given to the common belief of the faithful, another *locus* was at hand to fill the gap. This was the argument from the needs of political legitimism. It went thus: the maintenance of law and order, and the preservation of the Temporal Power in particular, would be impossible without a dogma of the Primacy; therefore the Primacy must be defined as an article of faith. This reads curiously today, but few hairs seemed to have been turned when it was expounded in the Council by such Neapolitans as Celesia of Patti, who saw in ecclesiastical authority the sole hope of preventing civil society from crumbling into ruins and the clergy from forming societies 'del clero emancipato';[30] or Salzano of Tanes *in partibus*, who believed that 'the dominant heresy of the present day is a denial of authority, which has so deplorably attacked civil society and the family itself'[31] — giving the reader a strong sense of *déja vu*. It was left to Gastaldi to put the argument in its crudest terms: 'At the present moment all authority is on the way to ruin. War is being waged today not only on royal but also on paternal authority. We must therefore safeguard that authority which comes before all others and which has the power to safeguard every other kind of authority: I refer to that of the Roman Pontiff.'[32]

Part of the trouble with Gastaldi, Salzano and others was that they suffered as much as any priest of today from a crisis of identity. None of them seemed quite sure if they were bishops of the Catholic Church or Senators of Ancient Rome. Gastaldi's was one of the few speeches which moved the Fathers to *plausus* — as well it might, for he managed to find room for Cyprian's dictum that the Emperor Decius preferred a rival to the Empire rather than a Pope in Rome; and Prosper of Aquitaine's 'quidquid non possidet armis, religione tenet'[33] This was always good for a cheer. As for Salzano — by the time he got to his peroration he was a Scipio speaking with the eloquence of a Ciceronian Philippic: beginning each successive paragraph with a thunderous 'Hannibalem non ad portas, sed intra moenia nostra habemus'[34] *Pastor Aeternus* was to be the last proud defiance of Imperial Rome: 'For my part, I fear neither revolutions, nor the violence of mobs, nor the power of nations, nor the anger of kings — nor Garibaldi or even the Devil himself.'[35] This was magnificent; but it was not theology.

Most fatal of all Italian attitudes at the Council was an almost complete insensitivity to the ecumenical mission of the Church. The Holy See had to triumph, Gastaldi leading the way: 'In my own personal opinion, the [Greek] Church is in especial and imminent danger of dissolution. When it realizes its complete and total collapse, it will come on its bended knees to the Roman Pontiff, the Vicar of Christ, begging once more to be folded to his bosom';[36] if they had no bread, they could eat cake. Vancsa of Fogaras, sole representative at the Council of the four Uniat Rumanian dioceses of Hungary, pleaded in vain for consideration to be given to the claims of ecumenism: 'Although I know that faith is above all a gift of divine grace, yet the reason and opportunity for accepting or rejecting it can be greatly speeded up or slowed down by the actions of men — and thereby all hope of conversion can in fact often, and humanly speaking, be rendered impossible. Those who work in the Lord's vineyard in the midst of the enemy will be convinced that this is nothing but the truth.'[37] Zinelli remained unmoved; there must be no weakness, and 'when the time of mercy comes, God will move their hearts: in the meantime, we must pray for them and define the truth without fear.'[38] Treviso was not, as it happened, in the midst of the enemy, and it has not been ascertained whom Zinelli had to fear.

Such was the theological outlook of those who spoke for a hierarchy both numerous and voluble enough to dominate the Council. How far this was shared by the rank and file of those who voted with the Majority is difficult to say. Few seemed interested enough in Chapter III to speak in favour of it in the Special Discussion. Only three favourable speeches came from hierarchies other than those of Italy, France and Spain. To the growing number of bishops living in the New World, the Far East and the Antipodes, there must have seemed little reason to fuss over the exact terms of the definition. Rome was too remote to impinge much upon their lives, for the steam revolution in communications had not yet reached its international completion. Some, perhaps, only wanted to get the thing over and done with — or at least to dispose of the Primacy and get down to the real business of Infallibility: both of which feelings were expressed admirably by Trucchi of Forlí, arguing that a quick definition of Infallibility would save a lot of trouble and enable the Fathers to get away.[39]

Curious though they may seem after the experience of Vatican II, the principles that can be described as Italianism were by no means alien to the secular thinking of the time. The rise of papolatry coincided with the growing political ascendancy of Bismarck's Prussia, and with its underlying Hegelian concept of the State as 'God walking on earth'. And the whole of Southern Europe was at that time under the spell of Prussia. Spain was looking for a Hohenzollern prince to bring it to heel and save it from itself; Piedmont looked to Prussia as its natural ally against the Austrians; and even Pius IX, incurably optimistic, had moments of hope that Bismarck would step in where France and Austria had failed, and stage a last-minute rescue of the Papal States. As to respect for public opinion — this had no useful function in the resurgence of Bonapartism in France and in the enlightened despotism of Franz Josef. Nor was it only in Curial circles that the Papal Primacy was looked upon as a guarantee of civil authority. The Protestant Guizot had told Manning in 1869 that Rome was the 'Centre of the European Order' and that the Council was 'the last great moral power, and may restore the peace of Europe'. Salvation, both in Church and State, lay in strong centralized governments, dominating unified and obedient populations. It was no mere coincidence that the definition of the Primacy came within the same twelve months which saw the proclamation of the German Empire and the unification of Italy; came shortly after the United States had asserted its unity in the Civil War; and was to be followed in a few years by Victoria's crown of Empire, and liberal England's brief excursion into Imperialism.

2. *The Missing Piece*

The remark of Mourret[40] that the infallibility question can be subdivided into three, may seem a peculiarly unexciting example of pedantic analysis. But it contains within itself some wisdom, and provides a clue to the inadequacy of the Primacy decree. Chapter IV of *Pastor Aeternus* had to face up to three sub-questions: is the Pope infallible? — when and how, in what circumstances and with what limits is he infallible? — is it opportune to make his infallibility a dogma? The Council did indeed ride rough-shod over the third of these questions, but gave clear and reasonable answers to the first two. It was, in fact, only by giving an answer to the second question and setting limits to infallibility by the magic phrase *ex cathedra*, that the decree was saved from becoming a nonsense. By contrast, the decree on the Primacy answered only the first of the three questions which the Fathers had to face. It defined a primacy of jurisdiction; it refused to define the limits of this jurisdiction; and was equally cavalier in its treatment of the opportuneness of the dogma. The result was as futile as appointing a General Officer Commanding to an unspecified army in an un-identifiable theatre of war; and as baffling as a jig-saw puzzle with one essential piece missing from the middle.

Since 1870, the Church has been left to fill in the missing piece with what fertility of imagination may be given to each one. And there has been no lack of imagination. The *fautores* of Italianism find no difficulty in conjuring up an image of 'unlimited' power, and this is apparently the theory behind those Curial operations which are causing such heart-searching in the Church today. It is worth recording that there was wisdom enough among the Fathers of Vatican I to foresee the present situation and to realize what a rod was being put in pickle by refusing to define the limits of papal jurisdiction. Rauscher of Vienna led off the Special Discussion by complaining that 'two powers which are "ordinary" in the same sense, cannot co-exist within the same diocese', and pleaded for 'words which cannot be twisted into a sense which is very different from the truth'[41] Bravard of Coutances complained that if the words of the second paragraph of Chapter III were taken literally, 'many people will consider bishops to be no more than Vicars-Apostolic'.[42] When the *Schema* came first into the hands of Goss of Liverpool, as phlegmatic an Englishman as ever covered an Ecumenical Council from the sunny shores of Cannes, it seemed that the papacy was being given a 'dictator's truncheon'.[43] Similar complaints of ambiguity came from Dupanloup, David of St. Brieuc, and Dreux-Brézé of Moulins;[44] also from Krementz of Ermeland who, in a resounding and minatory speech on the last day of the debate, compared the Fathers to the priests in I Maccabees 5 who fell in battle 'while, desiring to do manfully, they went out inadvisedly to fight'.[45] The analogy was not lost on the

Curia, and got Krementz into considerable hot water; but it
at least proved that, contrary to common opinion, prophecy
had not ceased with the age of the apostles.

At a distance of a hundred years, and with the thick folio
volumes of Mansi's *Concilia* not readily available in every
presbytery, there may be some excuse for imagining that the
absence of any mention of limits to papal jurisdiction in
Pastor Aeternus means that there are no such limits. But
Dogmatic Constitutions are like hire-purchase contracts:
they have their quota of 'small print' which it is dangerous
to neglect. This is to be found in the records of the five
debates on the Primacy, and one does not have to read
far into these before discovering that it was a common viewpoint of the Fathers that primatial power was not all-embracing, unlimited and able to do what it liked, but subject
to definite limits in its exercise. Whether those limits were
not only definite but definable was another matter — and
the ultimate decision was that they should not be defined
but left concealed in the mind of God and the Holy Father.

It seems indeed to have been somewhat of a surprise to the
Minority to find that the Majority were wholly in agreement
with them that the *plena potestas* of the Holy See was not
illimitata. Landriot of Rheims brought great erudition to bear
on this point during the first day of the Special Discussion.[46]
But he was tilting at windmills, and on the following day
Sala of Concepcion in Chile, the solitary spokesman of Latin
America and a speaker for the Majority, got up to agree
that it was wrong to speak of papal power as unlimited,
except in the sense denied by Conciliarism; it was, in fact,
limited by a variety of considerations, ranging from divine
law to human common sense.[47] Vérot of St. Augustine
attempted like Landriot to take the bull by the horns, only
to find it collapse in his grasp. In a speech of execrable
Latin[48] he proposed an additional canon that 'If anyone
says that the authority of the Roman Pontiff is so full that
he can do anything he likes, let him be anathema'.[49] Cardinal Capalti as President told him tartly that the Fathers
had not come to a theatre to hear jokes, and Vérot had to

sit down content with the knowledge that his 'canon' was so obviously true that even to mention it was an insult to the intelligence of the Council. Dupanloup seems to have found general acceptance for two neat analogies — that of the sea, which is always full but has limits, and that of the human body, which has a head but would be destroyed if the head overstepped its limitations.[50]

So much for the 'common view-point'[51] of the Fathers that there are limits to the exercise of the Petrine Primacy: the rub came when attempts were made to define those limits. Two of these have found their way into the final form of the Dogmatic Constitution, but one of these was disastrous and the other impossibly obscure. All other attempts at amendments perished without trace.

The first *Schema* of 21 January had made no mention of episcopal jurisdiction. The Minority protested that this omission seemed to leave the Church entirely under the sole pastoral responsibility of the Holy See. Their protest was met by the addition, in the revised *Schema* of 9 May, of what is now the third paragraph[52] of the third chapter, and which asserts that the jurisdiction of the papacy does not conflict with that of the episcopate. The intention was good and the effect catastrophic. When the two paragraphs are read together, they imply that each diocese is subject to two powers with identical jurisdiction: episcopal, immediate and ordinary. If taken at their face value, each episcopal Tweedledee is duplicated by a papal Tweedledum; and as the papacy was sufficient in itself, there seems no reason why redundancy notices should not be served on the episcopal Tweedledees.

Rauscher, as has been noted, seized immediately upon the point that two powers which are 'ordinary' in the same sense cannot co-exist within the same diocese. He proposed to avoid the dilemma by defining papal jurisdiction not simply (as the text of the second *Schema* had it) as 'ordinary', but as 'a principate of ordinary power'.[53] Zinelli of Treviso, on behalf of the Deputation of the Faith, gave this amendment the unusual accolade of a *valde placet*[54] and it was carried with almost complete unanimity.[55] Rauscher himself explained the meaning of his amendment as indicating that papal jurisdiction, while being what a canon lawyer would regard as 'ordinary', was nevertheless what any other human being, not versed in canon law, would regard either as 'extraordinary' or as being used in an 'extraordinary manner'.[56] Reading this, heads may be pardoned if they begin to reel, and one wonders who on earth, unless he be good Joseph Smith translating the Book of Mormon through miraculous spectacles, could guess that *ordinariae potestatis principatus* meant, in the language of Vatican I, 'extraordinary power'. Even when the opacity is penetrated, it cannot be said that Rauscher's amendment throws much light on the respective limits of papal and episcopal jurisdiction. The import of ordinary and extraordinary is still left undecided. All that can be said is that it is a positive assertion of the limitations of papal power, and that negatively it rejects any supposition that the Petrine commission was to manage every detail of diocesan life as far as the mental and physical stamina of a Pope allowed, leaving to bishops only what was left over after he had gone exhausted to bed.

If it is accepted that the Primacy can never become credible until its limits are defined, it is of considerable importance to note what suggestions were made, on the unique occasion of an Ecumenical Council, for the definition of those limits. It is also of importance to identify the reasons why the suggested amendments, often admittedly excellent, were rejected and never found their way into the text of the Constitution.

Had the Primacy been debated after, instead of before, the question of Infallibility, it seems probable that the resultant picture might have been very different. The debate on the latter question showed that a definition of limits to infallibility could not be avoided; and that the key to identifying these limits was to be found only in the purpose which *ex cathedra* pronouncements were meant to serve. Unfortunately, the question of Infallibility was so dominant in the minds of the Fathers both before and during the Council, that they came to the Primacy debate much less well prepared and often casual in their approach. Nevertheless, the records of the debate show that the Council did not lack men capable of identifying the purpose of the Primacy, and arguing therefrom to a definition of its limits. Pre-eminent among these was Monserrat of Barcelona: the ordinary jurisdiction of the Holy Father was that which he exercised 'when, by virtue of his principate, he makes provision for those matters which are relevant to the preservation of unity'.[57] In thus anchoring the Primacy firmly to the concept of unity, he was followed by Caixal y Estrade[58] and by the most moderate and gentle of the Italians, Abbot Zelli of St. Paul's Outside the Walls. Zelli's was, perhaps, the finest speech of the debate and would have been perfectly at home in Vatican II. He argued that the Primacy was a service; that the Church must not model itself on secular governments, either monarchic or democratic; and that the essence of the Primacy had been perfectly expressed by Cyprian as being given to Peter 'in order that it may be known that the Church of Christ and its teaching are One'.[59]

These were speakers who voted with the Majority. In this matter at least, they were of one mind with the Minority. But if both sides were agreed as to the purpose of the Primacy, it was left to the Minority to draw the logical conclusion that papal jurisdiction does not extend beyond the fulfilment of this purpose. The major premiss was put by Haynald of Kalocsa: the Church could only be harmed by the extension of papal authority to matters 'which the purpose of the Primacy does not make it necessary for him to do';[60] and the conclusion was tabled by the redoubtable Melchite Patriarch Gregory Iussef of Antioch in an amendment, framed in the form of a *tantum . . . quantum*, and restricting the jurisdiction of the Holy See to what was necessary for the unity of the Church: 'it extends only so far as hierarchical subordination and the unity of faith and communion require'.[61]

This amendment was soundly trounced. It was rejected

by *fere omnes*. But it is instructive to see the reasons given by Zinelli for its rejection: it was 'vague and ambiguous, and therefore dangerous in practice; for the limits to which pontifical jurisdiction extends seem to be left . . . to private judgement'.[62] This calls for thought. The sinfulness of private judgement does not seem to be recognized at the present day, and indeed St. Thomas More could hardly have been canonized if he had not set up his private judgement against the hierarchy of England (and Wales). Nor is the Infallibility decree considered dangerous, in that it leaves theologians to argue from private judgement what is *ex cathedra* and what is not. As to the alleged vagueness, it was at least sharp enough for any normal man to distinguish between major issues which affect the unity of the Church, and such questions as who should be a parish priest in the Diocese of Limburg and whether or not the canons of some obscure diocese in the English Midlands may sell off their old vestments.

The chance to fill in the missing piece of the jig-saw puzzle of the Primacy decree was thus lost. It became evident that the Deputation of the Faith, dominated by Italianism, did not want the piece filled in. Instead, it substituted the Mind of the Pope. Thus Zinelli, commenting on its behalf on an amendment put by Dupanloup, resisted any attempt to delimit the respective jurisdiction of Pope and bishops on the ground that the papacy could be safely left to delimit itself. As to the possibility of undue interference by the Holy See in diocesan administration, 'is there anyone', he asked, 'even in a dream, who could think of so absurd an hypothesis? I would beg you all therefore to keep quiet, put your trust in the self-restraint of the Holy See, and express no doubt that the authority of the Holy See will be a source of strength to the powers of the bishops and not harmful to them'.[63] Some historically-minded bishops of the Minority thought this anything but an absurd hypothesis, and they did not need to dream. They conjured up ghosts from the past: Nicholas V complaining that his own papal predecessors 'left other bishops no jurisdiction whatever';[64] and a Boniface II nominating, in an early example of croneyism, his favourite deacon to succeed him.[65] But Zinelli remained unmoved. The Primacy was credible enough to him without any definition of the limits of jurisdiction; it mattered nothing to him that it could not be taught credibly by those who fought on the frontiers of Catholic Christendom, and that the self-restraint of the Holy See was not immediately evident to Greeks who remembered the Fourth Crusade, to English Protestants who remembered Grosseteste's denunciation of the Curia, and to scientific humanists who remembered Galileo. The Twentieth Ecumenical Council was not as ecumenically-minded as all that.

3. *Re-stating the Primacy*

Reading the debates that led to the 1870 definition of the Primacy, it is difficult to avoid the impression that the Fathers had it in them to produce a much better document than they did. The one common view-point that they achieved, and which therefore can be taught as the doctrine of the Church, was that the purpose of the Primacy was the preservation of unity. This would seem to be all-important to any further restatement of the Petrine prerogative. It deserved a better fate than to be tucked away discreetly at the end of the second paragraph of the third chapter[66]. Paul VI, it may be noted, has given it the prominence it merits by characterizing the Primacy as 'the necessary principle of truth, charity and unity'. And, if it is at all accepted that our Lord commissioned Peter to be the shepherd of the whole flock, it means no more than that his pastorate is directed to the essential meaning of the Church — 'that they may all be one'.[67]

But it would be a brave man who, in this day and age, would suggest that divine revelation gives no warrant for the Holy See to do more than is strictly necessary for the preservation of unity. In 1870, when Haynald and Gregory Iussef made this suggestion, it was considered no worse than vague and dangerous. In the nineteen-seventies, and after the enormous changes that have come over the Church in the last hundred years, the same suggestion might seem at first

sight to put most of the 2260 *fonctionnaires* of the Curia out
of a job, which no Trade Union would agree to. Fingers
would also quickly be pointed to the repetition, at the beginning of the third chapter of *Pastor Aeternus*, of the Florentine
assertion that the Holy See has full 'power' to care pastorally
for, to rule, and to 'steer' the Church:[68] pastoral care surely
goes far beyond the preservation of unity, and would, for
instance, cover such activities of the Congregation of the
Clergy as forbidding laymen to preach at Mass in German
churches;[69] than which nothing could be more pastoral
and nothing less calculated to preserve the unity of the
Church. Moreover and on balance, in spite of bad mistakes,[70]
the activity of the Holy See during the past two millennia
has been beneficent and hardly deserves to be delegitimized.

This is a formidable barbed-wire barrier to cut through.
But it may become less formidable if it is realized that the
present issue is a re-statement of the Primacy as absolutized
by divine revelation, and that divine revelation is not the
only source which can legitimize the activity of the Holy See.
The Church, with the assistance of the Holy Spirit, is at
perfect liberty to erect institutions which are not found in
the Gospel. It can remain true that there is no divinely-
revealed warrant for the Primacy to go beyond the limits
of what is necessary for the unity of the Church, while remaining equally true that the consensus of the Church may
justify it in going far beyond those limits. The point has been
well put by a Jesuit theologian of the English province:
'the institutional element in Christianity, by which I mean
especially social structure and law, is not part of the Gospel'.[71]
The author goes on at the same time to allow that institutions
and ecclesiastical structures, even though not revealed in the
Gospel, are nevertheless the fruit of the Spirit.[72] To this it
may be added that there would be no sense whatever in
speaking of the Pope as the Patriarch of the West unless
some part of his jurisdiction were derived, not from divine
revelation, but from the very human consensus of the
Church. A Patriarchate is essentially man-made and
constructed to meet the needs of a given cultural unit for

co-ordinated government and reasonable uniformity. Since the Eastern Schism, the concept of the patriarchate has unfortunately disappeared in the West. In the minds of the faithful the two roles of the Pope as Primate and as Patriarch have become inextricably mixed, and the divine aura of the one has been unjustifiably extended to the other. But once they are sorted out, there need be no fear that the whole structure of the Latin Church will collapse overnight: the mission to preserve the unity of the Church is a standard fitting, vested in the successor of St. Peter; Curias are optional, and so long as the Church wants them, it can have them. They will find a much more secure basis for their activity in the willing consent of the People of God than in any dubious claims to be implicit in the Gospel. Such a distinction may help to solve some of the puzzles both of 1870 and of the present day. The Fathers of Vatican I were worried by the convincing historical evidence that former Popes had often acknowledged their subjection to canon law, not seeing that he could be subject as Patriarch if not as Primate. Today's puzzle is how our Lord could possibly have given to the Bishop of Rome specifically and exclusively as successor of St. Peter, a commission so enormous that it can only be discharged by large numbers of *monsignori* and bishops *in partibus*, none of whom by any stretch of the imagination could claim to be successors of St. Peter. The answer is the same: Peter was not commissioned to be a one-man Congregation of the Clergy.

This is so far a negative argument — that the Primacy could be re-stated in the terms of the Minority without denying the legitimacy of the powers now exercised by the Holy See. The starting-point for a positive argument may be found in what the Vatican II Dogmatic Constitution *Dei Verbum* has to say, about 'tradition': this, derived from the Apostles and developed with the help of the Holy Spirit, is perpetuated and handed on in the 'teaching, life, and worship' of the Church.[73] What has the 'life' of the Church to say about the Primacy? The answer is a matter for the historian. Historical instances thrown up in the course of the

1870 debates were surprisingly but significantly few. Dechamps of Malines quoted what he considered to be the clearest example known to him in the whole history of the Church of the plenitude of papal power: the action taken by Pius VII in 1801 when, to end the chaos created by the Civil Constitution of 1791, he made a clean sweep of the whole French Hierarchy, erecting new sees and filling them with new bishops. This was, he thought, a supreme instance of the 'extraordinary means' by which the Holy See can provide 'a remedy for extraordinary evils'.[74] Rauscher quoted the same example[75] and no other concrete instance was cited by the Fathers.[76] In the abstract, Caixal y Estradé considered that to delimit the jurisdiction of each bishop and to erect new sees and Vicariates Apostolic would be an exercise of the Petrine Primacy;[77] and the Syrian Metropolitan of Mosul, Cyril Behnam Benni, cited in the same sense a letter from Leo the Great to Anastasius of Thessalonica, designed to ensure that 'everyone should not claim every right for himself'[78] As far as the Fathers of 1870 were aware, it would seem that no examples of strictly primatial action could be cited except such as were concerned with preserving the unity of the Church. And these were even rarer than *ex cathedra* statements of dogma. By contrast, when Ramirez of Badajoz and Desprez of Toulouse wished to write into the Constitution that the institution of bishops all over the world belonged of divine right to the papacy,[79] they were given their due meed of praise by Zinelli, but told that this did not belong to the Dogmatic Constitution.[80] It was, in short, a matter of canon law.

It is not easy for those who live in the twentieth century to realize how restricted was the impact of anything resembling primatial action in the 'life' of the Church before 1870. The change in the activity of the Holy See since then is more than a non-historical mind can grasp. Up to that date, the Pope was also encumbered with the Temporal Power, and those who read the dull pages of Pastor will know how little time this left over for a Pope to indulge in pastoral problems. Intervention in diocesan life outside the confines of the Papal

States was rare. It was the exception, rather than the rule, for bishops to be nominated from Rome.[81] The Roman Congregations were pre-occupied either with the government of the Papal States, or with the routine administration of canon law: the *Congregatio Studiorum* was a Ministry of Education for what remained of the Patrimony of Peter, and the *S.C. Concilii* still operated under the brief given to it in 1564 to interpret the decrees of the Council of Trent.[82] The modern system of Apostolic Delegations had not yet even been conceived in the womb of time.[83] Wiseman considered it 'one of the rarest exercises of Pontifical authority' when Gregory XVI wrote a corrective letter to a German bishop.[84] To read the lives of nineteenth-century Popes is to enter another world. Papal days were spacious. Gregory XVI could take his daily walk from the Ponte Molle to the Tor di Quinto, patronize the arts, and spend a morning at the Venerabile, entranced with a beer machine imported from England. Pio Nono found time to go riding in the Alban Hills, could spend four months in 1857 touring his dominions, and write charades while the Piedmontese were pouring into Rome. The time was not yet when the window of the Papal bedroom was the first to light up before dawn, and the last to be darkened in the early hours after midnight.

Dei Verbum regrettably fails to say what happens to tradition when the 'life' of the Church goes off in a new direction. It is not therefore possible to say more than that the Minority's suggested statement of the limits to papal jurisdiction can be justified by the life-style of the Church up to 1870.

This is about as far as one can go in seeking help from the Minority of Vatican I. But there is help, also, to be found in at least one speech from the Majority, the importance of which can be appreciated in the twentieth century as it hardly could in the nineteenth. Reference has already been made to Abbot Zelli's plea that the structure of the Church should not be conceptualized in the terms of human governments.[85] At the time this passed unnoticed. His hearers had simply no other concepts to work with except jurisdiction and obedience. It was only in these terms that they could conceive of the Primacy achieving its purpose. Strong, centralized government was the only way to get things done, and the model for the faithful was to be found in the Light Brigade at Balaklava. The present age has different concepts to work with, and the Church could learn much from current managerial theory:[86] the goals of a society can be attained by means other than the 'classical' type of management, with its dominant leadership issuing detailed directives aiming at maximum efficiency, and enforced by coercion in an organization which runs like a machine on established lines. It took the brief pontificate of John XXIII to show that the goals of the Christian Gospel can be achieved by means far removed from classical management, and that bore all the marks of the 'charismatic' type: prophetic, inspirational leadership; a rejection of the *status quo*; and spontaneous, unpredictable decisions. And under him the Papacy became a symbol of unity far more effective than centuries of 'I command: you obey'.

Principle of Unity

Pastor Aeternus is all the poorer in that it knows no other form of *principatus* than the *potestas iurisdictionis*. This is an ignoble restriction, and any re-statement of the Primacy would do well to put jurisdiction in its proper and very minor place — as no more than one of several routes by which the Holy See may fulfil its mission. The Council of Florence used the term *potestas*, and Robert Murray has usefully remarked that the Greek εξουσια which it translates, is a term of much wider connotation: it 'does not have the connotation of jurisdiction over others, much less the power to impose force on other persons, but rather the holder's rightful freedom to act'.[87] Trouble comes when attempts are made to put these ideas into words. 'Authority', if taken in the Latin sense of initiative and moral leadership,[88] would have served, but authoritarianism has made it a dirty word. There is a variety of terms derived from the root of the Latin *primus*, not at all of which are serviceable. This word itself has acquired too weak a significance by its usage in the

Orthodox Church to describe the Bishop of Rome as *Primus inter pares*.[89] As to Vatican I's use of *principatus*, this on the one hand has too much an overtone of secular monarchy, and on the other is insufficient to distinguish the Primacy from the Episcopate: in the *Relatio* with which Pie of Poitiers introduced the General Discussion of *Pastor Aeternus*, he went out of his way to emphasize that bishops are in no way 'inferiors' in relation to the Holy See, and that they are the 'primary pastors of their churches . . . with the character and authority of princes'.[90] These are words of weight, delivered on behalf of the Deputation of the Faith, and making it difficult to fault the Orthodox description of bishops as *pares* of the Pope. The best available term would seem to be that employed by Paul VI in speaking of the Primacy as the 'principle' of truth, charity and unity, and which seems to have much the same sense as the description by Vatican II of the Roman Pontiff as the 'perpetual and visible source and foundation of the unity of the bishops and of the multitude of the faithful'.[91] Some hard spade work will have to be done if the faithful are to grasp the meaning of such terms as 'principle' and 'source', but the task should not be insuperable, given that generations of Catholic children have made light work of transubstantiation and hyperdoulia.

How far does the small print of Vatican I, with some help from Vatican II and a little common sense, justify a re-statement of the Primacy on these lines by those who have to preach from the pulpit, teach in schools, or engage in ecumenical dialogue? There seems to be authentication enough for emphasizing that, as a divine institution, the role of the Primacy is to preserve and make visible the unity of the Church, no more and no less. Conversely, it seems only common sense to take the emphasis off jurisdiction: primatial judgements and commands may be rarer in the lives of the faithful than infallible pronouncements, and they are kept in unity by loyalty and love rather than by being 'under' the visible Head of the Church.[92] But — when jurisdiction has been relegated to its proper place — can anyone go further and say what are the limits of this jurisdiction? The unfortunate teacher of Christian doctrine is here faced with more than a dilemma. If he says that the jurisdiction of the Primacy is unlimited, he is contradicting the consensus of the world's bishops at Vatican I. If he says that it is limited, but that nobody knows where the limits are, he (and the whole Church) will look a perfect ass. If he says, with the Minority of 1870, that it is limited to what is necessary for the preservation of unity, he will be out alone on the uncharted sea of unauthenticated doctrine. But someone has got to push out from the shore, even at the risk of being torpedoed before he has gone very far. In the present state of the Church one cannot wait for ever for the *magisterium* to fill in the missing piece that alone can make sense of the third chapter of *Pastor Aeternus*. The restatement needs making, and, if made, the dogma of the Primacy may prove no longer to be the 'block of granite that bars the way to any mutual understanding on the part of Christian Churches, a block that is so great that it seems that we can neither move it nor climb over it nor get round it'.[93]

NOTES

1 *Unitatis Redintegratio*, 6.
2 Cf. *Mysterium Ecclesiae*, printed *in extenso* in *The Tablet* of 14 July 1973, pp. 667–70, and esp. p. 668, col. 3; also in *The Clergy Review* for December 1973, pp. 950–62.
3 Allocution to the Secretariat for Promoting Christian Unity, 28 April 1967; cited in Suenens, *Coresponsibility in the Church*, London 1968, pp. 38–9.
4 *Structures of the Church*, ch. vii.
5 At least in England, typified by a letter-writer in the *Sunday Telegraph*, 23 April 1972, complaining that the aim of the Cardinal is to 'shackle the divinely-given plenitude of power'.
6 Cf. the *Sunday Times* Weekly Review, 6 October 1968, where Bishop Butler is interviewed by Muriel Bowen. The Mother of Parliaments is not, however, to be blamed for the Third Vatican Synod of 1971, for an account of which cf. J. F. X. Harriott, S.J. in *The Times*, 30 October 1971.
7 *The Tablet*, 18 March 1972, pp. 264–6: 'The Church in Spain wins through against the Curia.'
8 So G. A. Bologna, in *Concilium*, October 1971, pp. 142–3.
9 Cf. *New Blackfriars*, November 1972, E. Quinn: 'The End of her Latin' esp. pp. 512 and 514, citing Fritz Leist, *Der Gefangene des Vatikans*, Munich 1971.
10 *The Tablet*, 20 October 1973, pp. 1004–5, 'Bishop Kempf'.
11 *The Tablet*, 11 November 1972, pp. 1083–4, 'Threat of Break'.
12 Mansi, *Concilia*, iv(52), 1100D.

13 Cf. F. J. Cwiekowski, S.S., *The Ecclesiology of the English Bishops at the First Vatican Council*, Louvain 1971, pp. 472–3. Among the Minority he lists Clifford and Errington and Goss; he classifies Ullathorne and Grant as Moderates, and the two Browns, Turner, Roskell, Vaughan and Amherst as Moderate-Minority. But Goss covered the Council from Cannes, and Roskell from a villa fourteen miles out on the Appian Way. Seven remained for the vote: 3 for, 3 against, 1 *juxta modum*.

14 Central and Eastern Europe had, in 1870, approximately 70 million Catholics; the rest of Europe had about 110 million. Outside Europe, and apart from Latin America, there were perhaps another 21 million. Latin America probably had a civil population of over 70 million, but how many of these could be counted as Catholic is difficult to say.

15 Italy had some 336 bishops for a nominal Catholic population of about thirty millions.

16 Cf. Mourret, M., *Le Concile du Vatican*, Paris 1919, p. 146n.

17 On the Majority side, besides the 13 speakers from Italy, there were 8 from France, 7 from Spain, 4 from Ireland, 3 each from the U.S.A. and Latin America, 2 each from Switzerland and the Uniat Churches, 1 each from Germany, Belgium, Holland, Greece, England and the Far East Missions.

18 Karl Rahner and J. Ratzinger, *The Episcopate and the Primacy*, 1961, p. 472.

19 Mansi, op. cit., 608C.

20 Ibid., 409D.

21 Ibid., 46C.

22 'Uno Pius Minor est Deo': cited R. de Cesare, *The Last Days of Papal Rome*, London 1909, p. 170.

23 Cited Mansi, op. cit., 659D. Other citations came from a letter of Jerome to Damasus: 'sequor magistrum et iudicem Christum, quem nec video nec audio nisi in te' (ibid., 659B); and from a letter to Hilarius from the fifth century Council of Tarragona: 'nos Deum in vobis adorantes' (ibid., 659D).

24 Ibid., 326C. Lenti had listened to contradictions between Manning and Clifford as to England, Cullen of Dublin and McHale of Tuam as to Ireland, and Papp-Szilàgyi of Nágy-Várad and Bonnaz of Csanad as to Hungary.

25 Ibid., 664D.

26 For its recognition by Vatican II, cf. *Lumen Gentium*, 12.

27 Mansi, op. cit., 39A.

28 Ibid., 329A.

29 de Cesare, op. cit., p. 89.

30 Mansi, op. cit., 63A. One would wish very much to know more of this early instance of Clergy Lib.

31 Ibid., 414A.

32 Ibid., 617B.

33 Mansi, op. cit., 609B.

34 Ibid., 414A.

35 Ibid., 415A. Salzano had an endearing liveliness of imagination; in the course of his speech he traced Neapolitan belief in Infallibility back to St. Januarius of the Liquefying Blood.

36 Ibid., 617B.

37 Ibid., 694C.

38 Ibid., 1115D.

39 Ibid., 183A.

40 Mourret, op. cit., p. 95.

41 Mansi, op. cit., 541A.

42 ibid., 678C.

43 Cf. Goss, Letter to Newman, 28 March 1870 (Archives of the Birmingham Oratory, Vatican Council Collection), cited in F. J. Cwiekowski, S.S., *The Ecclesiology of the English Bishops at the First Vatican Council*, Louvain 1971: 'Nothing ever wounded the simplicity of my faith so much as the trickery with which I became acquainted on official intercourse with the Curia. The present Council, as a friend of mine observes, will change the patriarchal sceptre into a dictator's truncheon, and the Bishops who went to Rome as princes of the household to confer with their august Father will return like satraps dispatched to their provinces.'

44 Mansi, op. cit., 574A, 593D, 1092C–D.

45 Ibid., 690A.

46 Ibid., 564C.

47 Ibid., 579D. Magnasco, Vicar-Capitular of Genoa, dealt with the term 'absolute' in the same way as applied to papal power: it simply meant that this power was not subject to conciliar decrees (ibid., 625C).

48 This contribution to the Anthology of Anglo-Saxon Latin included an invitation to the Pope to come to the United States to preach and hear confessions, and concluded; 'sed immo campus in America vastus est, ut si aliqui ex Roma volunt ad nos venire certe iucundissimi erunt' (ibid., 589C). The last phrase defies translation unless it means 'they will be very welcome'.

49 Ibid., 591C.

50 Ibid., 573C and 575A.

51 For the significance of such common view-points, cf. Vatican II, *Lumen Gentium*, 25.

52 DB 1828.

53 Mansi, op. cit., 1089B, being the 21st Amendment.

54 Ibid., 1107A.

55 Ibid., 1118A: 'fere omnes admiserunt'.

56 Ibid., 541A: '(potestas) vel extraordinaria est, vel extraordinario modo in dioecesi agit.'

57 Ibid., 598A–B.

58 Ibid., 1080B: 'ad unitatem communionis in regimine universalis ecclesiae'.

59 Ibid., 626B–C, 626A–B and 627B (citing Cyprian, de Unitate Ecclesiae, cap. V).

60 Ibid., 669B–C.

61 Ibid., 1086A, being the 13th Amendment.

62 Ibid., 1103C.

63 Ibid., 1105D.

64 Ibid., 682B (Krementz).

65 Ibid. 587–BC (Vérot).

66 DB 1827.

67 John 17:21.

68 DB 1826: 'governing' would be too loaded a translation of 'gubernandi'.

69 For this episode cf. *The Tablet*, 13 January 1973, p. 43, reporting a letter from Cardinal Wright of the Congregation of the Clergy to Cardinal Döpfner.

70 No one can reasonably hold, as did Gastaldi in 1870, that no decree of the papacy can impede the salvation of souls, after the *volte-face* over the question of Chinese Rites, condemned in 1715 by Clement XI in *Ex Illa die*, and sanctioned by Pius XII in 1939.

71 Robert Murray, S.J., 'Authority and the Spirit in the New Testament', in *Authority in a Changing Church*, London 1968, p. 19.

72 Robert Murray, op. cit., p. 36.

73 *Dei Verbum*, 8.

74 Mansi, op. cit., 546A.

75 Ibid., 540B.

76 No one, curiously, mentioned the judgement given by Nicholas I in 862 of the rival claims of Photius and Ignatius to the Patriarchate of Constantinople.

77 Mansi, op. cit., 660B–C.

78 Ibid., 553C–D.

79 Ibid., 1088D (Amendment No. 18) and 1091B (Amendment No. 30).

80 Ibid., 1108A–B– 'laudat quam maxime scopum.'

81 Up to the beginning of the nineteenth century the nomination of almost all bishoprics outside the Papal States was under crown patronage. The first dent in this system was made by the Wars of Liberation in Latin America and the final blow was struck by the extinction of Hapsburg power in the First World War. The extension of papal patronage was also helped by the proliferation of bishoprics in North America, in the missionary territories of the East, and other areas where crown patronage had never existed.

82 According to historical notes in the current *Annuario Pontificio*; this Congregation became the Congregation of the Clergy in 1968, with Ufficio's I, II and III: supervising the whole of clerical life, whether intellectual and moral formation, temporal possessions, preaching or catechetics.

83 In the *Annuario Pontificio* of 1867, four prelates hold the title of Apostolic Delegate, but with functions very different from those of today. They were located in Greece, Syria, Persia and Egypt and functioned under Propaganda.

84 Wiseman, *Recollections of the Last Four Popes*, London 1858, p. 508.

85 Vide supra, p. 21.

86 Thus P. F. Rudge, *Ministry and Management*, London 1968. On pp. 32–3 he gives a useful conspectus of five types of management: Traditional, Charismatic, Classical, Human Relations and Systematic.

87 Robert Murray, op. cit., p. 32.

88 So used to describe the Augustan Principate in the *Monumentum Ancyranum*: 'auctoritate omnibus praestiti.'

89 For this usage, cf. Paul Evdokimov in *Concilium*, Vol. iv, No. 7 (April 1971), p. 126.

90 Mansi, op. cit., 33C.

91 *Lumen Gentium*, 23.

92 As in the English Catechism of Christian Doctrine, Q.95.

93 Cited R. Pesch, in *Concilium*, ut supra, p. 35, from H. Küng, *Die Kirche* (Okumenische Forschungen I, i), Freiburg-im-Breisgau, 1967, p. 545.

9

The 'wound in the right foot': unhealed?

Garrett Sweeney

THE title of this study is borrowed from Rosmini's *Five Wounds of the Church* and calls for some explanation. Almost half of the book is devoted to the 'Wound in the Right Foot, which is that the Nomination of Bishops is given up to the Lay Power'.[1] Rosmini develops his theme with a wealth of historical argument, and with no hesitation in making value judgements: Popes and Councils who leave the election of bishops in the hands of cathedral chapters are Good, and Popes and potentates who take them into their own hands are Bad. In the year 1832, when he completed his manuscript, the Church was quite evidently 'wounded' by the concentration in lay hands of the *jus patronatus*[2] over the vast majority of Sees in the Latin Church. Only a small number of cathedral chapters retained the right of election, and a bare handful of bishops outside the Papal States owed their appointment to the Holy See. In the course of the last hundred years there has been a drastic change in the situation. Of some two thousand Residential Bishops now in the Latin Church,[3] fewer than two hundred are subject to State appointment and fewer than twenty are elected by cathedral chapters. All the others, to a total of some thousand eight hundred, are Vatican appointments. Moreover, since 1917 this method of appointment has been the accepted rule of the Church — *Eos libere nominat Romanus Pontifex*.[4]

The system of State patronage in the past has produced many bishops of great distinction. But few would deny that the transfer of power to the Holy See is an immense improvement on the previous situation. The question nevertheless can still be raised: has the 'Wound' in the Church really been healed by this transfer? It is not a question which has as yet become acute. Some controversy on the subject appears from time to time, but always in a low key and with the consciousness that the present system of making episcopal appointments is extremely convenient. A good deal of bother and heart-searching is saved by leaving everything to the Vatican. But there are signs that in the near future the question may be pressed more hotly. The American Church, after paying half a million dollars for a diagnosis of its ills, got full value for money by learning from Andrew Greeley that the bishops should resign *en bloc* and that 'Representative governance in the church, including especially the nomination of the bishops by the dioceses in which they serve, is the absolutely essential requisite for the effective governance of the church'.[5] This was in the February of 1972. A month after the publication of the Greeley statement, the Curia showed that it was aware of some disquiet by issuing new 'Norms for the Appointment of Bishops'[6] which did little to satisfy anybody. The question can moreover now be seen as involving more than the niceties of canon law. It has theological implications of considerable importance, which are becoming more apparent as the ecclesiology of Vatican II slowly permeates the Church. The Code was a by-product of Vatican I. If 'The Church' is conceptualized as a single machine, with divine assistance concentrated at the top, and nothing more required of bishops than that they should operate the machine efficiently, it is entirely appropriate that they should be appointed from Rome. If, on the other hand, the Holy Spirit moves among the' churches' and 'teaching life and worship' develop at grass roots among the faithful,[7] while the bishop is regarded as truly the Head of his church (and heads have usually some power of thought),[8] it may well be considered that some form of localized appointment might be as appropriate to the age of Vatican II as papal appointments were to the age of Vatican I.

It is by no means the intention of this present study to attempt an answer to this question. Before it can even be discussed dispassionately, the historical genesis of canon 329 must be established. It would be folly to destroy anything until the reason for its existence has been ascertained. At the same time, and as the question has been prompted by Rosmini — who has been proved in so many respects to have had more than his share of the prophetical spirit — it will not be out of place to take note of the answer he would have given. It certainly never entered into his head that some day the Papacy would take to itself a universal right to appoint bishops. When, *en passant*, he mentions past instances of this responsibility being assumed by the Holy See, he does so only to deplore it. Thus, of the Avignon period when Popes 'reserved' elections to themselves: 'No one person, albeit invested with ever so high a dignity, can possess power commensurate with the extension of such a right as the election of all bishops throughout the world. Together with these world-wide reserves, the Popes assumed responsibility beyond their strength.[9] His concern was not so much that episcopal appointments had gone to the State, as that they had gone out of the diocese: 'From the first ages to the present time the Church has ever attached the greatest importance to keeping the old form of Episcopal election inviolable; that is to say, the assent of all, and the decision of the clergy'.[10] And his exposition of this particular 'Wound' ends in prophecy: 'England and Ireland, the United States and Belgium, elect Bishops freely; and assuredly God will not delay the restoration of a similar liberty to all Christian nations'.[11] In Rosmini's way of thinking, the 'Wound' would quite evidently not have yet been healed.

The search for an historical genesis to canon 329 should in theory begin with legal history. The Pontifical Commission, which Pius X set up in 1904 for the revision of canon law, was not a legislative body. Its brief, as set out in *Arduum sane Munus*, was 'to arrange in clear order and gather together the laws of the Church which have been published up to the present day, after removing those which have been abrogated or become obsolete, and adapting others more closely to the conditions of the present day where the need for this arose'. It had no powers to enact new legislation. Unfortunately, the search for legal precedents for this canon appears to end in a wild-goose chase. The most authoritative conciliar legislation is that of Lateran II in 1139. Its twenty-eighth canon decreed that all bishops must be elected by their cathedral chapters. This, especially during the *Ere Concordataire*, was honoured more often in the breach than in the observance. But the papacy seems to have considered it as in force — at least in areas where patronage could not be given to the State — right up to the middle of the last century, and Gregory XVI was the last Pope to erect a diocese in accordance with the Lateran decrees. From that time it became obsolete, and it evidently played no part in the genesis of canon 329. The second of the *Regulae Cancellariae Apostolicae* compiled under Urban V (1362–70) looks more promising. It 'reserved' all episcopal appointments to the Pope. But the trouble with this is that its juridical status is beset with difficulties. If anyone but an expert canonist can understand what 'reserves' are all about, they appear to have a built-in obsolescence: according to *auctores probati*, episcopal appointments can only be reserved when they become *causae majores per accidens* — the accident in the case of Urban V being the prevalence of simony, the rapacity of ambitious laymen, and a shortage of cash in the papal pocket at a time when deserving characters had to be rewarded. As soon as the accident disappeared, and 'that which was meant to be a remedy became soon an easy way for the Curia to raise money', the reserve became invalid and pre-existing law (which reserves did not abrogate) again became operative.[12] Rosmini perhaps got it right: 'Not that the Holy See has not a right to reserve elections to himself (*sic*), when any extraordinary cause requires it. The right to save the Church from peril must always exist. But it was the system of ordinary and universal reserves which raised all classes against the Papacy'.[13] Whatever the juridical standing of the Second Rule of the Chancery, it was obsolete long before the Pontifical Commission began its work. It was only late in the nineteenth century that Rome showed any signs of asserting a right to nominate all bishops. In short, to search for legal precedents for canon 329 seems a fruitless occupation. Its historical genesis must be sought elsewhere, in the peculiar vicissitudes of Church history during the century before its formulation.

The Papacy Reluctant: to 1829

The way in which the mind of the Holy See was working in the early years of the nineteenth century can be seen clearly enough in a series of Concordats by which successive Popes tried to reconstruct a shattered Church in the aftermath of (and even during) the Napoleonic Wars. The map of Europe was in a perfect mess, and while the Congress of Vienna did its best to bring some order out of the chaos by re-drawing State boundaries in favour of the winners, Pius VII was busy doing the same for what was left of the Church. All along the line of the Rhine, and with extensions into eastern Europe and southern Germany, the passage of armies had left a trail of broken-up bishoprics and impoverished dioceses. The immediate need was to put the Church back on its financial feet and reorganize dioceses in conformity with new lines of State demarcation. Pius VII approached his problems in a spirit of realism. His Concordat with Napoleon in 1801 was a strictly cash transaction, with no love lost on either side. The First Consul contracted to maintain a reconstituted French hierarchy and received in return the right to elect bishops for the new Sees and their successors in perpetuity.[14] Later Popes were to convince themselves that the *jus patronatus* was given only to princes who had deserved well of the Church.[15] Pius had no such illusions. Napoleon had dragged too many Popes backwards and forwards across the Alps too often.

Two further Concordats were made by Pius VII with Crowned Heads — warmer in tone but with the same tenor and the same motivation. That with Bavaria was concluded in 1817. The Wittelsbachs had long enjoyed the right of nominating to vacant bishoprics within their territories, but Ludwig had picked up the title of King in the course of the wars, and his dioceses had suffered under French occupation. Church-State relations needed redefinition. Financial security and legal protection were provided for the eight dioceses within the provinces of Bamberg and Munich, and this *utilitas . . . ad res Ecclesiae et Religionis* was the explicit reason for granting the Wittelsbachs a perpetual Indult to select the hierarchy of their kingdom.[16] In the following year (1818) a similar Concordat was made with Ferdinand I of the Two Sicilies, where ecclesiastical organization had been somewhat confused by the Parthenopean Republic and the short-lived monarchy of Murat. This Concordat was unusually expansive. The kingdom was the only constant friend that the Papacy had in the Italian Peninsula. They shared a common bond in being the two worst-governed States in Italy, and Pope and King took turns at finding refuge from revolution in each other's territories. Pius was so far from claiming for himself the nomination of bishops that he extended the royal patronage to Sees *ad quas majestas sua jure nominandi nondum gaudebat.*[17]

In making these arrangements, the Holy See was by no means giving altruistically away a right which it would have preferred to claim for itself. This is clear from the provisions made by Pius VII and Leo XII for Prussia, the Upper Rhine, Hanover and Belgium, where there were no Catholic monarchs to demand a *quid pro quo*. These territories contained some of the most ancient and powerful Sees in Christendom, many of which had formerly enjoyed temporal sovereignty in their own right. The dioceses concerned had been brought by the vicissitudes of war and politics into the jurisdiction of non-Catholic princes. They had suffered loss, but were not destitute. Given a certain degree of rationalization and readjustment of boundaries, they could be made financially viable. There was no possibility of State subvention, and therefore (except in the case of Belgium) no need for Concordats. The first of these new arrangements was made for Prussia in the July of 1821, and was promulgated in a Bull which had already been the subject of negotiations with the Prussian government and which therefore could be regarded as a quasi-Concordat. Eight dioceses were concerned: four on the Rhine within the province of Cologne, and four in the eastern territories of Prussia with Posen and Breslau as metropolitans. The provision for the election of bishops was that laid down by the Second Council of the Lateran in 1139. The right of designation was left quite simply and without reservation in the hands of the relevant cathedral chapters.[18] An exactly similar provision was made in the following month for the newly erected Upper Rhine Province, with an Archbishopric at Freiburg-im-Breisgau, and suffragans at Fulda, Limburg and Rottenburg — each of which, in that highly fragmented period of German history, lay within a different kingdom or duchy.[19]

It fell to the next Pope, Leo XII (1823-9) to arrange matters in Hanover, which at that time had a half-share in King George IV of England. Only two Sees were concerned: Hildesheim and Osnabrück. The necessary Bull was issued in 1824. It differed from those for Prussia and the Upper Rhine only in that the chapter, before making a final election, had to ascertain from the Hanoverian government that the proposed new bishop was *persona grata*.[20] This system of election is said to have been identical with that which had operated since 1806 in Ireland, which had a strong hierarchy of twenty-nine bishops divided between four provinces.[21] The Concordat with King William I of the Low Countries was concluded in 1827. He was a Protestant ruler whose newly constituted kingdom included six Belgian Sees which had previously been for a time under French rule, and had been subject to the Napoleonic Concordat of 1801. Here again there was no attempt to take the election of bishops into the hands of the Holy See: the job of filling vacant bishoprics was left in the hands of cathedral chapters.[22] One further act of Leo XII deserves remembrance. In 1828 he erected a new diocese at Basel. Up to that time Switzerland had had a small hierarchy of three bishops. The German-speaking diocese of Chur already possessed the right to elect its own bishop; for want of easily ascertainable information, the arrangement in the French-speaking dioceses of Sion and Lausanne-Geneva may be conjectured to have been the same. When Basel was erected (or re-erected) a Convention was made with the four Swiss Cantons concerned. Its provisions are of great interest and were extraordinarily liberal, even in a country which was so dedicated to autonomy and the principle of self-determination. The right of designating a bishop was placed in the hands, not of the whole chapter, but of an inner group of canons known as the 'Senate', and which by definition had to be representative of all four Cantons concerned. It was further stipulated that the See must be filled from the clergy of the same diocese.[23] The pontificate of Leo XII is thus of great interest. He neither gave the *jus patronatus* to any temporal power nor retained it in his own hands. So far as this pontificate is concerned, the twenty-eighth canon of Lateran II was still operative.

There is one more point of significance in the Bulls issued for Prussia and the Upper Rhine, and in the Concordat for Belgium. Each of these documents contains an injunction that the provisions of an Instruction issued by Urban VIII in 1627 should be observed. This Instruction is wholly concerned with the procedure leading up to the canonical institution of a new bishop by the Pope. Reference to it implies that there are two distinct stages in provision for a vacant bishopric: election, designation or nomination, which does not belong to the Holy See; and canonical institution — which does. The procedure was designed to ascertain a candidate's canonical fitness by means of a thirteen-point questionnaire. One of these required evidence of a university degree or an equivalent certificate from some recognized academy, and is of especial interest in that it forbids the candidate to be styled 'bishop-elect' . . . unless election by the chapter has already taken place'.[24] This use of Urban VIII's Instruction seems clear enough evidence that in the time of Leo XII, the Holy See considered that it was fulfilling its duty of guardianship over the Universal Church well enough by retaining the right of canonical institution rather than by claiming the right of election.[25]

Across the Atlantic, the early history of episcopal appointments in the United States was of an importance which deserves more attention than it has yet received. The infant church was in a situation for which there was no precedent. On the one hand, the possibility of vesting the *jus patronatus* in a President (as was to be done in Latin America) was ruled out by the separation of Church and State. On the other hand there were no cathedral chapters, and the second alternative method of nominating bishops could not apply. In the face of this situation the Holy See could only act with an uncertain touch, for the Napoleonic captivity covered the crucial period when an American Province was being organized with a metropolitan and four suffragans. But beneath all the confusion and uncertainty it seems still possible to discern a recognizable pattern of papal thought.[26]

The first bishop of the new Republic was elected in 1789 by the twenty-six priests who in that year were active in the United States. A nomination made in this way was the nearest practicable approximation to the legislation of Lateran II. Pius VI accepted it *de facto* if not *de jure* and instituted John Carroll as first bishop of Baltimore. Pius VII in the main followed the same line — but with notable exceptions which perhaps only served to prove the rule. In his time he instituted twelve bishops to the nine sees which were in existence before he died. Five of these were instituted on the joint nomination of bishops and clergy; in one case he rejected their nominee and substituted a candidate of his own choice; four were appointed *motu proprio* without any consultation with the American Church.[27] The discernible reasons for the papal intervention are pertinent. After the Pope had rejected the clergy's nominee to the new see erected in New York in 1808, the five bishops then in the country wrote to Rome asking that the right of nomination be given to the Archbishop of Baltimore and his suffragans. Their letter was sent in 1810, while the Pope was in captivity, and it is difficult to conceive what answer they could have expected. They got their answer some eleven years later, after four more bishops had been appointed *motu proprio* and the American hierarchy had complained that the Church in the United States was being made the victim of an Irish conspiracy. The answer was a simple refusal to give the Archbishop of Baltimore and his suffragans the right to nominate. By all the precedents of canon law the Holy See was right. Nomination by clergy — as had operated up to and including the erection of the American Province in 1808 — bore at least a resemblance to the legislation of Lateran II. The claim of a hierarchy to be exclusively self-perpetuating bore no resemblance whatever, was without precedent in the canon law of the Church, and had obvious dangers: the development of a closed shop of inbred bishops, chosen by croneyism. That was reason enough for the Holy See to reject the proposals of the American bishops. A second reason may be found in the local politics of the time. There was dissension between the Catholics of French origin and those from Ireland. The bishops leaned towards the French. Three of the five nominations they made with the concurrence of the clergy were of French origin. By contrast, all five bishops appointed by Pius VII himself came from Ireland. It seems clear that in over-riding nominations from the United States he was influenced by an Irish lobby in Rome, operating in the interests of its fellow-countrymen.

Nevertheless he took some note of the disquietude in the American hierarchy. He could hardly have done otherwise. With the single exception of John England of Charleston, the five bishops sent by the Pope across the Atlantic from Ireland proved disastrously ill-chosen. In June, 1822, he agreed that the American bishops should have a right of 'recommendation' to vacant sees. Thus was introduced into the Church the combination of local recommendation and papal appointment which, owing to the pnenomenal growth in numbers and importance of the American hierarchy, was ultimately to become a pattern for the Universal Church and obliterate the combination of local nomination and papal institution decreed in 1139 by Lateran II.

Leo XII made no change in this system. Indeed he could not. To operate the Lateran decrees, as his predecessor had done in Prussia and the Upper Rhine, and as he himself was to do in Hanover, the erection of cathedral chapters was a prerequisite. But on this point the American hierarchy was adamant. From 1833 the Holy See pressed it to establish a capitular organization, giving as one reason that the clergy would thereby gain a voice in the election of their bishops. The pressure met with no response. The bishops of the United States had no intention of sharing power with their priests. The furthest they would go (and this after the First Plenary Council of Baltimore in 1852) was to accept 'consultors' chosen by themselves. Notwithstanding all this, Leo showed in practice that he did not think it was the business of the Holy See to pick bishops. All five appointments to American sees made in his pontificate seem to have been made in accordance with the recommendations of the local hierarchy.

The impression given at this time is very definitely that the last thing the Holy See wanted was to get involved in selecting bishops for the Universal Church. Leo XII in particular seems to have been conscious of no other legislation than that of Lateran II. Canon 329 would have filled him with dismay. If the Papacy ever picked bishops beyond the limits of its own temporal States it was because it had to. Thus to the south-east and in the Ottoman Balkans, eight little dioceses had survived in Greece, left behind in the islands by the Crusades and the Frankish domination. Another five survived in Albania. The average Catholic population of a Greek diocese scarcely reached 4,000, and the corresponding figure in Albania was perhaps 6,000. These were all in the midst of Muslim or Orthodox populations and no government was interested in the selection of men to govern dioceses of such profound insignificance. They were too weak and disorganized to look after themselves. As far as can be ascertained, the Holy See filled the gap and got on with the job. The situation in the Russian and Polish territories of the Romanovs was similar but of greater importance. After the third partition of Poland in 1795, Pius VI had sent Lorenzo Litta as Apostolic Delegate to reorganize the six Polish dioceses that now belonged to Russia, and the five struggling Latin dioceses that existed in Byelorussia and the Ukraine. The whole episode is a remarkable example of the vigour with which the Papacy could act, even when at its lowest ebb, and of the expert diplomacy which it had at its command. Litta's arrangements were promulgated in 1798 in a Bull which began with an expression of the Pope's present misery: *Maximis undique pressi calamitatibus exules angustiati afflicti, ac omni fere humana ope destituti*;[28] but the arrangements were thorough and showed an enormous grasp of the intricate details of the Russian and Polish situation. Their only interest in the present context is that Litta himself, as Apostolic Delegate, made appointments to the Sees he found vacant.

The year 1829 is a good moment to take stock of the distribution of the *jus patronatus* throughout the Catholic world. It was at this time that Rosmini was identifying his 'Wound in the Right Foot'; and it was up to, but not beyond this time that there are clear indications that it was not the mind of the Holy See to take part in episcopal elections itself but rather to leave this where possible to the local church as prescribed by Lateran II — deviations being accepted only when it was urgently necessary to hand patronage over to the temporal power. At the death of Leo XII there were approximately[29] some 646 Ordinaries in the Latin Church. Of these, no fewer than 555 owed their appointments to the State: in the Two Sicilies (113 dioceses), France (86), the Hapsburg dominions (82), the States of the Church (70), Sardinia and the Italian duchies (67), Spain and its possessions (61), the Spanish-speaking republics of Latin America (35), Portugal and its possessions (24), the Empire of Brazil (9) and Bavaria (8). Some form of election by cathedral chapters or the equivalent obtained in Ireland (29 dioceses), the German

Sees of Prussia, the Upper Rhine and Hanover (14), the United States (11), Belgium (6), Switzerland (4) and possibly Canada (3): a total of sixty-seven. Direct appointment by the Papacy was probably confined to the Russian territories (11 dioceses), Greece (8) and Albania (5) — twenty-four dioceses in all. It would evidently have been impossible at that date to say that 'the Roman Pontiff nominates bishops without restriction'.

The Pressure of Events: 1829–1878

The fifteen-year reign of Gregory XVI (1831–46) made no material change in the situation. There are no Concordats to record. One feature of this pontificate was a marked acceleration in the erection of new dioceses in the New World and in the British possessions overseas: six in Latin America, ten in the United States, five in Canada and four in Australia. This was of importance for the future, rather than for the present; for the Sees in English-speaking areas were soon to be transferred to papal patronage and their proliferation added considerably to the spiritual power of the Holy See. The Australian hierarchy, founded in 1842, was the last to begin its life under the 'Irish' system of episcopal appointment.[30] More remarkable still was the erection of a new diocese in Switzerland with the provisions of Lateran II for the election of its bishops. The diocese was that of St. Gall, formed by separation from Chur. By a Convention of 1845, Gregory agreed that the bishop-elect must be a priest who had worked for a considerable time in the diocese; that he should be approved by the *Supremum Consilium Catholicum* of the Canton; and that he should be elected by the cathedral chapter.[31] Confidence in the ability of a local church to manage its own affairs could hardly have gone further. But this was the end of the line. No later Pope was to show respect for the decrees of Lateran II.

This was not the only line which was coming to an end. Pius IX, succeeding Gregory in 1846, was to be the last Pope to pin his faith on State patronage. Concordats came once more into fashion. The first of this series was made with the Tsar Nicholas I in 1847. It established an unusual form of patronage. New bishops in the Romanov territories were to be chosen conjointly by Pope and Tsar 'd'après un concert prealable'.[32] How this concert worked out over the 1,500 miles between the Vatican and St. Petersburg is not clear and the results were not entirely happy. Twenty years later three of the eleven bishoprics and fourteen of the twenty suffraganates were still vacant.[33] The next Concordat was made in 1851 with Bolivia, and provided a prototype for a whole series by which Pius IX attempted to bolster up the Church in Latin America. Church-State relations in this area were causing anxiety. When the Wars of Independence came to an end in 1822, the Presidents of the new republics had taken to themselves the *jus patronatus* previously held by the Spanish Crown, and had written this into their brand-new constitutions.[34] But by the middle of the century the first flush of enthusiasm had worn off, a succession of unstable governments had failed to cope with growing economic distress, and the Church began to appear in the role of scapegoat. The wealth of the Church — which in Mexico was said to amount to between two-thirds and three-quarters of the real wealth of the country — was an obvious target for criticism and in every republic there was resentment at the forcible collection of the ecclesiastical tithe. The response of Pius IX was uncompromising. He sought to perpetuate the privileges of the Church by Concordats which embodied the interdependence of Church and State in the most extreme form. That with Bolivia began with the statement that Roman Catholicism was the 'Religion of the Republic', went on to define ecclesiastical control over education and to specify the endowments of the Church, and then stated explicitly that in return for these benefits the President was given 'the patronage or privilege of presenting'.[35] The irony of such a Concordat was that Bolivia was precisely the type of country to reduce to absurdity the Pope's reliance on State patronage. In the century and a half that followed independence, it had a record total of two hundred and fifty revolutions, successful or unsuccessful;[36] and very soon after the Concordat it came under the rule of its most celebrated *Caudillo*, President Mariano Melgarejo (1861–71): described as 'cruel, crude and ignorant' — a drunkard, womanizer and public concubinary.[37] This was the man to whom the selection of his country's hierarchy had been entrusted at the time of Vatican I. The bankruptcy of the system should have been evident.

For all this, Pius IX was committed to his policy and pressed it home. Concordats in almost identical terms were concluded with Costa Rica and Guatemala in 1852, with Honduras and Nicaragua in 1861, and with San Salvador, Venezuela and Ecuador in 1862.[38] There was no Concordat with Mexico, but it seems possible that the Pope had a momentary hope of stabilizing Church-State relations in that troubled country under Hapsburg leadership. He was on good terms with the Hapsburgs and in 1855 had made a Concordat with Franz Josef which confirmed his Apostolic Privilege of electing all the eighty-two bishops of his vast dominions.[39] Seven years later the chance seemed to arise of seeing a Hapsburg on a Mexican throne. President Juarez' Constitution of 1857 had separated Church from State and confirmed previous decrees for the secularization of education and the confiscation of ecclesiastical property. Pius denounced these decrees as null and void, the customary civil war broke out, most of the bishops fled the country, and Mexico defaulted on its external debt. In 1862 a combined French, Spanish and British expedition sailed to Vera Cruz to enforce payment, and the French stayed on to install Franz Josef's brother Maximilian as Emperor of Mexico. How far the Pope supported this ill-fated enterprise is not clear, but he evidently counted on its success: in a Consistory of 16 March 1863, he announced a reconstruction of the Mexican hierarchy, with two new provinces and seven new dioceses. But Maximilian met his end before a firing squad at Querétaro on 19th June 1867 and there was to be no Hapsburgization of Latin America.

At almost the same time and on the very doorstep of the

Holy See, the logic of events was beginning to force the Papacy to overcome its long-standing reluctance to be bothered with the election of bishops. The story is simple. Cavour and Garibaldi between them gathered the patronage of the whole Italian peninsula into the hands of Italy's first king, and then dumped it on the Vatican. The growth-point lay in the Kingdom of Sardinia. The victory of Magenta in the early June of 1859 enabled the King to ride into an ecstatic Milan and add to his modest dominions the nine Lombard Sees which had previously been under the patronage of the Hapsburgs. Later in the same month, the battle of Solferino led to the plebiscites which added the Grand Duchy of Tuscany (with 22 Sees), the Duchy of Modena (with 5) and the Duchy of Parma (with 3) to the Kingdom of Sardinia. The next move lay with Garibaldi. The target was the Kingdom of the Two Sicilies, whose hierarchy of 113 dioceses was the largest in the world at that time. Garibaldi's Thousand freelanced their way through Sicily, crossed the Straits of Messina, occupied Naples, and in the October of 1860 the whole kingdom was annexed by plebiscite to Sardinia. On the same day the papal territories of the Marche and Umbria voted themselves likewise into the Sardinian kingdom. When Vittorio Emmanuele II was proclaimed King of Italy in the March of 1861, only the Patrimony of St. Peter and the Veneto remained to be absorbed. The Veneto fell bloodlessly in 1866 in consequence of an attempt by Franz Josef to persuade the Italians not to help the Prussians — who did not need their help anyway — in the Seven Weeks' War which ended at Königratz. The eleven Venetian Sees brought the total in Italian hands up to 167, and when the Piedmontese stormed through the Porta Pia in 1870 the whole of Italy, with its 237 dioceses, was in Victor Emmanuel's hands. No earthly king had ever been faced with so many bishops to elect.

Fortunately for the ultimate good of the Church, the Italian government was among the most liberal in Europe and had a profound aversion to bishop-nominating. The principle of 'a free Church in a free State', enunciated by

Cavour in the March of 1861, became the basis of the Law of Guarantees which the Italian Parliament offered to the Papacy in 1871. Pio Nono rejected it as a whole, but began, by what has been called an 'unspoken compromise', to operate that part of it which gave to the Holy See the appointment of all the bishops of Italy.[40] It is some measure of the unprecedented nature of this development that a new Commission of five Cardinals had to be created to cope with Italian appointments. The Holy See was as yet far from claiming a universal *jus patronatus*, but was at least becoming mentally conditioned to taking responsibility for appointments upon itself.

If the pressure of events was responsible for the transfer of patronage in Italy from Crown to Papacy, it was pressure of a different sort which did much to induce the Holy See to take to itself once for all the appointment of the English-speaking hierarchies which came under the jurisdiction of Propaganda. One of the puzzles in the history of episcopal nominations is that authors who deal with the subject speak of the selection of bishops in these areas being made at first locally, and then — although no significant change in ecclesiastical law can be found — speak of a transfer to the papacy of the right of nomination in the later years of the nineteenth century.[41] There was indeed no significant change in the law, but there was a change in the way the law was administered. A system of recommendation, such as had been introduced in the United States in 1820, could have whatever weight the Holy See cared to give it. Under Leo XII and Gregory XVI, who ignored recommendations only in exceptional circumstances, it became virtually equivalent to a right of nomination. By contrast, Pius IX could treat recommendations as no more than suggestions, to be ignored at will.

An important indication of how this administrative change came to pass can be found in the early history of the Australian hierarchy erected by Gregory XVI. The British government insisted that this hierarchy should be firmly English in character, and Propaganda could think of nothing more English than Downside, to which the Australian mission was therefore entrusted. The Abbot of Downside chose John Bede Polding, O.S.B., to be first bishop of Sydney, where he arrived in 1835. His see became metropolitan in 1842 and five more sees were added in the same decade. All the new bishops were appointed in accordance with Polding's recommendations.[42] But they represented a vision of a Benedictine Australia which was quickly to fade. The Catholic population was overwhelmingly Irish in origin; it wanted Irish priests, not English Benedictines; and these in turn wanted Irish bishops. They were soon to get what they wanted. What has been described as 'Irish ecclesiastical imperialism'[43] was at that time coming to its apogee. Cardinal Cullen in Dublin had an extraordinary influence on the Roman Curia. He listened to the woes of the Irish clergy in Australia and, using his paramount influence with the Holy See, from 1865 secured the rejection of Polding's nominees and the appointment of his own. As it is not unknown for the Holy Spirit to blow among the upper branches of family trees, it was no surprise to find that the next five bishops appointed to Australia were all relatives or personal friends of Cardinal Cullen.

This triumph of Dublin over Sydney recalls the success of the Irish lobby in the affairs of the American hierarchy in the later years of Pius VII. It seems evident that the centralization of power in Rome was at least accelerated by Irish influence; and without this centralization there could have been no 'Irish spiritual empire'. But Pius IX's own autocratic bent had a lot to do with it. 1865 was also the year in which he set aside the candidates chosen by the Westminster Chapter and substituted Manning. The hierarchy of England and Wales, erected in 1850, had agreed to the establishment of cathedral chapters — as the American hierarchy had not. Nevertheless the right of nomination was not conceded to the new chapters; they were given at most the right of recommendation. How much attention or inattention was subsequently to be paid to their recommendations would make an interesting study.

The Claim Asserted: 1878–1918

The pontificate of Leo XIII had the character of a water-shed in the Church's history. It was a gentle watershed, and at times it was difficult to predict which way the streams would flow. Leo could momentarily look back to the days of Pius IX, as when he allowed the President of Ecuador to retain the right of appointing bishops in a revised Concordat of 1881.[44] Three years later he was showing a respect for capitular rights in Switzerland that would have been appropriate to the days of Lateran II. The occasion for this was the necessity to replace a bishop at Basel. The Pope himself nominated a successor, but was at pains to reassure the Chapter that he would not use this as a precedent to abolish their rights.[43] On the other hand, there are two Latin American Concordats from this period which contain the first public assertions of the papal right to nominate. Guatemala had just emerged from an acute attack of anti-clericalism in which Church property had been sequestrated and sold. Leo made a new Concordat with this republic in 1884. Those who had bought Church property were to be left undisturbed in their possession of ill-gotten goods; but there was to be no right of nomination for the President as there had been in 1852. Provision for Guatemala's one and only See was to be made by the Pope *motu proprio*.[46] A Concordat with Colombia in 1884 made the claim in more explicit terms and in a formula which was to become common in the years that followed the Code: 'the right of nominating to vacant Archbishoprics and Bishoprics belongs to the Holy See'.[47]

But the most significant developments of this pontificate were taking place in France. The acquisition of patronage in Italy had provided a precedent for the take-over by the Papacy of the right of nomination in a country where it had previously been exercised by the Crown. But it was a limited precedent. Italy was on the papal doorstep, and no great mental adjustment was necessary when the Pope began to provide bishops for Gaeta in the old Kingdom of the Two Sicilies. It was only thirty-three miles up the road from Terracina in the Papal States, which had always got its bishops from Rome. Moreover the Pope was himself an Italian and the Primate of Italy. The choice of bishops had been at least kept within the family. It was a different matter to extend the papal *jus patronatus* to the Eldest Daughter of the Church north of the Alps. No one in 1870, with memories of Gallicanism behind him and French opposition to the Vatican decrees before him, could have foreseen that thirty-five years later the French would accept and positively welcome the appointment of their bishops by Rome.

That this came to pass was due to a series of events which were closely parallel with those in Italy in the previous period. The anti-clerical radicalism of Gambetta and Waldeck-Rousseau did as much to increase the spiritual influence of the Vatican as the liberalism of Cavour.[48] Under continual harassment from a government which penalized their schools, broke up their religious congregations, and finally sequestrated Church property, the French Catholics underwent a spectacular conversion to ultramontanism. Leadership was lacking, they were deeply divided among themselves, and in their distress they turned to Rome. Strong leadership could hardly have been expected of bishops who were paid officials of the State. However much 'irré-prochable dignité' might be locked in their bosoms, it needed considerable strength of mind to speak out of turn when, as happened in 1903 to the Archbishop of Besancon and the Bishops of Nice and Séez, the immediate penalty was the loss of salary and an end to any expectation of future promotion.[49] As to internal divisions, the main line of demarcation lay between those who clung nostalgically to monarchism as an Article of Faith, and those who were prepared to 'accept 'the Republic; but almost any issue could provide an excuse for further dissensions. Lacking leadership and unity within, the French Church sought to find it in the Pope. The newly defined Primacy provided a ready-made solution to all difficulties. The pre-1870 situation was exactly reversed: it was not now the Pope who was relying on the French to preserve the Temporàl Power — it was French Catholicism which was relying on the Pope in its struggle for survival.

A personal cult of Leo XIII arose. His Silver Jubilee in 1888 was celebrated with especial enthusiasm in France. Pilgrimages to Rome came into fashion and had an enormous vogue. Thanks to the initiative of Père Picard and the Augustinians of the Assumption, trainloads of pilgrims went off through the new tunnels under the Alps. Leo was consulted about anything and everything, from the Boulanger escapade to the vexed question of whether a law of penal taxation on the religious should be fought in the Chamber of Deputies or in the courts. In these, as in other cases, he told the French Catholics to make up their own minds. But even so he found it necessary to issue no fewer than five Encyclicals directed especially to France. His every word became law: 'Le pape nous demande d'accepter la République', wrote the Editor of *La Croix* on 25th May 1892, 'acceptons-la'. Ultramontanism reached its peak when the Abbé Perriot proclaimed in the *Ami du Clergé* that when the Pope asked the French to accept the Republic he was speaking infallibly *ex cathedra*.[50] Both Gambetta and Waldeck-Rousseau based their anti-clerical campaign on the charge that the French Catholics could not be good Frenchmen, because they took their orders, even in political matters, from abroad[51] — and the Catholics of France did their very best to justify the charge.

Leo XIII did not survive to see the outcome of the struggle. He died in 1903. Two years later, on 9th December 1905, the separation of Church and State in France became law, and the Napoleonic Concordat of 1801 was a thing of the past. From that moment Pius X took upon himself the responsibility of filling the Sees that fell vacant, and the French Catholics, mentally conditioned by their new-found ultramontanism, accepted this as the most natural thing in the world. When Portugal followed suit in 1911, separating Church from State after the abolition of the monarchy, Crown patronage in Europe was restricted to Spain, Austria-

Hungary, Bavaria, and (in collaboration with the Holy See) the territories of the Romanovs.

This was the historical background against which the Pontifical Commission for the Revision of Canon Law, set up by Pius X in 1904 by *Arduum sane munus*, began its work. There might have been no usable juridical precedents for a law on the appointment of bishops, but there was a good deal of hard fact. An estimate of the hierarchies subject to appointment by Rome on the eve of the Code shows just short of 700 dioceses involved — more than had existed in the whole Latin Church in 1829. The list of countries included Italy, Belgium, Holland, England, Scotland, Ireland, France, the U.S.A., Canada, Newfoundland, a minority of the Latin American Republics and Australia.[52] By contrast, Crown or State patronage was reduced to Austria-Hungary, Bavaria, Spain and some of the republics of South and Central America, totalling some 170 dioceses in all. The number of Sees where capitular election was the rule had dwindled to 18, all of them in Germany and Switzerland.

Exactly what went on in the minds of Cardinal Pietro Gasparri and his Commission when they drafted canon 329 may never be known in this world, but their canon was certainly a close enough expression of the factual situation of their time. Had they known it, a few more months would have made the approximation closer still. It would be improper for Providence to operate through worldly wars, but it still can manage to act in the oddest of ways. The timing of the Code was perfect. Benedict XV promulgated it on 27th May, 1917. The Romanovs had already disappeared, taking their 'concert' with them. But no one at that moment of the war would have been prepared to bet on the defeat of the Central Powers. The Code came into force on 19th May of the following year and, six months later, on the night of the 7–8 November, the Wittelsbachs abdicated, to be followed on the 11th by the last of the Hapsburgs. That was the end of Crown patronage in Central and Eastern Europe. Ludwig's Indult and Karl's Apostolic Privilege were left behind and no one thought it worth while to pick them up.

The republican governments who succeeded Kings and Emperors had little interest in Catholic bishops and no desire whatever to appoint them. There was a power vacuum, and canon 329 was ready to fill it. The claim of the papacy to nominate bishops without restriction had become a reality. No one in any case was likely to challenge that claim. Europe at that moment was too preoccupied with its ten million dead.

Canon 329 *Accepted*

No new legislation of such crucial importance to the Church can ever have been accepted with so little fuss and so complete an absence of demur. The Catholic mind was no doubt prepared for it. The Holy See had already acquired a widespread *jus patronatus*, if not in law, at least in practice. And it must have seemed to many, who had little opportunity to enquire into the meaning of the 'fullness of power' that Vatican I had attributed to the Pope, that Rome could take to itself whatever powers it wished. But there can be little doubt that — however far it was from the intention of Pietro Gasparri to carry out a *coup d'Eglise* — the timing of the Code had a lot to do with it. 1918 was not a good year for canonists and theologians. The aftermath of a Great War was no time to scrutinize a Code of Canon Law. The struggle for existence was all-absorbing: thought could come later, when bellies had been filled.

The new hierarchies which arose amid the ruins of the Hapsburg, Romanov and Hohenzollern dominions found the Holy See a welcome alternative to their former masters. With independence came also a numerical increase in strength. Poland has now a total of 26 Ordinaries, Jugoslavia 23, Czechoslovakia and Rumania 12 each, Austria 9 and Hungary 8. The pontificate of Pius XI (1922–39) brought a fresh rash of Concordats, and as most of these were concluded under the aegis of Gasparri as Secretary of State it was only to be expected that they should embody the new provisions of the Code. In three cases (Latvia in 1922, Czechoslovakia and Rumania in 1927), this was done by implication, in that the Papacy undertook to consult the relevant governments before making a definitive appointment.[53] In other cases the papal right to nominate was stated explicitly, the standard formula becoming 'appartient au Saint Siège' or 'steht dem Heiligen Stuhle zu' — as in the Concordats with Poland in 1925, Lithuania in 1927, Austria in 1933, and Ecuador in 1937.[54] The Concordat with Bavaria, made in 1933 while Eugenio Pacelli was Nuncio in Munich, gives the Holy See 'volle Freiheit' in its choice of bishops.[55]

The traditional rights of cathedral chapters in Prussia and the Upper Rhine might have proved a problem to the acceptance of the new legislation, but diplomacy found a way. Eugenio Pacelli, at that time Nuncio in Berlin, negotiated a revised Concordat with the Weimar State of Prussia in 1929. It produced a face-saving compromise by which the final say nominally remained with the cathedral chapters, while their freedom of choice was drastically restricted: the canons sent a list of candidates to Rome, but additions could be made to this by the Prussian hierarchy, and then the Holy See picked out three names from the entire list and sent these back to the relevant chapter for a final choice.[56] A similar Concordat for the Upper Rhine was made with Baden in 1932.[57] Much the same arrangement obtains, by virtue of the 1933 Concordat with Austria, in the diocese of Salzburg: the election of a new Archbishop remains nominally in the hands of the cathedral chapter, but the canons have to choose from a list of three selected by Rome.[58] Capitular election without restriction appears to survive in at least three of the Swiss dioceses and in the Czechoslovakian diocese of Olomouc.[59] This brings up to 18 the number of dioceses which retain some vestigial remains of the legislation of Lateran II.

Portugal, where the situation had been obscure since the Separation of Church and State in 1911, was brought completely into line with the new Code by a Concordat concluded in 1940.[60] A year later there was a new Concordat with Spain which modified the royal patronage in much the same way as capitular rights had been modified in Germany. The process of election begins with a list of six candidates chosen by the Nuncio in consultation with the government; from these the Pope selects three, and the final choice is left to the Head of State.[61] Oddly enough, the one party which might be supposed to have the deepest interest in episcopal elections — the Spanish Church itself — seems to have no legal standing in the process.

In the current year (1975) there are some 2,000 Ordinaries in the Latin Church.[62] Crown or State patronage operates in about 175 of these, all concentrated in Spain or six of the Latin-American republics. Capitular patronage, in a form which almost always reduces it to co-patronage with the Holy See, survives only in 18 dioceses of Central Europe. The *jus patronatus* of Rome now extends to the remaining 1,800 dioceses of the world as compared with 700 in 1917 and with 24 in 1829. This represents an enormous increase in what may be called the 'spiritual power' of the Papacy — its ability to ensure that local churches shall always conform, for good or for ill, to the thought and policies of the Vatican. Whether this system will endure is up to the Church to decide. The one hard fact to bear in mind is that canon 329 has no roots deeper than the historical circumstances of the late nineteenth century and the cogitations of the Commission which produced the Code in 1917. It is not an absolute. It is a child of its times. And times can change.

NOTES

1 Antonio Rosmini-Serbati, *Of the Five Wounds of the Church* (trans. H. P. Liddon), London, 1883, 133–298.
2 The *jus patronatus* could extend to other offices, but it was *par excellence* the right to designate bishops; and it is in this sense that the term is used in various Concordats. It is sometimes defined in legal texts as the right of 'naming, presenting, designating or electing' a new bishop; and it should be noted that the English word 'nominate' does not convey the full sense. The selected person was not one of several candidates, but the Bishop-elect.
3 For the purpose of the present study, only Ordinaries of the Latin Rite will be taken into consideration.
4 Canon 329 2.
5 *National Catholic Reporter*, 18th February 1972, 15.
6 Summarized in *The Clergy Review*, December 1972, 967–9.
7 *Dei Verbum*, 8.

8 *Lumen Gentium*, 27.
9 Rosmini, *op. cit.*, 167–8.
10 *Ibid.*, 143 n.1.
11 *Ibid.*, 296. The inclusion of 'England' is puzzling, for this country had no Ordinaries until two years after the book was published.
12 *Dictionnaire de Théologie Catholique*, S.VV. *Causes Majeures* (cols. 2039–42); *Election des Evêques* (col. 2270); *Réserves* (cols. 2441 & 2445).
13 Rosmini, *op. cit.*, 239.
14 Mercati, *Raccolta di Concordati*, Vatican Press, 1954, I, 562–3 (Arts. 4 and 5).
15 So Leo XIII in a conflict with the Italian government over the patronage of Chieti: Mourret, *Histoire de l'Eglise Catholique*, Paris 1924, Vol. IX, 25.
16 Mercati, *op. cit.*, I, 594 (Art. 9).
17 *Ibid.*, I, 634 (Art. XXVIII).
18 Mercati, *op. cit.*, I, 653; Bull *De Salute Animarum*.
19 *Ibid.*, I, 670: Bull *Provida Solersque*.
20 *Ibid.*, I, 701: Bull *Impensa Romanorum Pontificum Sollicitudo*.
21 So J. B. Sägmüller, *Lehrbuch des katholischen Kirchenrechts*, Bd. 1, Freiburg i. Breisgau, 1914, 3 Aufl. 335, who describes this as the 'irische Wahlmodus'. For the documentation of this statement he refers to H. Brück, *Das irisches Veto*, 1879. Stutz a.a. 0.50f., 168f.
22 Mercati, *op. cit.*, I, 705–6 (Art. III).
23 *Ibid.*, I, 713 (Art. 12).
24 *Bullarium . . . Editio Taurinensis*, Turin 1868, Tom. xiii, 585.
25 There is one notable instance in 1850 of the Pope refusing canonical institution to a man elected by a cathedral chapter. The canons of Mainz had elected Leopold Schmidt, Professor in the University of Giessen and suspected of indifferentism. Pius IX withheld institution. The chapter asked him to nominate a substitute and his choice fell on the great von Ketteler. The system worked.
26 The analysis which follows is based on Edward J. Ryan's contribution 'The Holy See and the Church in the United States', in L. J. Putz (ed.), *The Catholic Church, U.S.A.*, London, 1958. This in turn draws heavily on C. F. McCarthy's article 'The Historical Development of Episcopal Nominations in the Catholic Church of the United States (1784–1884)' in *Records of the American Catholic Historical Society*, 38:297–354.
27 Information on the nominations of the remaining two, Louis Dubourg of New Orleans in 1815 and Edward Fenwick of Cincinnati in 1822, has not been available to me.
28 Mercati, *op. cit.*, I, 538.
29 To achieve complete accuracy in these figures would require an excessive expenditure of time without substantially affecting the overall conclusion.
30 This is at least the implication of a statement by Sägmüller (*op. cit.*, 334 n. 6) that the Australian hierarchy came under papal patronage in 1866.
31 'Jus electionis novi episcopi penes Capitulum residet'; Mercati, *op. cit.*, I, 748 (Arts. 7 and 8).
32 Mercati, *op. cit.*, 755.
33 The vacancies are recorded in the *Annuario Pontificio* for 1867. The standing of the mysterious suffraganates is not clear. They appear to have been auxiliary bishoprics with local titles taken from Poland and Russia instead of from the parts of the infidel.
34 Thus in the constitutions of Colombia (1824) and Venezuela (1830). In Brazil the former rights of the Portuguese Crown were taken over by the Emperor; not that this meant very much, for Brazil was so undeveloped in 1822 that it had only one bishop.
35 The Latin text, fuller than the Spanish, reads: 'jus patronatus, seu privilegium designandi seu praesentandi'; Mercati, *op. cit.*, I, Suppl. 5.

36 The calculation was made in 1971 by W. Carter, *Bolivia—A Profile*, London, 1971, 39.

37 W. Carter, *op. cit.*, 44–5.

38 In all of these it is the 7th Article which covers the right to nominate bishops: Mercati, *op. cit.*, I, 802 (Costa Rica); 814 (Guatemala); 937 (Honduras); 951 (Nicaragua); 962–3 (San Salvador); 973 (Venezuela); 951 (Ecuador). Haiti's President also got the right to nominate bishops by a Concordat of 1860 (*op. cit.*, I, 930), but the five proposed Sees were still vacant in 1867.

39 So Mourret, *op. cit.*, IX, 18. The requirement of a royal *exsequatur* was satisfied by posting up Bulls of Nomination in obscure cathedral sacristies for the King to look at if he ever wanted to: thereby showing that the Holy See was as expert as any English University in 'deeming' to be true that which is not.

40 Mercati, *op. cit.*, I, 825.

41 Thus Sägmüller, *op. cit.*, p. 334 and n.6., states without explanation that the Holy See exercised *libera collatio* in Australia only from 1866.

42 The statement of P. O'Farrell, *The Catholic Church in Australia*, London, 1969; p. 57, that Polding 'appointed' them all is an evident terminological inexactitude.

43 The phrase is O'Farrell's, *op. cit.*, p. 133. It is not unjustified, for Cardinal Moran of Sydney could speak of an 'Irish spiritual empire'; *ibid.*, p. 135.

44 Mercati, *op. cit.*, I, 1007 (Art. XII).

45 *Ibid.*, I, 1028 (Art. 2).

46 *Ibid.*, I, 1019 (Clause 7).

47 *Ibid.*, I, 1055; in the Spanish text: 'el derecho de nombrar . . . corresponde a la Santa Sede'; in the Latin: 'Jus Archiepiscopos et Episcopos . . . constituendi est Sanctae Sedi proprium et peculiare' (Art. 15).

48 What Montalembert said about the French Revolution at the Malines Congress of 1863 could equally well have been said about the *Risorgimento* and about French radicalism: 'You made the revolution of 1789 without us and against us, but *for us*, God wishing it so in spite of you'. The Vatican has often been slow to recognize its true friends: Cavour never became a Knight of St. Gregory and no medal *Bene Merenti* was ever pinned on Garibaldi's red shirt.

49 The 'irreproachable worthiness' is Mourret's judgment (*op. cit*)., IX, 83) on the nineteen bishops appointed 1875–92 while Mgr. Czacki was Nuncio in Paris — making the point that State patronage did not work out all that badly. The three bishops got into trouble by organizing a petition against the Law of Associations (*op. cit.*, IX, 186).

50 Mourret, *op. cit.*, IX, III.

51 So Gambetta, in his Romans speech of 1878, attacking the 'milice multicolore, dont la patrie ne repose plus que sur la dernière des sept collines de Rome' (Mourret, *op. cit.*, IX, 59). But this was how the French were thinking of themselves. Mourret, publishing in 1924, seemed to find nothing objectionable in Waldeck-Rousseau's description of the Church as, 'une société d'hommes dont le siège et la direction sont fixés à l'étranger, puisque son siège est à Rome et que son chef est le pape' (*op. cit.*, IX, 160).

52 Sägmüller, *op. cit.*, 333–4. He includes Portugal among countries where nominations were made by the Crown, but cancels this in a footnote(333, n. 5) to the effect that this right could not be exercised since the separation of Church from State in 1911. New Zealand should be added to the list of countries wherein episcopal appointments were made by the Pope.

53 Schöppe, *Konkordate seit 1800*, Frankfurt am Main/Berlin, 1964, 292 (Art. XI: for Latvia); 377 (Art. V: for Rumania); 501 (Art. IV: for Czechoslovakia).

54 *Ibid.*, 322 (Art. XI: for Poland); 284 (Art. IV: for Lithuania); 304 (Art. IV: for Austria); 88 (Art. 1: for Ecuador — the Spanish formula being 'Corresponde a la Santa Sede la eleccion de Obispos').

55 *Ibid.*, 49.

56 *Ibid.*, 65 (Art. 6).

57 *Ibid.*, 39 (Art. III).

58 *Ibid.*, 304 (Art. IV). There is the further anomaly in Austria that the nomination of bishops for Seckau (Graz) and Gurk (Klagenfurt) are nominated by their metropolitan, the Archbishop of Salzburg (Eichmann-Mörsdorf, *Lehrbuch des Kirchenrechts*, Bd. 1, Paderborn 1953, 5 Aufl., 399).

59 Eichmann-Mörsdorf, *op. cit.*, 399. The Swiss Sees he names are Basel, Chur and St. Gall.

60 Schöppe, *op. cit.*, 360 (Art. X).

61 *Ibid.*, 441. This Concordat was confirmed in 1853 (*ibid.*, 483). For the Concordat which conceded the 'patronato regio' to Ferdinand VI in 1753, cf. Mercati, *op. cit.*, I, 425 (Clause 5).

62 The *Annuario Pontificio* for 1975 gives 2,219 for the total of 'Residential Sees' in the whole world, but from these the Uniats must be deducted. It also lists 1,980 Titular Sees, of which no account has been taken in this study.

10

St Edmund's House: an embodiment

Garrett Sweeney

On 20th March 1973 a body representative of the Catholic
Church in this country did something rather uncharacter-
istic of the church which it represented. It signed away
assets of considerable value in Cambridge and handed them
over for the establishment of a small postgraduate College in
the University. More precisely: the legal Association known
as St. Edmund's House, clerically-dominated and clerically-
orientated, dissolved itself and handed over its property and
funds to a new Association for the general purposes of promoting education, learning, religion and research in the
manner appropriate to a Cambridge College. The judgement of posterity can sometimes be capricious in its appreciation of surprising acts of self-denial. Lest St. Edmund's
House be given the treatment that Dante gave to Celestine
V's *gran rifiuto*, some attempt must be made to leave for
posterity an account and explanation of what happened.

The beginning of the story dates to 23rd April, 1896. On
that day the community of students known as St. Edmund's
House took up residence in Cambridge. On 2nd November
of the same year it moved to the present site on Mount
Pleasant. Its status in the University was at that time as low
as it possibly could be — a lodging house operating under

licence from the Lodging Houses Syndicate. It compensated for its lowly status by inordinate ambition. This was the precipitate of the very varied motivation of the three men who had done most to promote the venture. The 15th Duke of Norfolk, who provided the funds, had begun with a simple desire to overcome the disabilities (imposed formerly by the State, latterly by the Church) which prevented Catholic students from reading for Cambridge degrees; he ended by trying to establish a Catholic College with the status accorded at the present day to an Approved Foundation. Bernard Ward, President of St. Edmund's College, Ware, provided the students. What he wanted was the affiliation of his own college to the University, with a branch house in Cambridge where his men could keep their last six terms before graduation. Anatole von Hügel, younger brother of the better-known Friedrich and Curator of the Museum of Ethnology and Archaeology, provided expertise in University legalities and procedures and added some hopeful dreams. He had begun by trying to establish a Catholic chaplaincy and ended up with some vision that St. Edmund's House might be to England what the Parisian *Institut Catholique* was to France.

Inordinate ambition had an early setback. On 12th May 1898 the Senate rejected by 463 votes to 218 a grace for the recognition of the House as a Public Hostel. But enough sympathy and support had emerged during the preceding discussions to keep hope alive. For the next twenty-eight years St. Edmund's continued to operate under licence from the Lodging Houses Syndicate while at the same time leading an embryonic collegiate life. Its constitution had been constructed on lines suitable for a Public Hostel and enjoined it to seek that status; its Head was known as Master; its students developed their own para-collegiate organizations; their numbers grew slowly but in due time exceeded the limit allowable for a lodging-house. When this point was reached, the House achieved a modest enhancement of status within the newly-invented category of House of Residence. This brought it out of the purview of the Lodging Houses Syndicate, but gave it no other powers than that of enabling students to keep term. By the close of the Mastership of John Petit (1934–46) some twenty years later, St. Edmund's had at least the makings of a college: the buildings had been doubled and the number of students was approaching forty. The Master felt that the time had come to revive the attempt to secure recognition as an Approved Foundation. He calculated that there were, usually dotted about Cambridge in small houses, about a hundred Catholic clergy and religious, male and female. He planned to gather them all under the aegis of St. Edmund's House, make provision for tutorial care and supervision and seek collegiate status. But there were no ecclesiastical takers and the project of 1946 was still-born. The urge nevertheless remained. It was insistent and within the next two decades was to find at least the beginnings of satisfaction.

Twelve years later and in very different circumstances, thoughts of seeking recognition came again to the surface. John Petit's proposals had in one respect been well ahead of their time: they would have made St. Edmund's House the first mixed College in Cambridge. But in other respects they had been hardly of a kind that could have won support in the Council of the Senate. The time for exclusively clerical establishments under tight episcopal control had gone. The atmosphere which had produced his plan was rapidly dissipated during the long Mastership of Raymond Corboy (1946–64). Student numbers rose to fifty; laymen were admitted in significant numbers; more building was undertaken; the atmosphere of the House became open and expansive. The line of development was contemporary and congruent with a Catholic academic movement of the mid-fifties which gave it further force and direction.

This movement, as shall later be noted, had its roots in the history of the early nineteenth century. Its manifestations were irregular but recurrent: often frustrated and sometimes successful. One such manifestation appeared in 1958. A group of Catholics teaching in the English Universities used the summer issue of the *Dublin Review* in that year as a symposium of dissatisfaction. The general theme was that the

Catholic Church in this country had a need for exact scholarship and higher learning; had an obligation to promote it; and, in proportion to its numerical strength and material resources, was failing to do so. The contribution of Dom David Knowles from Cambridge thus summarized the situation: 'it can scarcely be in doubt that Catholics today in England make a poorer show in scholarship and in the academic world than they do in almost any other activity of educated men'; and he applied this particularly to the clergy. These feelings were shared and voiced by other men of weight and distinction: Professors Beales and Parker of London and Armstrong of Liverpool; also in ecclesiastical circles by Abbot Christopher Butler of Downside and Archbishop Beck of Liverpool. (They had been shared, too, by Lamennais and Rosmini early in the nineteenth century, by Newman and the *Rambler* circle in the middle, and by the modernists at the end.) This weight of opinion led to action. A Catholic Conference on Higher Education was held at Strawberry Hill, Twickenham, in the September of 1958. Archbishop Beck delivered an inaugural address which brought matters to a head: 'I wonder whether, in fact, we can help to put matters right unless we have somewhere in the country, somewhere in our educational system, a Catholic Institute of Higher Studies. The ideals we talk about, the atmosphere we wish to cultivate, will remain disembodied and nebulous unless they can be housed and localized, given a body in which to exist and act.' The concept of 'embodiment' was to be basic in the further development of St. Edmund's House, towards which the Archbishop's speech might have been thought to be pointing an invisible finger.

The Conference took up the idea of a Catholic Institute and forwarded it for consideration by the hierarchy at its October meeting of the same year. The bishops received the proposal favourably and agreed that an Institute should be formed and based on St. Edmund's House. Through their influence, an anonymous benefactor came forward and placed in the hands of the Cardinal of Westminster enough money to fund two or three initial Fellowships. In the July of 1960 a Committee in Cambridge set to work on a legal constitution for the project. Its first thought was to gain for the Institute the standing and facilities which it needed by incorporating it in the House and then, with this added academic weight, seek recognition as an Approved Foundation. But this first thought had to be abandoned after a preliminary conversation with the Registrary left no immediate hope that recognition would be granted. The work of the Committee then entered on a period of protracted negotiations which it would be tedious to narrate. To put it briefly, the Committee advocated the establishment of a new and autonomous Governing Body formed from men of sufficient academic distinction to give the Institute the standing it needed in the University. As against this, most of the hierarchy insisted that the Institute should operate under the existing Governing Body, which had not been selected on grounds of academic distinction. The two points of view proved irreconcilable, the hierarchy held the funds, and in the March of 1964 the newly-appointed Archbishop of Westminster announced that the proposed Institute would not be established in Cambridge.

The whole incident was disappointing, but not fruitless. It had revived once more the feeling that the House could not always be content to be a passive recipient of the University's teaching and was destined itself to take an active part in the world of learning. It had also revived a conscious urge to seek collegiate status and revealed the weaknesses in the constitution of the House. It was at this propitious moment that a change in the Statutes of the University enabled St. Edmund's to gain some satisfaction for its long-standing ambitions.

The change in Statutes was designed to meet a situation created by the rapid expansion of the University in the aftermath of the Second World War. The existing Colleges could no longer provide a congenial environment for the increased number of postgraduate students, and the number of Teaching Officers far exceeded the Fellowships available. The Bridges Report of 1962 suggested a remedy. It recommended the establishment of new colleges and societies for postgraduates. The Council of the Senate worked on this Report and came up with a recommendation that the University should recognize a new category of collegiate institution to be called an Approved Society. This differed from an Approved Foundation in that its recognition could be withdrawn by the Senate without the necessity for a long and complicated legal process. The category was admittedly experimental. It seemed tailor-made for St. Edmund's House. Even before the necessary amendment to Statutes had become law, the Governing Body had successfully applied for provisional recognition as an Approved Society. The amendment was approved by the Queen in Council on 29th January, 1965. From that date the House was empowered to matriculate and present for degrees its own postgraduate students — an enablement which was subsequently widened to include certain categories of undergraduates. It had crossed the magic line between collegiate and non-collegiate status.

At this level St. Edmund's House was to function for the next ten years. It organized itself with the necessary College Officers, elected some twenty Fellows, augmented its buildings and brought student numbers up to sixty. In short, it made a modest but genuine contribution to the solution of those problems of University life which had been considered in the Bridges Report. It was growing, and in consequence it had growing pains. These should be seen in the light of the remarks, quoted above, of Archbishop Beck at the 1958 Conference of Higher Studies. The move to collegiate status had been driven on by the conscious need of academically-minded Catholics in this country to house, localize and give body to their ideals. The drive had not yet been exhausted. Embodiment, if it is to be effective, must be permanent and secure. An Approved Society had no guarantee of permanence and no final security. Its status was admittedly experimental and revocable. It was asking a lot of Fellows that they should commit their fortunes to an institution which lacked legal permanence; and it was asking the impossible to expect anyone to donate the funds necessary for the development of the House if it was liable to come to an untimely end. These were disadvantages inherent in the very nature of an Approved Society. There was the further disadvantage in the particular case of St. Edmund's House that its 1897 constitution was a very old wineskin and its collegiate existence a very new and heady wine. If only on the grounds of remoteness, its Governing Body was incapable of taking the frequent and urgent decisions needed by a Cambridge college.

After some four years' experience of operating as an Approved Society, the Master and Fellows came to the conclusion that the House could make no progress, and indeed could hardly continue to exist, unless it took a further step forward and attempted to achieve recognition as an Approved Foundation. In practice, this meant amending the Memorandum and Articles of Association which made up the constitution of 1897. The basic need was for a Governing Body which would both safeguard the Catholic purposes of the foundation and at the same time have academic standing with the University. Negotiations to this effect lasted from the summer of 1969 to the spring of 1973. At last, on 23 March 1973, an Extraordinary Meeting of the Association accepted a new constitution which had already been passed by the Council of the Senate as suitable for an Approved Foundation. The essence of the new formula was that the Governing Body should be an Association so composed that at one and the same time a majority of its members would be drawn from the Senate of the University, and no less a majority would represent the interests of the Catholic Church. After allowing a year to test the practical working of the amended constitution, application was made for recognition as an Approved Foundation. There was no opposition. At noon on 8th March 1975, St. Edmund's house achieved the status for which it had been founded seventy-eight years before.

So much for the story of what happened.[1] It remains to explain why it happened. What was it that justified the foundation of a Catholic-related postgraduate College in Cambridge with funds which the Church desperately needed for purposes which might have appeared more practical and down-to-earth?

Anyone who has the leisure and patience to read through the bulky files in the archives of St. Edmund's House which record the negotiations will find that initially the Master and Fellows based their case on the classical principle that an institution which neglects the chance to go forward will inevitably go back; and that, in this particular case, it would have been impossible to halt retrogression this side of extinction. The argument was pragmatic. But the long period of negotiation gave time for deeper considerations to become formed and conscious. It is at this deeper level that one must look for the motivation of those who stuck doggedly to the task of bringing St. Edmund's House once for all into the University. Their motives found articulate expression only rarely in the minutes and papers of the various negotiating committees. Motivation was most often a matter of aspirations and hopeful dreams, the realization of which could be predicted only by a gambler's calculation of the odds. This was not the stuff to make a debating point among hard-headed men. The proceedings of committees turned largely on legalities and practicalities. From time to time there was a parting in the sea of words, and a momentary glimpse given of the aspirations which flowed underneath — seen at least long enough to find some mention in the written records. Thus there can be found a documented desire for an end to the isolationist spirit that had characterized the Church of the nineteenth century, and for the collaboration of Catholics and non-Catholics in the common project of a University College; also to make an act of confidence that the laity were competent and committed enough to maintain the Catholic character of the House without clerical supervision. Then, as the exigencies of debate forced the House to look into its own past, there was added a strong current of historical sense. The question of St. Edmund's House was seen as one particular instance of a general problem that for nearly two centuries had faced the Catholic Church both in England and on the Continent and was recurrent in its history: whether or not it needed to take up a vested interest in university life and on what terms it could do so. In the light of this historical consciousness the re-foundation of St. Edmund's House took on a significance greater than that of a private enterprise undertaken by a group of Cambridge dons and academically-minded bishops. It brought the whole question into the context of a wider academic movement of European Catholicism, convinced of the Church's need for exact scholarship and higher learning, and seeking constantly to embody its aspirations in diverse institutional forms appropriate to each country's university system. Only in this context can the final development of St. Edmund's House be fully understood.

This continental movement had arisen from a situation created by the French Revolution. Until its outbreak, universities had been an integral part of the life of the Church in those countries which remained in communion with the See of Rome. Their character was as Catholic as anything could be at that time. They were an accepted fact of the ecclesiastical scene. Canon Law presumed that they existed and were readily available: thus Urban VIII's Instruction of 1627 required that a bishop-elect should have a university degree or some equivalent. After the Revolution and the subsequent Napoleonic reforms the Church could no longer take universities for granted. On the French-speaking continent and in part of the Germanic world they had lost their Catholic character. How profoundly this loss affected the whole development of ecclesiastical history was realized only gradually. Newman saw it quite clearly by the middle of the century: 'This age of the Church is peculiar, — in former times, primitive or medieval, there was not the extreme centralization which now is in use. If a private theologian said anything free, another answered him. If the controversy grew, then it went to a Bishop, a theological faculty, or to some foreign University. The Holy See was but the court of ultimate appeal. Now, if I, as a private priest, put anything into print, Propaganda answers me at once. How can I fight with such a chain on my arm? It is like the Persians driven to fight under the lash. There was a true private judgement in the primitive and medieval schools, — there are no schools now, no private judgement (in the religious sense of the phrase), no freedom, that is, of opinion. That is, no exercise of the intellect. No, the system goes on by the tradition of the intellect of former times.'[2]

Recovery began in Germany. It took the form of specifically Catholic Faculties of which the first was established at Tübingen in 1817. Münster, which had ceased to be an ecclesiastical state in 1803, gained a Catholic Faculty of Theology in 1818; another was established at Giessen in 1830. Thus, as Munich had never lost its Catholic character, the German-speaking Church — even without the Austro-Hungarian Empire — had four university institutions to service its needs. Three of these moreover had the stimulating experience of living in co-existence with Protestant Faculties. The result was impressive. Tübingen alone produced Drey, Möhler, Hefele and Funk, and Döllinger could gather a hundred theologians of distinction to his Munich Congress in 1863.

Conditions in France were very different. The Napoleonic system of an all-embracing State University had survived the Bourbon Restoration. Within this system there was no way of giving 'body' to any Catholic intellectual revival — no room for any institution comparable to the Catholic Faculties of Germany or to Belgium's University of Louvain, soon to be restored. Revival was slow in coming. Its initial impetus seems to have come from three events of 1830: the July Revolution, the Belgian movement of Independence, and the appearance of *l'Avenir*. The abdication of Charles X was a moment of truth for the Gallican-minded hierarchy of France. Bourbon patronage was no longer a possible option. If there were to be any Bossuets and Fénelons in the future, the Catholics of France would have to produce them without any help from the State and its University. At the same moment Catholics had joined forces with Liberals in Belgium

to secure the liberation of their country from Dutch hegemony, and the lesson was not lost on the French: much in
the Liberal programme could be absorbed into the life of
the Church, and educational freedom was part of it. Belgium
independence moreover brought in its train a bonus that
could be thought exemplary. In the December of 1833 the
University of Louvain, suppressed by the Revolutionary
armies in 1794, once again opened its doors. It was a Catholic
University, assisted indeed by a Liberal government, but
nevertheless independent. The Belgian Church had found
its own way to embody its intellectual aspirations. Louvain
rapidly recovered its international reputation in the world of
learning; it was hardly a coincidence that at the same time
its clergy became recognized as second to none in respect of
educational standing, numerical strength and missionary
zeal.

In France itself many trains of thought were set off by
Lamennais' periodical, *l'Avenir*. The condemnation of its
Liberal Catholic ideals by the Encyclical *Mirari Vos* of 1832
delayed their authoritative acceptance for more than a
century but failed to stem their propagation and their
effectiveness on the life of the Church. Lamennais realized
early that his work depended upon an intellectual revival
which could hardly be expected at the seminary level of
clerical education: 'Everything has changed around you;
ideas have taken and continue to take new directions;
institutions, laws, morals, opinions, nothing resembles what
our fathers saw. Of what use is the most intense zeal without
knowledge of the society in whose midst it must perform. We
must learn with another method and learn more; with
another method, to understand better, in order not to fall
behind those for whose guidance we are responsible.'[3] This
was written in 1829. A year later Gerbet was inspired in the
pages of *l'Avenir* with a vision of France's Catholic intellectuals leading Europe along the road of progress while the
Papacy kept it firm in faith.[4] The vision was to endure.
Lacordaire, who had collaborated with Lamennais before
the condemnation, made it his own in 1841 in a conference

which he preached in Notre Dame on the Vocation of the French Nation. The immediate effect of this was to inspire a group of young men with so great an enthusiasm for higher learning that they went off to Lyon and founded an *Institut Catholique*. Weak though this was to remain for many years, it was nevertheless a first attempt to find a practical embodiment for the intellectual aspirations of Catholic France. If the State University system left no room for Catholic Faculties as in Germany, or for a Catholic University as in Belgium, there was nothing for the French to do except found an independent Institute and hope that at some future date it might find its way into the full pattern of university life.

Three decades later this came to pass. In the July of 1875 a revision of the educational laws made possible the establishment of private universities. Before the end of the year there were Catholic Universities at Angers, Lille and Lyon; Paris followed in 1876. These were genuine *studia generalia*. They each began with Faculties in Law, Letters and the Natural Sciences. Theology and the Sacred Sciences came later. Although their right to use the title of University and grant their own degrees was taken away from them by the law of 1880, they had come to stay. They had acquired teaching officers and students, they had proved themselves capable of teaching to university level, and the Church had invested money in them. The intellectual movement of French Catholicism had found a 'body' which needed care and nurture and the hierarchy of the country had made a commitment to the academic life which it could hardly fail to honour. It mattered little that after 1880 the title of University had to be given up. Paris and Lyon carried on as Catholic Institutes, Lille as a Catholic Faculty, and Angers ultimately recovered the title of Catholic University of the West. The work was carried on, even though degrees had to be obtained by State examinations. There was one weakness in this French form of the embodiment of academic ideals. These para-Universities were under immediate episcopal control, and each was governed by the bishops of the region it was intended to serve. Had they been autonomous the history of the modernist crisis might have been far different. It needed a man from an English University to see this: 'It is no doubt the case that some of the modernists were too much under the spell of current (evolutionary, immanentist, or pragmatic) fashions of thought and, when driven to extremes by oppressive measures, advocated ideas that would be difficult, if not impossible, to reconcile with historic Christianity, but this was after they had been made more or less desperate by the Church's refusal to look in the face the questions they had raised. It is an unwarranted assumption that they would have gone to such lengths if they had been treated by the authorities with respect and understanding.'[5] But there was to be no respect for Loisy and no understanding: the *Institut Catholique* could not provide him with the temperate 'free air' that Hans Küng was to find in Tübingen. The matter went on both sides to extremes that would have been impossible in an autonomous university.

While the French Catholics were founding their own universities, Cardinal Manning was opening his University College in Kensington.[6] This may appear at first sight to be an event of profound insignificance in the academic history of Europe. In itself it was: it never attracted more than sixteen students and after its brief existence of seven years it ended in bankruptcy. It was in no sense an attempt to satisfy a strong need for higher education felt by English Catholicism and its motivation was in fact precisely the opposite. What Manning wanted was to head his flock away from the universities in general and from Oxford in particular. If the College at Kensington has any significance whatever it is by way of reaction. That it had to be established at all was a side-effect of the need for academic progress that English Catholics felt as much as their continental brethren and its failure showed that this need could not be satisfied in the way of Manning's choice.

The year 1848 is memorable for various reasons. In the Catholic history of England it is to be remembered for the first appearance of the *Rambler*, a periodical intended by

John More Capes, its first editor, to be 'an organ of lay converts'.[7] It was to be more than that. Richard Simpson, who became editor in 1858, believed that his periodical was the heir to an indigenous tradition of scholarship and that it recommended itself 'to the remnants of the old parties of Lingard and Milner who had education enough to follow the advance of knowledge among Catholics abroad and Protestants at Home . . .'.[8] To these two academic streams flowing from the old Catholics and the new Oxford converts there was added a third when the young John Acton joined Simpson as assistant editor in 1858. He had studied under Döllinger during the years 1850–57 and could thus connect the *Rambler* up with the intellectual movement of continental Europe. Thus the *Rambler* became a focal point in an English movement 'to re-habilitate Catholic thought in a non-Catholic world'.[9]

Simpson himself also had links with the continental movement. Montalembert had taken over the direction of *Le Correspondant* in 1855 and four years later Simpson wrote for him a contribution which shows that he shared Newman's dissatisfaction with clerical learning and his belief that the rot had set in with the Revolution: 'our priests brought back a tone and a manner which savoured of the salons of the Faubourg St. Germain and an intelligence that might recall Bossuet and Fénelon. They were independent gentlemen . . . The strength which then mainly consisted in the force of individuals must now be sought in discipline and organization; a clergy of a different calibre, of different education and different origins must make up for individual want of weight by corporate union, by unquestioning obedience to absolute direction and by administrative unity.'[10] Newman himself took no part in the direction of the *Rambler* until he reluctantly accepted the editorship in 1859. It would be otiose to labour the point that he shared its views on academic distinction as an integral need of the Church. Let it suffice to quote a fine appreciation of his ideals from the recent editor of one of his major essays: 'Newman's abiding vision was that, in the dark days that were approaching and

have now inevitably come upon us, the fullness of the
Catholic idea demanded that the intellectual layman become
religious and the devout ecclesiastic intellectual. He had
hoped that it was his vocation to bring about the means by
which this might be achieved — by his University, his school,
his house at Oxford, and his support for the work of the
Rambler. But it was not to be so. His was that greater vocation still: to witness, by the way he met and mastered the
indifference, hostility, persecution and tardy recognition of
his Catholic life to the very embodiment of that ideal he had
devoted his life to foster: the practice of the saintly intellect'.[11]

In 1864 the ideals for which the *Rambler* had stood came
up against the English hierarchy and — administratively
and in practice, if not in principle and in theory — were
rejected. At their Low Week Meeting of that year, the
bishops resolved that parents should be discouraged from
sending their sons to Oxford or to Cambridge. Even so, this
resolution needs to be glossed. Both Wiseman and Ullathorne (then Bishop of Birmingham and second only to the
Cardinal in influence and reputation) seem to have been
ambiguous in their attitudes. Each of them at various times
was to be in serious conflict with the *Rambler*. But Wiseman,
if the first biographer of his successor is to be believed, had a
basic sympathy with its ideals: 'No one knew better than he
did how grievous was the loss suffered by English Catholics
from the want of University education. They were everywhere placed at a disadvantage in the race for life. Their
intellectual inferiority as a necessary result of the lack of
higher training was a reproach to the Catholic Church. It
was more and worse: it was a danger to Faith; for in the
higher walks of literature, in philosophy, in science Catholics
occupied a lower intellectual ground . . . That Catholics, in
that day of abounding grace, when so many of the noblest of
the sons of Oxford were returning to the Church, should be
trained once more in the Universities raised by their forefathers, was to Cardinal Wiseman like the beginning of the
fulfilment of the desire or dream of his heart. The proposal
to found a hall or college at Oxford, under exclusively

Catholic management, enlisted at first Cardinal Wiseman's warmest sympathy.'[12] As far as sympathy went, Wiseman was not alone. Ullathorne had shown his sympathy with a return to Oxford in his correspondence over Newman's purchase of a site near Worcester College in 1864 and the proposal to establish an Oxford Oratory; and 'many of the bishops were known to be in favour of Catholics going to Oxford and Cambridge; unless as a necessary alternative a Catholic University was founded.'[13] As the bishops present at the Low Week Meeting were unanimous in declaring that a Catholic University was impracticable, this could only mean that they were quite simply in favour.

Such sympathy as there was could not stand up to Manning's hard line and determination. He was at this time Provost of the Westminster Chapter and dominant over the failing Wiseman. Through his Archbishop he was able to persuade the hierarchy to give up dreams of a Catholic presence in the historic universities of England. But he was able to persuade them only by assuring them that a Catholic University was about to be founded as an alternative. Ten years later, now Archbishop of Westminster and clear of the labours and anxieties of the Vatican Council, he could at last honour the pledge he had given in 1864. The University College at Kensington was the result. Various reasons have been given for its rapid failure — the inadequacy of its Rector, the failure to enlist the services of Newman, the exclusion of the Jesuits. But it also ran counter to the principle that a Catholic academic movement can only embody itself in the form of University life appropriate to the country in which it finds itself. An English University and its Colleges must be autonomous. The College at Kensington was not. In *Anglican Difficulties* Newman had written: 'it is the property of life to be impatient of any foreign substance in the body to which it belongs.'[14] Manning's College was a foreign substance. It could not fail to be extruded from the English academic scene.

St. Edmund's House has perhaps a valid claim to be the outcome of those same forces which on the Continent had

produced Catholic Faculties, Universities and Institutes of
repute. It was nevertheless an outcome with a difference. A
Cambridge College can indeed be a suitable embodiment for
the academic aspirations of English Catholicism but it must
also have a degree of autonomy enjoyed only imperfectly by
some of its continental counterparts. Therein lay the rub.
The value of autonomy is not easily grasped in ecclesiastical
circles. That it was finally found acceptable is to be explained not only by the need to conform to the traditions of the
universities of this country, but also by the peculiar logic of
English Catholic history. Parallel movements on the
Continent had never had to face such a barrier against
intellectual development as Manning had erected in
England. His episcopate of twenty-seven years had been long
enough to mould his bishops, clergy and people into a shape
which was his own and not that of Newman or indeed of
Wiseman. That shape was magnificently pastoral and
practical. It was therefore not so much anti-intellectual as
un-intellectual: the Catholic poor for whom he lived and
worked had little use for Wiseman's *Horae Syriacae* and neither
had he. It was long before this barrier broke down and when
it did so there had grown up a desperate desire for some
indication, if not a guarantee, that it would never be re-
erected. A generation, not unbelieving and certainly not
unhopeful, looked for a sign that the Church in this country
was prepared to pledge its resources, personnel and reputation to the cause of academic progress. The possibility of
re-founding St. Edmund's House as an autonomous College
came opportunely to provide such a sign, and the sign was
given.

This account of the genesis of St. Edmund's House as a
College in the University of Cambridge has kept reasonably
within the bounds of history. It has tried to show why certain
men acted in a certain way. Whether they were right or
wrong in their persistence is for the theologian rather than
the historian to discuss. Is a vested interest in university life
integral to the Catholic idea? Some indications towards an
answer have emerged in the course of the historical narrative

— Newman's need for the free 'exercise of the intellect' and the comments of Mignot and Vidler on the possible outcome of the modernist crisis if only authority had reacted less sharply; if justified, these suggest that universities have at least the virtue of providing somewhere where fools can be suffered gladly. In general, the indications point to a theory of balance on lines developed by Newman in his Preface to the third edition of the *Via Media*. From the threefold office of Christ as Priest, Prophet and King, it follows that Christianity must be 'at once a philosophy, a political power and a religious rite . . . As a religion, its special seat is pastor and flock; as a philosophy, the Schools; as a rule, the Papacy and its Curia . . .'[15]. From this standpoint it was possible to recognize that tension between the intellectual and political elements in the Church was unavoidable and even salutary: 'Arduous as are the duties involved in these three offices, to discharge one by one, much more arduous are they to administer, when taken in combination. Each of the three has its separate scope and direction; each has its own interest to promote and further; each has to find room for the claims of the other two, and each will find its own line of action influenced and modified by the others . . .'[16]. Friedrich von Hügel was equally aware of the need to keep in balance what he called the 'Three Elements of Religion' (the mystical, the intellectual and the institutional) but was much less optimistic that the balance could be kept. He recognized 'the causes and reasons that are ever tending to produce and to excuse the quiet elimination or forcible suppression of one or other of the elements that constitute the full organism of religion'; and among them he cited the phenomenon that 'the Institutional easily tends to a weakening both of the Intellectual and of the Emotional.'[17] In short, tension between the Church Authoritative and the Church Academic was, to von Hügel, one of the facts of ecclesiastical life that have to be lived with. But he was speaking from the experience of his own peculiar times.

Such ideas have been given respectability and authority by the documents of Vatican II, if only by the insistence of

Lumen Gentium that the prophetic office is not confined to bishops and clergy but extended to all the laity. A prophet who has no place to prophesy is but a prophet lost; and it is perhaps on such lines that can be constructed a theory of university institutions as integral to the life of the Church. If such ideas meet general recognition it will be because the Church has recognized in our own time that the development of Christian thought and all that is meant by 'tradition' can be 'housed and localized, given a body in which to exist and act' in corridors other than those of power and authority. Discoveries of this sort do occur from time to time in the history of the world. Tacitus recognized one such discovery when Galba succeeded Nero and the 'secret of empire' was revealed. His words almost exactly fit the present case: *evulgato imperii arcano posse principem alibi quam Romae fieri.*

NOTES

1 For further details, cf. a typescript *History of St. Edmund's House*, completed to 1976 and deposited in the archives of the House. *An Abbreviated History of St. Edmund's House* was privately printed for the House in 1976.

2 J. H. Newman, Letter to Emily Bowles, 19 May, 1863; *Letters and Diaries*, xx, 447.

3 *Des Progrès de la Révolution et de la guerre contre l'Église*, Paris, 1829, 276–7; cited J. Tracy Ellis, *The Catholic Priest in the United States*, Collegeville, 1971, 4. Even so respected a person as the Jesuit General John Roothaan could say of the sacred sciences in 1832 that 'everything has been reduced to a mountain of erudition which conceals an abyss of emptiness and vague uncertainties' (cited ibid., 97, n. 3.) In the same year (1832) Rosmini was completing the manuscript of his *Five Wounds of the Church*, in which the poor quality of clerical education, and the prevalence of what he described as minced-meat theology, are described as the second of these wounds.

4 Gerbet, in *l'Avenir*, 28th December 1830 (cited A. Vidler, *Prophecy and Papacy*, London, 1954, 178, n. 117): 'C'est la grande mission de tous les écrivains catholiques, et surtout des écrivains français. Si Rome est le centre immobile de la foi, la France est le foyer de l'activité intellectuelle de l'Europe.'

5 A. R. Vidler, *The Church in an Age of Revolution*, London, 1974, 188–89. In his *Variety of Catholic Modernists*, C.U.P., 1970, 104, Vidler quotes a similar judgement on the work of Pius X made by Archbishop Mignot of Albi in a letter to von Hügel written in 1914: 'He crushed many souls whom a little goodness would have kept in the right way.'

6 Purcell, *Life of Cardinal Manning*, London 1896, ii, 498, gives the October of 1874 as the date of opening. Manning himself, in a brief historical note on the venture which he wrote in 1887, dates the opening to 1875 (op. cit., ii, 502).

7 Damian McElrath, O.F.M., *Richard Simpson 1820–1876, A Study in XIXth. Century English Liberal Catholicism*, Bibliothèque de la Revue d'Histoire Ecclésiastique, Fascicule 55. Louvain, 1970, 50.

8 Notebook G in the Simpson Collection, Downside Archives; cited McElrath, op. cit., 70.

9 J. Coulson, Introduction to J. H. Newman, *On Consulting the Faithful in Matters of Doctrine*, London, 1961, 2.

10 Cited J. Coulson from the Downside Abbey Archives, op. cit., 44–45.

11 J. Coulson, op. cit., 47–48.

12 Purcell, op. cit., ii, 288–89.

13 Ibid., ii, 290, n1. Ullathorne's correspondence with Newman and others over the Oxford question is cited ibid, 292–99.

14 J. H. Newman, *Difficulties felt by Anglicans in Catholic Teaching*, (4th ed.) London, 46.

15 J. H. Newman, *The Via media of the Anglican Church*, (3rd. ed.) London, 1877, xl.

16 Ibid., xli. A good example of the 'Schools' modifying a Papal 'line of action' may be seen in the story of 16th. century teaching on usury; cf. J. T. Noonan, *The Amendment of Papal Teaching by Theologians*, in (ed.) C. E. Curran, *Contraception: Authority and Dissent*, London, 1969, 41–75.

17 F. von Hügel, *The Mystical Element of Religion*, (2nd. ed.) London, 1923, i, 65.

The Contributors

JOHN COVENTRY S.J. has been Master of St. Edmund's House since July 1976. Born in 1915, he was Rector of Beaumont 1956–58, Provincial of the English Jesuits from 1958 to 1964, and subsequently for many years a Lecturer at Heythrop College. His latest book, *Christian Truth*, was published in 1975.

ADRIAN HASTINGS is a Lecturer in Religious Studies at the University of Aberdeen. Born in 1929 and ordained in 1955, he studied at St. Edmund's House 1957–58 and was a Research Fellow of the House from 1974 to 1976. His recent books include *Christian Marriage in Africa* (1973), *The Faces of God* (1975), and *African Christianity* (1976).

J. DEREK HOLMES was born in 1935 and ordained in 1960. He read History at Cambridge and then became Dean and Research Fellow of St. Edmund's. He has contributed to editions of Newman's essays *On the Inspiration of Scripture* (1967), *Newman's University Sermons* (1970) and *The Theological Papers of John Henry Newman on Faith and Certainty* (1976). At present he is Lecturer in Church History and Director of Studies, Ushaw College, Durham.

RAYMOND LAHEY was born in Canada in 1940. Since 1968 he has held appointments as Associate Professor of Religious Studies and Principal of St. John's College in the Memorial University of Newfoundland at St. John's. He has been associated with St. Edmund's House as a member since 1966 and while engaged in research has lived in the House for several periods. A Catholic priest, he is a Consultor of the Archdiocese of St. John's. He has written several articles on theology and church history, specialising in the Malines Conversations.

NICHOLAS LASH was born in 1934. He is a Fellow of St. Edmund's House, of which he was Dean from 1971 to 1975, and a University Assistant Lecturer in Divinity. His recent publications include *Change in Focus* (1973), *Newman on Development* (1975) and *Voices of Authority* (1976).

HUGH A. MACDOUGALL was born in Nova Scotia in 1922. He is presently Professor of History at Carleton University, Ottawa. He was a member of St. Edmund's House as a graduate student from 1957 to 1960 and a visiting Fellow in 1969. He is the author of *The Acton — Newman Relations* and *Lord Acton on Papal Power*.

BERNARD SHARRATT was born in Liverpool in 1944 and educated at Upholland College. He was a research student and then a Research Fellow at St. Edmund's House from 1968 to 1971. Since then he has been a Lecturer in English and American Literature at the University of Kent at Canterbury. An editor of *Slant* in the 1960s and a contributor to many periodicals, he is currently working on a book on Marxism and literature.

INDEX